Beyond Fact

Nonfiction for Children and Young People

compiled by Jo Carr

American Library Association

Chicago, 1982

Acknowledgments

p. 7. From *Four Women in a Violent Time* by Deborah Crawford. Copyright © 1970 by Deborah Crawford. Reprinted by permission of Crown Publishers.

p. 9. From *The Old China Trade: Americans in Canton 1784–1843* by Francis Ross Carpenter. Copyright © 1976 by Frances R. Carpenter. Reprinted by permission of the publishers, Coward, McCann & Geohegan, Inc.

p. 11. From *The Great Constitution: A Book for Young Americans* by Henry Steele Commager. Copyright © 1961 by Henry Steele Commager. Reprinted by courtesy of the Bobbs-Merrill Company, Inc.

p. 46. From *The Story of Life: From the Big Bang to You* by Kim Marshall. Copyright © 1980 by Kim Marshall. Reprinted by permission of Holt, Rinehart & Winston, Publishers, and the Sterling Lord Agency, Inc.

p. 52. From a review by Marion P. Harris, Boston University in *Appraisal: Science Books for Children* 12, no. 2:33 (Spring 1979). Copyright © 1979 by the Children's Science Book Review Committee. Reprinted by permission of the publisher.

p. 85. "How" from *Feathered Ones and Furry* by Aileen Fisher. Copyright 1938, 1965 by Aileen Fisher. Reprinted by permission of Thomas Y. Crowell Company.

p. 94. Text excerpt from *Strange Footprints on the Land: Vikings in America* by Constance Irwin. Copyright © 1980 by Constance Irwin. By permission of Harper & Row, Publishers, and Curtis Brown, Ltd.

p. 94. From *Blood Feud* by Rosemary Sutcliff. Copyright © 1976 by Rosemary Sutcliff. Reprinted by permission of the publishers, E. P. Dutton, Inc., and Oxford University Press.

p. 128. From *Where Was Patrick Henry on the 29th of May?* by Jean Fritz. Copyright © 1975 by Jean Fritz. Reprinted by permission of the publishers, Corward, McCann & Geohegan, Inc., and Russell & Volkening, agents for the author.

p. 135. Specified excerpt from pp. 102–108 in *Woman against Slavery* by John Anthony Scott. Copyright © 1978 by John Anthony Scott. Reprinted by permission of Thomas Y. Crowell Company.

p. 149. From *Nothing Is Impossible: The Story of Beatrix Potter* by Dorothy Aldis. Copyright © 1969 by Dorothy Aldis. Reprinted with permission of Atheneum Publishers.

Library of Congress Cataloging in Publication Data
Main entry under title:

Beyond fact.

Includes bibliographical references.
1. Children's literature—History and criticism.
I. Carr, Jo, 1923-
PN1009.A1B47   809'.935   82-1601
ISBN 0-8389-0348-7 (pbk.)   AACR2

A child is not a vase to be filled
but a fire to be lit.

——Author unknown

Contents

Preface

You can always tell a fine nonfiction book by reading it aloud. If children listen with hushed attention and then fight to take the book home, it's a winner.

What is the great appeal of such a book? Take William Kurelek's *A Prairie Boy's Winter* for instance. Do the children love it because they want to find information about Manitoba? Yes, partly, but they could learn about Manitoba by reading the encyclopedia, after all. They must be responding to some exceptional quality in the book, most likely to the rich paintings and detailed prose that have been masterfully blended. William Kurelek, a fine writer who is also a fine artist, has created a book that will not easily be forgotten.

Outstanding books like *A Prairie Boy's Winter* deserve greater recognition than they ordinarily receive. Evidence of this neglect is not hard to find:

Only six nonfiction books have won the Newbery Award since it was founded in 1922, and five of those were biographies.

Children's literature courses give very little attention to the evaluation of nonfiction

Teachers rarely read nonfiction aloud to their classes or encourage children to read factual books for their personal enjoyment

Children's librarians in the public library do not often make a practice of reading nonfiction books before they order—or after, for that matter—although they do read fiction

Even the most literate parents never think to read a nonfiction book to their children at bedtime

Bookstores do not stock anywhere near as many nonfiction books as they do fiction, even though far more nonfiction books are published each year.

So we find a consistent, if unconscious, denigration of nonfiction for children, as Milton Meltzer has pointed out in his *Horn Book* article, "Where Do All the Prizes Go?" All too often these books have been considered for their content alone, earmarked exclusively for "curriculum support" and neatly categorized for some useful purpose. It is no wonder that quality cannot be recognized from such a limited perspective.

The utilitarian approach to children's nonfiction contrasts sharply with the serious treatment of nonfiction for adults. While John McPhee and Barbara Tuchman find their books not only reviewed in serious review journals but stocked in bookstores, nobody reading these journals or wandering into the children's part of a bookstore would even be aware of Olivia Coolidge or Laurence Pringle. Yet both write extremely well. Their combination of scholarly detail and straightforward prose is nonfiction writing at its best. Certainly they deserve the same critical attention that is paid to someone of equal competence who is writing in the adult field.

It is for these reasons that I have compiled this collection of essays. I would like to stimulate interest in nonfiction writing for children. In addition, I would like to explore the meaning of quality in nonfiction writing for them. The contributors to this collection have presented their views of what constitutes "the best." By discussing the demands of their craft, by telling us what to look for in our quest for excellence, they may be able to educate us in critical evaluation.

Is there any doubt that we need informed critical judgment in order to deal with the vast number of books being published in the United States each year? When some books are as poor as the "Berenstain Bears" book on nature and some are as beautiful as Anne Ophelia Dowden's book on herbs, we need to become almost aggressively selective. Only then can we be effective, not only in buying the best books, but also in persuading children to read them.

Before going on, we need to consider the sticky problem of terminology. Although nonfiction in Dewey's classification includes plays, poetry, folk literature, and story collections—all more appropriate to discussions of imaginative literature than has been intended here—the term is useful simply because most of us assume it refers only to factual writing. So, with some misgivings, I shall be using "nonfiction" here, rather than the more accurate term "informational writing."

While terminology is sticky enough in discussing nonfiction, age levels are even stickier. Although the age of the readers of the books being discussed ranges from kindergarten through grade 8, age-level distinctions are very fuzzy indeed. Denise Wilms reveals in her article "Out in Space" how difficult it is to distinguish between an adult book and one intended for children. Yet the division is no less drastic for being arbitrary. Try to persuade an adult—especially a high school student—that a book from the children's room might be valuable. Most of us who have served both adults and children agree with John Rowe Townsend that the arbitrary dividing line has indeed hardened into a barrier.

Adults, on their side of the barrier, are the losers. They might be surprised to find that a book written for children is livelier than an adult book on the same subject, and with no sacrifice in scholarship. Franklyn Branley has said that it is only when he must explain a subject to children that he realizes he doesn't understand it at all. So the successful children's writer may be forced to refine his or her thinking to the point of absolute clarity. The result may be, in a way, a distillation of the subject. In addition, the imaginative use of graphics in many children's books further clarifies, as well as enhances, that subject. Many books for adults seem abstruse and dull by comparison.

In discussing fine nonfiction books, for whatever reader, I do not include textbooks. The focus here is on trade books, those nonfiction books that offer a stimulating extension of school work or pleasure reading for its own sake. The only exception is some editorial comment on the mind-boggling implications of Frances FitzGerald's analysis of American history textbooks, *America Revised.*

All the articles, with two exceptions, cover nonfiction writing exclusively. The exceptions are two articles in the controversy section, one by the Council on Interracial Books for Children, and the other, a reaction to the principles of the Council, by Nat Hentoff. Both articles are concerned with children's literature in general, rather than nonfiction writing in particular. But, since the discussion in both articles covers nonfiction as well as other kinds of literature, I have chosen to include them. The implications of CIBC policy in terms of intellectual freedom are too serious to ignore in any discussion of nonfiction writing for children.

Finally, I would like to express my gratitude to Margery Fisher, whose name appears many times in the pages that follow. It was her seminal book on nonfiction writing, *Matters of Fact,* that initially sparked my interest in nonfiction. Having always been a confirmed fiction reader, I was not prepared for the glued-to-the-page fascination with which I began reading about mummification in ancient Egypt, the discovery of DNA, and the explanation of black holes. These books, and many others on every conceivable subject, have opened up a world for me. As the articles in this collection will show, they can do the same for children.

Nonfiction Writing:

Books as Instruments of Intelligence

To care for good reading, to keep on with good reading because you care for it, means that little by little this backgound takes on substance in the mind, and unconsciously every new subject contemplated, studied, or enjoyed enlarges and enriches it. From every book invisible threads reach out to other books; and as the mind comes to use and control those threads the whole panorama of the world's life, past and present, becomes constantly more varied and interesting, while at the same time the mind's own powers of reflection and judgment are exercised and strengthened.

——Helen Haines[1]

Writing the Literature of Fact

Jo Carr

Teacher. Scholar. Promoter. Artist. Reporter. Catalyst. Philosopher. A fine nonfiction writer is really all of these but is teacher and artist, most of all.

First, consider the nonfiction writer as teacher. After this, as artist. A writer who is a teacher must be able to explain something so clearly that the reader, or student, can understand. So the nonfiction writer–as–teacher must be able to command techniques of clarification—understandable language, tightly structured organization, analogy, illustration, metaphor, scholarly documentation—while respecting the intelligence of the reader and stimulating curiosity. In addition, the nonfiction writer must structure information to support or explore a perceived idea or principle, thereby giving significance to what could be in the hands of an inept expert merely a range of footnoted facts.

These techniques for clarifying complex subjects, for collecting facts and illuminating them, are basic. They are so important that a separate article on science writing in this book is devoted to them. Although the observations in that article have been confined, of course, to science writing, they actually apply to history and biography as well. Historians and biographers also must interpret facts according to their perceptions, formulating either deductively or inductively principles that clarify the subject.

But what about the author whose writing transcends clarification, one who reaches "beyond fact" to write what John McPhee has called "the literature of fact"? What qualities do we look for in a book that is so powerful we never forget it?

Perhaps the qualities we look for are the same as those we find in a great teacher. Most of us have been lucky enough to know at least one such teacher, and we never forget that person. Although Miss Lyon or Mr. Brown, or whoever it was, may have initially riveted our attention through breadth of knowledge and lucidity, eventually the appeal becomes more potent. We discover ourselves mesmerized by a dynamic personality or a far-reaching mind, or both. Persuasive charisma and vast knowledge combine so effectively that we end up thinking or feeling in a completely new way. We remember these teachers because their teaching changed us significantly. They gave us, not just information, but knowledge, or at least access to knowledge.

The effect of an outstanding nonfiction book is like that. Truly inspired and masterfully written, it can lead us, by way of facts and beyond facts, to awakened understanding.

What does a teacher actually do to achieve this? What does a writer actually do? These are difficult questions. What they do and how they do it are probably as various as the people who teach and write well. Still, even while acknowledging this, we can perhaps suggest some ways in which they are alike. There are at least two characteristics common to fine nonfiction writers that can be measured by their effect on the reader: first, like the best teachers, they make us think deeply. And second, like the best teachers, they make us feel deeply. The stimulation of thinking is obviously vital. A good nonfiction book, as it marshals facts, should create a challenge. It should encourage a child to think—to relate one fact to another and test a familiar idea against a new idea—until at last he or she is able to weave a pattern of increased understanding. What begins as idle curiosity should end as independent thinking.

When we recognize what other ideas children are absorbing, or not absorbing, during their school years, independent thinking seems precious indeed. With the publication of Frances FitzGerald's analysis of American history textbooks, *America Revised,* we must acknowledge that textbook publishers, by trying to appeal to everyone and offend nobody, have too often reduced ideas to homogenized pulp. Unlike discovery texts in science, history textbooks are written "not to explore but to instruct—to tell children what their elders want them to know about their country. This information is not necessarily what anyone considers the truth of things. Like time capsules, the texts contain the truths selected for posterity."[1]

Who is doing the selecting? Now we come to the scary part. Textbook publishers, who in turn have been instructed by school boards responsible for text adoption, are basically deciding how we should think about our country. Through the power of their blue pencils, editors have become "the arbiters of American values, and publishing companies the Ministries of Truth for children."[2]

Some trade books, of course, are guilty of even worse oversimplification than textbooks. Some handle facts so irresponsibly as to convey untruths and sensationalism. But the best trade books are always challenging and thought-provoking. It is by way of these books that we are able to offer children an open marketplace for ideas of all kinds. Children, as well as adults, should be free to confront each side of the debate on nuclear power, to read the British version of the American Revolution, to consider the pros as well as the cons of communism. What we really want to do is to start the wheels of the mind turning by means of books. In other words, we want to teach children how to think, not what to think. This idea has been pursued further in the article "The Problem with Problem Books."

Teaching children how to think involves exposing them to a great deal of information, many ideas, and different interpretations of those ideas on a level that they can understand. This means that writers not only have to be informed, they must actually be authoritative at the outset.

Let us look at two examples of such sound scholarship.

Linda Grant De Pauw has written a thought-provoking book called *Founding Mothers* (Houghton, 1975) that is concerned with women at the time of the American Revolution. Her scholarship is impressive; her coverage of the subject so authoritative and written with such imaginative insight that the reader is almost compelled to seek more information about this time in our history.

The reader is similarly motivated after reading *The Visionary Girls* (Little, 1973) by Marion Starkey. In this instance the documentation required to produce an adult book strengthens this simpler book for young people and the story of the Salem witch trials emerges as the drama that it actually was.

There are, of course, volumes and volumes of comparable scholarship on nonfiction shelves, waiting to offer children real intellectual stimulation. Such books, combining scholarship with the imagination of the creative artist, endorse the truth of the statement attributed to Rabelais, "a child is not a vase to be filled, but a fire to be lit."

Thinking, then, is important. Intellectual content is basic. Yet strangely enough, so is feeling. Emotion too can be well expressed through the imaginative use of fact. In writing what we call "literature of fact"—as opposed to writing "plain fact"—the author probably proceeds from intellectual mastery of the subject to conviction and enthusiasm, in all likelihood a natural development after reading widely and thinking deeply about that subject. This kind of keen enthusiasm, passion if you will, is then transformed through imagination until the reader's passion is awakened in response. The author must care deeply about the subject, or the reader won't care at all.

Passion, then, can be an energizing force in writing. Elaine Moss, a British authority on children's books, says that it is crucial. Asked once what she thought of a book that had been given one of the *Times Educational Supplement* (TES) nonfiction awards, she said that she thought it wasn't a book at all; it was television in print. She then went on to lament what she called "journalism" in children's nonfiction, a kind of superficial treatment of a subject, usually visually seductive, that is churned out by a group of editors. The result: a child going flip-flip-flip with the pages, much as he or she goes flip-flip-flip from one simplified idea to another on a mass-produced television program. Unfortunately many works of nonfiction in this country bear the same mark of institutional writing that Elaine Moss has noted in England. Barbara Tuchman, eloquently castigating books that are written without personal enthusiasm, says that an author's passion is essential if there is to be, as there must be in all good writing, "a pulse beat on the printed page,"[3] the beating of the pulse on the page that keeps the book alive long after its author has turned to dust.

All the contributors to this collection confirm Barbara Tuchman's belief in the importance of individual enthusiasm, the value of the writer's "personal voice" that has been described by Milton Meltzer as a "quality of vision."[4] Zena Sutherland underlines it. Margery Fisher considers it basic. Olivia Coolidge makes it a reality with biography. Their views become especially significant when we consider the current proliferation of publishing conglomerates, bookstore conglomerates, book distribution conglomerates. It is no wonder we are dismayed when a conglomerate of writers threatens to replace the individual author!

For an example of conglomerate writing, consider the "special award for an outstanding series of books on engineering and technology" given by the New York Academy of Sciences to Viking Press in 1978. These books, which explore the intricate workings of machines and airports and space technology and television production, are absolutely fascinating. They are, in fact, perfect examples of books that clarify complex subjects in an entertaining way. Without any question there is an important place for books like these. But we do need to ask ourselves the same question to which Elaine Moss responded in considering the TES award. Can such books be considered literature? Here is an example of the writing in *Jet Journey*, one of the books in the series, the work of two authors and nine contributors:

> Aircraft accidents are rare. Air travel is one of the safest forms of transportation in terms of numbers of people hurt for distance traveled. In 1977, figures show .387 accidents (.061 fatal accidents) per 100,000 landings.[5]

The New York Academy of Sciences in its award is recognizing legitimate and important strengths in these books; but the quality of literary distinction that we are seeking obviously is lacking. The limitation of institutional writing like this will be further accentuated later when we contrast the selection quoted above with examples of vivid writing from *Ishi, Last of His Tribe* and two other well-written books.

Naturally not all kinds of facts lend themselves to imaginative interpretation. It would be hard to produce an almanac, for instance, that could be described as anything but "institutional." On the other hand, many so-called "reference" books contain facts so imaginatively assembled that we sense the enthusiasm of the editor behind tremendous scholarly effort. *The Encyclopedia of American Facts and Dates* (Crowell, 1966) by Gordon Carruth comes to mind, as do the "Everyday Life in . . ." books by the Quennells (Putnam). Edwin Tunis, an outstanding historian and illustrator, has also given ample evidence of his own personal commitment to his work as artist and writer. His books, although primarily reference books, are fine examples of facts magically transformed in a way that Paul Murray Kendall has beautifully described:

At best, fact is harsh, recalcitrant matter, as tangible as the hunk of rusty iron one trips over and yet as shapeless as a paper hat in the rain. Fact is a cold stone, an inarticulate thing, dumb until something happens to it. . . . Fact must be rubbed up in the mind, placed in magnetic juxtaposition with other facts, until it begins to glow, to give off that radiance we call meaning.[6]

It is someone writing with passion and enthusiasm who is most likely to produce books that will give off this kind of "radiance."

Intellectual content and passionate enthusiasm then, might be considered essential characteristics of the nonfiction writer whose books are as memorable as the seminars of our most memorable teachers. But these qualities are not enough. A book qualifying as "literature of fact" must be written by someone who is not only a teacher but also an artist. Gifted writers work with facts as sculptors work with clay—or artists with paint, composers with melody, poets with words—to give meaningful form to their perception of things.

The next question is "how?", and the answer is fairly crucial in determining when nonfiction writing qualifies as "literature." How do writers capture the reader's interest and hold it? How do scholars make a subject that could be dry as dust so intriguing that the reader can't bear to put down the book? The author's wisdom and enthusiasm, crucial as they are, obviously do not weave this kind of spell. A spell is woven only when the writing is equal to the task of communicating that wisdom and enthusiasm, only, in other words, when the author's style is good enough.

We might look at style as Rae Goodell does in her book *The Visible Scientists* (Little, 1977). She uses the term "Pied Pipers" to describe certain outspoken scientists whose dynamic writing has captured the imagination of the public. Perhaps "Pied Piper" is a term we might also use to describe our most gifted nonfiction writers. They play a tune, and the melody is so lively that we must follow. The tune they play is their way of writing, their genius with words.

The tune is nothing if not elusive, heaven knows, and "how" questions are nothing if not daunting. One way to analyze the "how" of the writer's magic, the notes in the piper's tune, might be to look carefully at the result. Perhaps if we examine examples from the work of "literary" nonfiction authors we can determine what they have in common, what range of writing techniques succeed in giving moving expression to personal vision.

Let us start with this excerpt from *Four Women in a Violent Time* by Deborah Crawford:

Penelope was left on the beach with her husband, whom others had pronounced all but dead. The night came on; crouched beside Kent she slept fitfully. She must have known by then that she was going to have to face the New World as a widow.

But there are times when one's fears, great as they are, may be rendered pale by the onrush of reality. For in the morning came events more terrible than this pretty, sheltered young bride from Holland could possibly have imagined. In the morning the wild men came.

She saw little—three or four men with feathers sticking up from shaved and coppery heads; then their arms were swinging down upon her with knives and with something she was to learn later was a tomahawk.

One blow of this weapon and the dying young man was dispatched. Penelope was deftly scalped; a knife slashed into her shoulder, and another stroke drove into and across her abdomen.

Then they left her for dead.[7]

The foregoing isn't "just like a story." It is a story, and a good one. There is nothing like this kind of suspense—to say nothing of real drama—to keep the pages turning.

Here is a selection from a book by another author:

Suddenly the storm was over, and the sun broke through. When we forced open the front door against the hailstones that had piled up on the porch, we beheld an unbelievable sight. What had been just a few minutes earlier a spring day with green grass, trees in full foliage, and lettuce and radishes growing in the gardens, was now the most beautiful winter scene imaginable! The trees, completely stripped, stood naked against the sky as in January. White, glistening hailstones covered the ground like new-fallen snow. . . . After a quick survey of the damage, grandmother Gordon, who had prayed aloud during the storm, quietly gathered hailstones from the back porch and made herself a cup of ice water.[8]

This selection from *A Nickel's Worth of Skim Milk: A Boy's View of the Great Depression* by Robert J. Hastings also tells a story.

Narrative, then, offers scope for the author's imaginative insight. When, in addition, the narrative features a person, especially one with whom we can strongly identify, then we are truly hooked. What must it have been like to be scalped? What was the old grandmother thinking when she looked at the havoc outside? Had her prayers been answered or not? We automatically react this way to stories about people, it seems, and even more forcibly when the people are "real."

Even writers for adults depend on narrative. If John McPhee, in *Encounters with the Archdruid,* had tried to present his ideas in straight exposition, we would have been overwhelmed in our efforts to understand them—not just overwhelmed, bored! Instead, there we are, sharing a hazardous voyage down the Colorado with David Brower, then director of the Sierra Club, and a rancher named Floyd Dominy, a worthy opponent on environmental issues. With McPhee as referee, the two battle it out. David Brower: "Emotionally, people are able to look only two generations back and two generations forward. . . ." Floyd Dominy: "Nonsense, nonsense, complete nonsense."[9] In such dramatic scenes as this McPhee habitually uses people as vehicles for abstract ideas, with stories about them carrying the reader from one idea to the next. If storytelling works this well for John McPhee—considered by almost everyone today as the top writer of adult nonfiction—no wonder it succeeds for Deborah Crawford and Robert J. Hastings and for all the other writers of children's nonfiction who use it so imaginatively.

This is not to say that the use of narrative is always justified. We need to beware of the writer who starts a book with the story of an archeologist who, after bravely enduring months of scorching desert heat, cries "Eureka!" as he finally unearths a valuable artifact, this moment of drama being followed by two hundred pages of boring exposition about the life-style of the ancient people who had produced that rare object. Or the type of science writer who introduces information about turtles by telling a story about a mother turtle with her three babies and the exciting adventures they had on the way to the water's edge. The artificial grafting of story to information with the transparent intent of capturing the reader's attention is so obviously manipulative that children are quite right to feel insulted by it.

Narrative is only one of the piper's tunes. What is the appeal in the following selection from *Ishi, Last of His Tribe*?

> When Ishi came down the ladder pole, the warmth rose to meet him: warmth from the fire and reflected warmth from the low bark-covered walls. There were many smells in Mother's house in winter—the bite of smoke, the sharp spice of burning pine and baywood; hot resin; green and drying grass and bark; meat broth; still-warm bread; and the different smells from the baskets which sat in a neat circle on the upper house level: dried salmon and deer meat and bulbs and fruit; pelts and rugs and blankets. And there were the smells of tobacco and medicines and herbs which hung in bunches along the walls.[10]

And in this one from *Museum People: Collectors and Keepers at the Smithsonian* by Peggy Thomson?

> I liked the noisy excitement of [the Smithsonian], even just stepping around the edges the way I did, when the totem poles and heavy machinery and cannon were set in place. . . . But then I like the quiet excitement, too, in other parts of the buildings—the absorption and sense of purpose—where people were stitching sails or stirring rice paste or sketching pollen under a microscope, and where curators were writing in cubicles piled ceiling-high with books, maps, specimens, and stacks of print-outs from the computer.[11]

And what about this selection by Francis Ross Carpenter from *The Old China Trade: Americans in Canton, 1784-1843*?

> What a sight! Long before seeing the warehouses and long before catching sight of the shops, the temples, the beggars, the mansions, he would see the waterfront. No waterfront in the world was like it. The harbor was choked with boats. Some were family affairs with as many as three generations on board, the youngest tied perhaps to a ring on the inside

to keep him or her from falling overboard. They laughed a lot among themselves as they artfully shoveled rice in with their chopsticks and shared their tea. Frequently it was just such a boat with just such a family that carried the cargoes down to Whampoa, where the American vessels lay, the water slapping at their empty hulls as they awaited a cargo. . . . To add to all that excitement, joss paper was lighted and thrown flaming into the river for a sacrifice to the gods of wind and waves. If a vessel were leaving, it might be given a send-off with baskets of exploding firecrackers from other ships. And everywhere there was shouting and there was the din of gongs, summoning up good spirits to protect the men at sea. Nowhere else had there ever been such a water-front.[12]

What do these passages have in common? Compare them to the passage from *Jet Journey*, quoted earlier, and the power of vivid description is obvious. Unlike the writing in *Jet Journey*, these are replete with fasci-nating detail, graphic images, and sensual appeal. The selection from *Ishi* is all smells, almost as redolent as Wilbur's barn. That of the Smith-sonian is sights: totem poles, microscopes, cubicles "piled ceiling-high. . . ." And the scene at the Canton waterfront is both sounds—shout-ing, the din of gongs, exploding firecrackers—and sights—boats, temples, flaming joss paper.

What is more, you are there in every scene. You can imagine just what it must have been like. And you identify with the people being de-scribed: You are climbing down the ladder pole with Ishi; you are one of those Americans on the empty vessels, absorbing the sights and sounds of that incredible harbor, as their cargo is being loaded; you are along-side the author, peering into the museum's cubicles and moving about its exhibits. The writer's vision becomes your vision, the storyteller's story your story. This must have been what Paul Murray Kendall meant when he said that "fact must be rubbed up in the mind . . . until it begins to glow, to give off that radiance we call meaning."[13]

Now try reading aloud Hal Borland's description of October in *The Golden Circle: A Book of Months:*

October is a time of far and misty horizons that beckon, a time of crow-caw and jay-jeer, before the slash of sleet or the gentle fall of snow. It is frost creeping down from the hills in moccasin-quiet feet to dust the valleys with glitter, of wind skittering down the road in a scuffling of leaves, of owl hoot and fox bark in the moonlight.[14]

The author's sentences, rhythmic and rich in imagery, achieve a kind of grace that is extended by the magnificent illustrations of Anne Ophe-lia Dowden. In writing like this, our Pied Pipers seem to spin words with such beauty that their style becomes almost poetry. For a more compre-hensive discussion of poetic power in nonfiction, read Zena Sutherland's article, "Science as Literature," included in this compilation.

Some excellent literature of fact is distinguished by qualities that are unrelated to language. Look, for instance, at *Peter Pitseolak's Escape from Death* (Delacorte, 1978) by Peter Pitseolak. The text of this auto-biographical account of an Eskimo's ordeal on floating ice is appropriately simple, but it is the primitive pictures that embody the excitement and drama of survival.

Read also *A Northern Nativity* (Tundra, 1976) by William Kurelek. Notice how the rich paintings project the message of the nativity as it might have been received during the Depression years of the 1930s in the remote areas of Canada. Let the mood of the book capture your imagination, as the idea for it must have captured the imagination of the author-artist.

The foregoing two examples demonstrate beauty of artwork in combination with beauty of language, yet another manifestation of good literature. With so many talented artists illustrating and writing children's books, it is hardly surprising that they have brilliantly applied their pens and brushes to the pages of nonfiction books.

So far, then, we have discussed imaginative storytelling, masterful description, eloquent style, and graphic excellence. Now for the last selection:

> Most nations don't have to be made. They are there already. They have always been there. No one had to *make* France or England or Denmark. You might say that history made them. They don't have any "fathers" or any "birthday."
>
> The United States is different. Remember how Lincoln put it in the Gettysburg Address: "Our fathers *brought forth* on this continent a new nation."
>
> This is just what they did, too: They brought it forth; they almost invented it. What had been thirteen Colonies became thirteen States, and what had been thirteen States became the United States of America.
>
> Of course, it wasn't all that easy. After all, how does one go about *making* a nation? It isn't like making a cake, you know, or a table; Just follow the directions, and presto! there it is. No one had ever *made* a nation before. There were no directions.[15]

These are the words of Henry Steele Commager, speaking about the origins of *The Great Constitution*. He hit upon a single concept with which to give his book dramatic focus. Who had ever before thought of comparing the "making" of a nation to the making of a cake or a table? What an extraordinary thought! But how right it is! Once one has thought about our founding fathers in this way, one understands in a flash something significant about our country. Pages and pages of straight facts could never do it so well.

The technique of applying this kind of pivotal concept, what might be considered an extended analogy, is one that many writers use to unify their ideas. It was used by Linda De Pauw to discuss the "hidden heroines" in the Revolution; by William Kurelek in his refrain about the Holy Family, "If it happened there, why not here? If it happened then, why not now?"; by Gerald Johnson to compare the United States to a person growing to maturity in his trilogy *A History for Peter* (Morrow, 1959, 1960); by Marion Downer to link the maturing of a culture to the development of design in her book *The Story of Design* (Lothrop, 1963).

Storytelling skill, descriptive power, vivid prose, graphic excellence, and sharply defined focus—these are only some of the writing techniques that distinguish gifted nonfiction writing. You can probably discover many more the next time you reread your favorite book on the discovery of the Dead Sea Scrolls, the history of the Bayeaux Tapestry, or whatever.

In the final analysis, however, these techniques are only superficially significant. They are clues only. A writer is outstanding for reasons far more complicated than can be neatly summarized in a discussion like this. Perhaps we should look at nonfiction writing in this way: good nonfiction writers, like all teachers who know their subject well, distill from their knowledge a significant view of the world. But it is how the author communicates this insight that is crucial. In literature of fact the teacher's insight is vividly illuminated by the writer's art.

Introduction to
Matters of Fact
Margery Fisher

What is non-fiction? As a composite word it has official though not yet published existence. So far it has been traced back to 1909, and examples of its use are being collected currently for the next printed supplement to the Oxford English Dictionary. It is still not a term that can stand up to close examination. For that matter, neither can "fiction." Historical novels are normally classified as fiction, when they are neither wholly nor materially so. Even if we call them "stories" rather than "fiction," it is still clear that they have some right to be classified as information books.

The distinction between fiction and non-fiction is no clearer if we

Adapted from chapter 1, pages 10–16 of *Matters of Fact: Aspects of Non-fiction for Children* by Margery Fisher. Copyright © 1972 by Margery Fisher. By permission of Thomas Y. Crowell, Publishers, and Hodder & Stoughton.

use the terms "information books" and "stories." A great many fact-books make use of incident fiction, and who could argue that fiction had no element of fact? The distinction between fiction and non-fiction is blurred and constantly shifting, but we still use it and need it. We have to accept the convenience that lies behind this naïve generalisation for very young readers:

> There are shelves of books in a library. The story books are called fiction. Other books, not stories, are called non-fiction. These are books about history, nature and hobbies.

Like so many general terms, "non-fiction" represents a compromise with some sense in it.

As a commercial distinction, it is necessary to help with the marketing and the library classification of commodities available in enormous numbers. It is irrelevant that the category of non-fiction is often rendered meaningless for various reasons by authors, critics and readers. In a more important sense, the terms fiction and non-fiction express *intention* in a broad way. It is true that some children may look for and extract nothing but facts from a novel by Cynthia Harnett, while others may become so deeply involved in a history of the invention of the wheel or of church music that facts become a springboard for emotion. Looking at it from the writer's point of view, however, we can see that there is a distinction, a very flexible one, between writing a story and writing an information book. In a novel the story—the fiction, perhaps I should say—comes first and has priority; facts, of whatever kind, exist to support it. The writer of an information book sets out to help towards knowledge, and the techniques he uses, which may well include story-telling, will be subordinate to this end.

It is the writer's business to provide a book which a child *can* use himself, whether in private or in the atmosphere of a classroom, to discover something new or to confirm what he already knows. The fact that the reader is young will impose certain limitations and responsibilities. Beyond the literary obligations which any writer faces in regard to any kind of readership—obligations to be accurate, to be clear in explanation, to be stimulating, to pursue a logical arrangement of his material—he must be aware of the age and aptitude of his readers in a broad way, just as a teacher or a parent selecting books must take into account in a relative way a writer's choice of vocabulary and of facts, as well as the illustration and design of a book as a whole.

But there is more to an information book than its technical aspect. Each one should contain fact, concept and attitude. Any book that is not a mere collection of facts (and many of them are only this) has an end in view, a generalisation towards which the facts are arranged. This final concept might be a statement of the result of victory or defeat, in a book of historical fact, or the definition of the end-product of a process and its use in a book of technology, it might be the summing-up of the purpose of an institution or a public service, or the pronouncement of an abstract idea.

Behind the generalisation that concludes, or should conclude, an information book lies the attitude of the writer. In some cases this may be a visible partisanship—as for instance in Frank Knight's *The Dardanelles Campaign* or Bruce Catton's study of the American Civil War, *This Hallowed Ground*. The enthusiasm of an expert discernible in a book on a sport, a pastime, a hobby, is in itself an attitude. Flatness of style, perfunctory writing, flabbiness in generalisation, all denote the lack of an attitude and promise ill for any book. A writer's conviction has an immediate effect on the reader, whether it is to invigorate and stimulate interest or to communicate a prejudice.

A writer's attitude is often revealed in his terminology. Natural history books provide a useful example here. In any index of this category certain words are likely to recur—Wonderful, Marvellous, Oddities, Miracle, Secrets. What attitudes do these indicate and how should we regard them?

Anyone who chooses to write about natural history has the responsibility for communicating a scientific attitude. To indicate that nature is "wonderful" is to suggest that to the writer the world of nature, in which he properly includes his own existence, is something that excites him and something that he feels could excite the reader. The child's sense of wonder is two-fold. He notices with a lively interest and he also wonders—that is, he wants to know and he asks questions. Whether his interest is stimulated by reading a book or by using his eyes when he is walking in city or country, "wonder" implies an attitude that is potentially active. It leads to discovery and knowledge. "Wonderful" is a word that denotes the observer and his state of mind, not the observed; it need not interfere with a scientific attitude.

But—"marvellous"? What does this imply? Surely, that there is something inexplicable in nature, something involuntary, something different. Such an attitude is basically unscientific. Whether it is devoted to a single subject (spiders, a cat having kittens) or to a region of behaviour (animal navigation), the business of a natural history book is to relate facts to a pattern of life in which humans participate as animals and which they should understand because they are part of it. However informal the approach, however simple, a natural history book for the young belongs to the science of biology. To suggest that the food-catching mechanism of a mussel or the egg-depositing behaviour of a cuckoo is "marvellous" is to make nonsense of the whole process of evolution. This pre-Darwinian attitude is discernible today also in the words "miracle" and "creature," though these may be used without any conscious intention. Words like this are enough to lead a young reader to accept the author's anthropomorphism as a matter of course.

An equally dangerous attitude may be detected in the *avoidance* of certain words. Scientific principles and terminology need not be daunting to young readers. It does not make it easier to see the natural world in perspective, for instance, if the term "animal" is used for "mammal," as it almost invariably is in information books. Alan James in *Animals* (1969) even goes so far as to explain that "usually when we say 'animals' we are talking about *Mammals*" but he still decides "we shall use the word 'animal' all through the book." His reasoning eludes me. It is not pedantic to suggest that the proper terms should be used in the simplest book. Children read books like this to sort information, and to sort properly they must be given the proper categories and terms to work with.

Formally or informally, an information book sets out to teach. To conceal this entirely natural aim, authors writing in many categories use the ubiquitous word "fun" as a smoke-screen. In this respect, trends in non-fiction have followed trends in education, not always with advantage. The move away from a captive audience and set classroom lecturing, healthy though this move certainly is, can lead to trivial studies as easily as to original and exciting work. A superficial permissiveness in the classroom is reflected in the throw-away manner of some information books. An advertisement for a junior travel series announces "a series of guides for young people with a completely original approach. The books are fun to read and the authors have concentrated on amusing the reader, while the educational aspect is left to look after itself."[1] The book advertised on the occasion was *Let's Look at Austria* by Gwynneth Ashby. I wonder how the partition of Austria in the past or her fate in World War II could be made to seem "amusing"; in fact, the author does not try to fulfil this promise except by being evasive at this stage of her survey.

Children are invited to have fun with coloured paper and with time, with collage and with paleontology. How disconcerting for them to discover that a book recommends them to *use* mind or hands, and how surprising, too, to open a book like *Mr. Budge Buys a Car* and to find that Gareth Adamson has made technicalities into fun without saying so and without demeaning himself or his readers.

Learning has always been fun in the sense of exciting, invigorating, stimulating and entertaining, but it has never offered to be effortless. The delight in discovery goes far deeper than "fun." A title that uses the word "quest" or "discover" or "look at" picks up and uses the energy which boys and girls are ready to exercise if they are helped to do so. The writer who respects his readers will call upon them to exercise their minds as well as their hands; no better exercise-machine for the intellect has yet been devised than a book. A teacher wrote recently:

> Activity can too easily mean filling jam jars with water, weighing sand, measuring the playground, making cardboard models of Jerusalem or papier-maché models of this year's school camp. Why so frightened of books? They are friendly things, willing to be picked up or discarded at any time without reproach, able to be copied, absorbed, read and reread,

looked at, skipped, pondered over—are completely at the disposal of the user. They do not cut one's finger as scissors can, nor stick one's cuffs with paste; they do not form gritty patches on the floor like sand, nor wet messes like water. The world's books contain the world's knowledge. Surely it is worth everyone's while to help children to learn how to use them.[2]

This demurely humorous rallying call to teachers may be extended to writers, publishers, reviewers and readers. I write in the belief that for learning, as for teaching, books are still and always an irreplaceable tool.

Historical Backgrounds

Evelyn L. Wenzel

Before the eighteenth century, so few books had been published exclusively for children that there was no need to establish a definition for informational books. Indeed, it is all but impossible to distinguish such books from books for school instruction or moral exhortation. According to Mrs. E. M. Field in her history of children's literature published in 1892:

> The history of children's literature . . . is parallel, and sometimes interwoven, with that of children's *education*.[1]

Mrs. Field traces the beginnings of books of instruction to Aldhelm (656–709 A.D.), a monk who prepared in dialogue form the first book of instruction for the monastery schools;[2] to the Venerable Bede (673–735 A.D.), another monk who recorded all that was then known of natural science, natural history, botany, and astronomy;[3] and to Alexander Neckham (1157–1217), a professor at the University of Paris whose *De Utensilibus*, a Latin reading book for children, told about household equipment, food and cooking, poultry yards and barns, spinning and

From *Time for Discovery*, compiled by Evelyn L. Wenzel and May Hill Arbuthnot. Copyright © 1971 by Scott, Foresman and Company, pp. 252–59. Reprinted by permission of Evelyn L. Wenzel.

weaving, the sciences of farming and navigation, and the work of scribes and priests.[4]

Far better known and more enduring for both British and American children was *Orbis Pictus* (the world illustrated), by a Moravian bishop, John Amos Comenius (1592–1670). It is usually cited as the first picture book for children. Originally written in German and Latin and translated into English in 1658 but retaining the parallel Latin text, it was used as a textbook throughout Europe until the late 1700s and reprinted in the United States in the early 1800s. It qualifies as a milestone in the history of children's books because it was a first successful effort to devise a way to teach children more effectively and interestingly through the close association of words and pictures. The content was "informational," mostly natural history. "The word of sensible things drawn; that is the Nomenclature of all Fundamental Things in the world and actions in life reduced to Ocular Demonstration."

British books of the eighteenth century

During the eighteenth century a few books appeared that bore some resemblance to informational books as we think of them today. Although still heavily didactic, these books represented a great step forward, partly because of the efforts of John Newbery, an energetic and innovative seller of books and patent medicines. The amply worded titles in the following list give some idea of the content of early informational books and, in a few cases, of their techniques for entertaining as well as instructing.

1726 Isaac Watts, *The Knowledge of the Heavens and the Earth Made Easy or the first Principles of Geography and Astronomy Explained*

1736 Thomas Boreman, *A Description of a Great Variety of Animals, and Vegetables . . . especially for the Entertainment of Youth*

1759 John Newbery, *A Pretty Book of Pictures for Little Masters and Misses; or, Tommy Trip's History of Birds and Beasts; with a familiar Description of each in Verse and Prose*

1761 —————, *The Newtonian System of Philosophy, adapted to the Capacities of Young Gentlemen and Ladies, and familiarized and made entertaining by Objects with which they are intimately acquainted*

1786 Mrs. Sarah Trimmer, *Fabulous Histories; designed for the Instruction of Children, respecting their treatment of animals.* Later published under the title *The History of the Robins*

John Newbery's *A Little Pretty Pocketbook*, first published in England in 1744, is truly a milestone publication, in that it tried to engage children's attention and through various devices make more palatable the instructive nature of the content.

The name of Isaac Watts is more famous than the title of the book that appears on this list. It was an early work, written during the time he served as a tutor. Apparently very little of Newbery's concern for the entertainment of children rubbed off on Mrs. Sarah Trimmer, whose zeal for the education of poor children in Sunday schools led her to gain their attention by introducing Father and Mother Robin, Robin, Jr., Dicky, Flapsy, and Pecksy and then to use the characters to impart moral instruction that included, of course, kindness to animals.

Nineteenth-century travel books

Not until well into the nineteenth century did American publishing go beyond reprinting and/or revising British books for children. The most ubiquitous informational material of this period was the travel series, with an essentially similar basic pattern: a family or an adult escorting a group of children takes a series of trips to a foreign land (usually several countries of Europe); the children are instructed by the adult who, of course, attends to morals as well as to mind.

In 1827, Samuel Goodrich initiated the travel series in this country with the first *Peter Parley* book. It was intended to provide more wholesome and interesting fare for children than the "violence-filled" fairy tales and the dull accounts of history and geography, both of which Goodrich lamented. His preface to *Balloon Travels of Robert Merry and his Young Friends over various countries in Europe*, edited by Peter Parley (New York: J. C. Derby & Co., 1855) reveals his intentions:

> The purpose of this volume is to entertain and instruct the reader by carrying him, in imagination, with a party of adventurers in a balloon, over the most interesting portions of Europe. . . . It is hoped, too, that the occasional passages of moral instruction, given in the conversations of Robert Merry, may be useful, by imparting sound morals and good manners. Peter Parley, Editor

The nature and quality of the entertainment and instrument will interest modern readers:

> We may consider the mind as a garden. If we would have it free from dangerous plants and poisonous weeds: if we would have our garden of the soul blooming with fresh and healthful flowers, we must sow it over with the seeds of beautiful and pure thoughts, derived from the society of good people and from good books. (p. 23)

> [comparing France with America] . . . we not only furnish a refuge for those who can escape from these lands of bondage, but our influence tends to shed light upon the world at large. We are impressed by being an American as we travel old, worn, and seedy Europe. (p. 99)

Goodrich was followed by other writers whose combined efforts resulted in hundreds of volumes of such instruction. Many of those who published these books in the latter half of the nineteenth century contributed also to children's magazines such as *St. Nicholas* and *Youth's Companion.* The following list[5] gives a few of the better-known authors along with the first book of each series and the dates of the first and last volumes:

1827-1860   Samuel G. Goodrich, *Tales of Peter Parley about America.* Boston: S. G. Goodrich

1840-1858   Jacob Abbott, *Rollo's Travels.* Boston: W. Crosby & Co.

1872   Charles Asbury Stephens, *Left on Labrador; or, The Cruise of the Schooner Yacht "Curlew."* As recorded by "Wash." Boston: J. R. Osgood

1875-1885   Horace Scudder, *Doings of the Bodley Family in Town and Country.* New York: Hurd & Houghton

1879-1894   Thomas W. Knox, *The Boy Travellers in the Far East, or Adventures of Two Youths in a Journey to Japan and China.* New York: Harper

1880-1895   Hezekiah Butterworth, *Zigzag Journeys in Europe, Vacation Rambles in Historic Lands.* Boston: Estes & Lauriat

1881-1886   Edward Everett Hale, and Miss Susan Hale, *A Family Flight through France, Germany, Norway and Switzerland.* Boston: D. Lothrop

1883-1892   Elizabeth Williams Champney, *Three Vassar Girls Abroad. Rambles of Three College Girls on a Vacation Trip through France and Spain for Amusement and Instruction. With Their Haps and Mishaps.* Boston: Estes and Lauriat

While the pattern—described in Zim as "erudite expert and his juvenile straight man"[6]—was similar, there were differences from series to series in content and tone. The Bodleys, for example, were a family of father and mother and three children, all reasonably lifelike, who moved from town to country where the children learned in both casual and contrived situations from various adults. When Nathan sprains his ankle, father, in an unsubtle effort to make the boy thankful that his injury was no worse, recalls from his travels a man with no arms painting with his toes, and mother describes two deaf-and-dumb children talking with their hands. On July 3, the family drives in a carriage through the Bunker Hill area of Boston, where they see two boys, one dressed in a navy uniform, the other in an army uniform, whereupon the family give three cheers "for our Army and Navy," and father lectures in history-book fashion on the Battle of Bunker Hill, with questions occasionally inserted by the children. There are touches of humor, the print is large and clear, and the plentiful black-and-white illustrations make the book look much like a "storybook."

Knox's *Boy Travellers: Russian Empire* (1887) devotes 505 pages to the travels of Dr. Bronson, Frank, and Fred. The author qualifies himself in the beginning by stating that he "has been three times in the Russian Empire, and much of the country described . . . was seen and traversed by him." While the print is fine and the pages forbiddingly solid, there is evident an attempt to tell about things that would interest young people and to be reasonably objective. Knox tries to show the differences in a foreign land but not, in Peter Parley fashion, as inferior to our own. When the boys are curious about the surrender of passports in the hotel, Dr. Bronson explains how sensible this precautionary measure is, because the Russians do not have the problem (as in America) of guests leaving sometimes without paying the hotel bill. When they eat in a Russian restaurant, the boys learn both how to make cabbage soup and how to eat it.

Virginia Haviland, who made a careful study of the travel series of the nineteenth century, attributes their rise to the stimulation to travel in this country and abroad occasioned by the development of the steam-powered ship and the transcontinental railroad. As to the reasons for their fall, she says: "Most of these pseudo-fictitious books taking young Americans abroad waned in popularity. . . . Such informational story-telling was connected all too easily with school lessons."[7]

History and science books of the nineteenth century

The travel series was not the only kind of informational material published in the nineteenth century. After the Civil War, American book publishing for children flourished. Richard L. Darling calls attention to the large number of history and science books—in addition to the travel series—published in this period.[8] T. W. Higginson's *Young Folks' History of the United States* (1875) was one of the most widely reviewed and extolled histories of this time. Butterworth, Scudder, and Hale wrote or edited historical books as well as travel series. In 1871-1872, Jacob Abbott produced a four-book science series: *Heat, Light, Force,* and *Water and Land,* sugar-coated in much the same style as his travel series. Two well-known British authors addressed themselves to botanical subjects: the books of Mrs. Margaret Gatty (*Parables from Nature,* 1855, and *Worlds Not Realized,* 1857) and of Mrs. Juliana Horatia Ewing (*Mary's Meadow* and *Our Field,* 1886) were published in the United States and were widely read. Darling quotes a review of *Parables from Nature* that attests to both its scientific and moral fitness:

> These parables . . . are so pervaded by fidelity to nature both in spirit and in fact, and so fitted to inspire that tender reverence in which children of the present day are sadly deficient, that they could not but do good.[9]

Arabella B. Buckley produced *The Fairy-Land of Science* (D. Appleton & Co., 1879), a title likely to be nauseous to the modern reader, but the book was reviewed in *The Nation* by a gallant Harvard physics professor who found her method fascinating and described her book as "a graceful attempt to show the forces of energy as fairies."[10] A British author, Forbes E. Winslow, wrote the *Child's Fairy Geography: A Merry Trip Round Europe* (1880), which was reviewed in *The New England Journal of Education* as "a charming specimen of the 'sugar-coated educational pills!' "[11] The periodical *Popular Science Monthly,* founded in 1872 to promote interest in science, reviewed a select few of children's science books.[12]

Nineteenth-century reviews of children's books

Darling's study of reviews of children's books during the sixteen years following the Civil War provides fascinating material that merits careful examination for what it might yield about informational books. Reviews of these books—some of them critical—are plentiful and look forward to the twentieth century rather than backward. His conclusion to Chapter 3, "Types of Children's Books," might, out of context, be mistaken for an account of children's book publishing today:

> Never before had children had books in such quantity nor dealing with such a variety of subjects. Never before had there been books of such quality either, but along with the truly excellent books there came great quantities of inferior books. With those books that provided delight and entertainment to children, while maintaining high moral standards, came others that, in order to entertain, were ever more wild and extravagant in incident, arousing complaints that they demoralized the children.[13]

Darling's finding that children's book reviewing of this period was far better than had been realized suggests the possibility that the informational material, too, might be more varied and interesting than commonly thought.

Beginnings of the modern informational books

In the first two or three decades of the twentieth century, influences begun in the preceding century continued, new ones emerged, and change slowly but surely came about until gradually there began to appear informational books recognizable as modern to us. What were some of the influences that eventuated in informational books as we know them today?

For one thing, improvements in illustration processes made possible, first, the production of informational books for very young children, and, second, the interweaving of pictures and text, especially important in informational material. During the early 1900s E. Boyd Smith produced several picture books that reflected the factual, real world of the farm and seashore (*Chicken World* and *The Farm Book*, 1910; *The Seashore Book*, 1912) and the events of the past (*The Story of Pocahontas and Captain John Smith*, 1906). Cecil Aldin, whose specialty was puppies, illustrated *The White Puppy*, 1917, and *The Mongrel Puppy Book*, 1912.

Advances in printing processes opened up new possibilities for the interweaving of text and illustration. Up to this time, colored illustrations on "shiny" pages were inserted into the frontispiece and then into the book at intervals. Black-and-white illustrations, usually small, were used at chapter heads and inserted rather formally and mechanically into the text. The 1920s and 1930s saw the beginnings of increased flexibility in the use of illustration and color, which reached full flowering in the 1940s, when illustrations, both black-and-white and color, became an essential part of the "informing" process in books for children of all ages.

In 1921, Lucy Sprague Mitchell wrote her *Here and Now Story Book* for preschool and early school-aged children, and along with it publicized her conclusions that young children are more interested in the world of "here and now" reality than in that of fantasy. She recommended, therefore, that children's earliest literature be about the real world—the "magic" of plumbing and electric lights—rather than fairy tales of kings and princesses in the faraway and long ago. The controversy flared up and burned steadily through the 1930s. While the argument centered primarily on the issue of whether to give or not give fairy tales to young children, it accorded new importance to informational material. If children were, indeed, little realists, interested in and endlessly curious about the natural and physical world immediately available to their senses, then information in books about this world should be given to them. And it was, in great quantities. Young children were the chief benefactors, for the picture book was ready and waiting to be put to new uses.

As early as 1900, *Four-and-Twenty Toilers*, a picture book written by E. F. Lucas, illustrated in color by Francis D. Bedford, and originally published in England, was brought out in the United States. Its full-page illustrations depicted very realistically and in great detail occupations such as shipbuilder, cobbler, engine driver, veterinarian, miller, knife-grinder, gamekeeper, and stevedore. The verse form used, presumably to engage young readers' attention, does not completely distract from the informative nature of the content:

> To make the Keeper's moleskin vest
> A hundred moles have died,

Edel's *Henry James*, Richard Ellman's *James Joyce*, Quentin Bell's *Virginia Woolf*, Henri Troyat's *Tolstoy*, George Painter's *Proust*. Or consider those who create literature as they write about science and nature: Rene Dubos, Rachel Carson, Lewis Thomas, Loren Eiseley. And what about such historians as Bruce Catton and Barbara Tuchman?

Even some of those commonly dismissed as journalists have proved their medium can be raised to literature. John McPhee's books have excited national attention. One critic has said that McPhee "is a journalist who writes of fact with that full measure of literary distinction that some associate only with fiction or poetry." McPhee was praised for his "Balzacian zest for detail" and "his gift for portraiture that enables him to capture real people as memorably as any novelist does his imaginary one." Another critic said that McPhee "is above all a craftsman . . . a reporter who makes art. He writes pieces that are as complex as novels, as meticulous as scholarship . . . in prose that is humorous, elegant, economical."

Look at the subjects of the dozen or so books McPhee has published. He has written of "basketball and tennis, oranges and firewood, wilderness and city, physics and engineering, art and education, men who build bark canoes and those who build unique flying machines, people who dwell in New Jersey's Pine Barrens and those who inhabit cabins on the tributaries of the Yukon River." Most of these are topics you might find in junior book catalogs almost any season. In such a setting they would be indifferently treated as "information" books or "fact" books. And there is truth in that description: McPhee prides himself on being "loyal to the lowliest of fact." But between the covers of his books readers encounter more than facts.

His books belong in the category of "The Literature of Fact," which is the title of a writing course he gives. As William Howarth, Professor of English at Princeton, has suggested, if McPhee were a novelist, poet, or playwright, his books would all be on the library shelf labeled American Literature, instead of scattered under such headings as Science, Sports, Recreation, History, Education. Why are they not catalogued as American literature? Because no one has a proper name for his brand of factual writing. Everyone calls his work nonfiction, a frustrating label for it does not tell what McPhee's books are but what they are *not*. "Since 'fiction' is presumably made up, imaginative, clever, and resourceful, a book of 'nonfiction' must *not* be any of these things, perhaps not even a work of art. If the point seems a mere quibble over terms," Professor Howarth goes on, "try reversing the tables: are Faulkner's books on Mississippi 'non-history' just because they are novels?"

Now what is the main thing being said in all this praise of McPhee's work? It can be reduced to a three-word sentence I have already quoted: "He makes art." The verb "makes" is all-important. Art does not begin when the artist chooses his subject. It is what he does with it, what he *makes* out of it, that counts. And here I pick up on another phrase quoted earlier: "McPhee is above all a craftsman." Which means he has superb technique.

Mark Schorer, literary critic and himself the creator of excellent fiction and biography, gets at it this way: "When we speak of technique we speak of nearly everything. For technique is the means by which the writer's experience, which is his subject matter, compels him to attend to it; technique is the only means he has of discovering, exploring, developing his subject, of conveying its meaning, and, finally, of evaluating it. And it follows that certain techniques are sharper tools than others, and will discover more; that the writer capable of the most exacting technical scrutiny of his subject matter will produce works with the most satisfying content, works with thickness and resonance, works which reverberate, works with maximum meaning."

But some may discount what I am saying when it comes to writing nonfiction for young readers. Such writers of nonfiction, they think, simply go out to find the facts, and then type them up. Don't the facts speak for themselves? Wolves are wolves, aren't they? Abe Lincoln is Abe Lincoln, the American Revolution is the American Revolution. "But the facts *never* speak for themselves," the critic Jacques Barzun insists. "They must be selected, marshaled, linked together, given a voice." Fit expression, he goes on, is not "a mere frill added to one's accumulation of knowledge. The expression *is* the knowledge."

If the writer cannot find the language to express what he thinks he has to say, then whatever he is after is simply not there on the page. His work begins to exist only through his craft. Lacking craft, many books of nonfiction contain nothing but dead words, words which serve no purpose beyond the stale repetition of the most rudimentary kind of fact.

Perhaps if I were to take apart a piece of my own nonfiction, showing what I have tried to do and how I went about doing it, it might throw some light on what I have been talking about. My example is *Never to Forget: The Jews of the Holocaust*.

Why did I want to write it? The impulse came from a pamphlet reporting a study of American high school textbooks. "Their treatment of Nazism was brief, bland, superficial, and misleading," said the author of the study. Racism, anti-Semitism, and the Holocaust were either ignored or dismissed in a few lines. Nor were college textbooks much better. As far as young people were concerned, "darkness hid the vilest crime ever perpetrated by man against man."

By one of those remarkable coincidences, an editor at Harper and Row had read the same pamphlet at about the same moment, and concluded Harper's must try to fill that hole. Knowing my other books on Jewish history, she approached me just as I was about to look for a publisher.

This was to be a book for young readers. I assumed they would know little or nothing about the Holocaust and what gave rise to it. And I wanted this to be a book for Gentile as well as Jew. While writing about black history, I had learned you couldn't deal with black Americans without dealing with white Americans. Black life and white life in America are profoundly affected by one another. Their experience is inseparable. It seems obvious, but for a long time people on both sides didn't see it. So too with Jew and Gentile in the Holocaust. I knew the book couldn't be for Jews alone. It had to be a book for non-Jews too.

The work of scholar-specialists on the Holocaust is enormous. They have been digging deep for the facts and publishing their monographs in the academic journals or in volumes few adults and even fewer young people would ever read. So too with the Holocaust studies of the philosophers and theologians. They have been trying for decades to grapple with the meaning of this cataclysmic event. Then there are the memoirs of survivors of the Holocaust—men and women whose bodies and spirit bear the scars of that racial fury.

I read for a long time in the forbidding masses of sources material. To include everything was manifestly impossible. I had to be concerned with selection, deletion, emphasis, proportion. I had to find a form and a voice that would enlarge the reader's experience, deepen it, intensify it.

First of all, I had to catch the young reader's attention. After several wrong starts I came upon what felt like the right beginning—that day in my own experience when, back in 1930, as a high school boy and a Jew, I first saw the shocking front-page news of Nazis in brown uniforms marching into the German parliament and shouting "Deutschland erwache! Jude verrecke!" ("Germany awake! Jews perish!") History became immediately personal to me at that moment. And would for my readers too, I hoped. The opening goes on to foreshadow the consequences of Hitler's brief twelve years of power. And pointing to the horror of the Holocaust, asks how could it have happened? What does it mean?

The preface decided upon, the problem now was how to organize the facts and ideas scattered through my stacks of 3x5 slips—the thinking that goes into it, the fretting, the worrying, the doing and the undoing, the snipping and patching—all to get the ordering of the parts right. Chronology, the simple and direct movement from point A in time to point Z, is the easy temptation, and of course I played with that approach. But chronological order can be terribly tiresome. The other kind of order is topical. I could arrange the history of the Holocaust by subjects. I knew what I wanted to single out; the ideas would fall readily into a series of topics—but then the book would read like a string of essays. This was history after all, the passage of events through time. To eliminate the time sequence would be to throw away the power of narrative. So in the end I combined the topical with the chronological. Each of the book's three main parts stresses a single theme, while at the same time chronology moves the story forward. The arrangement I finally worked out imposed a form upon the book.

The theme of Part One, covering five chapters, is anti-Semitism, with its development traced through time. Who were the Jews as a historical people? Why did anti-Semitism grow in Europe and what part did the Christian church play in it? How did anti-Semitism change its character so that from a religious issue it turned into a racial one? Why did it take hold in Germany and what part did it play in the rise of Nazism and Hitler's taking of power? The theme is carried from the ancient world up to the eve of the Second World War.

Part Two deals with the war itself and Hitler's use of it to seize the continent's Jews and destroy them. Eight chapters trace the step-by-step measures taken to that end.

In Part Three, I use five chapters for the single topic of the Jews' resistance to their fate. A conclusion I came to from my research was that wherever there was oppression, resistance of some kind emerged. The Jews, counter to the old calumny, did not somehow murder themselves. Almost a third of the book—the action moving back and forth in time—traces the great variety of means by which the Jews carried out the watchword of their resistance: "Live and die with dignity!" Here I was able to compare the behavior of the Jews with the behavior of non-Jews, when both were under the stress of the greatest terror, hunger, and humiliation.

So much for one aspect of the problem of form. There is another element of the book, its most important, I think, which accomplishes what nothing else could. Since I am not one of the Jews who experienced the ghettoization, the transport trains, the labor camps, the death camps, I could write about them only from a remote distance. I chose therefore to make the story immediately personal by telling it in the words of the people who lived it. I drew upon original sources—diaries, journals, letters, memoirs, notebooks, eyewitness accounts, testimony given at hearings and trials, official documents, even the songs and poems people wrote to voice what they were going through. This firsthand testimony is woven into the narrative which carries the reader from the beginning to the end. Terrible and complex as the events were, they can be brought within the range of understanding if the reader is helped to see them from the inside. If a reader can be made to feel, to care, he or she will be much more ready to understand. So the men, women and children who lived the experience speak of it directly to the reader in their own words.

With young readers as my primary audience, I wanted much of the testimony to come from boys and girls, or to be about them. There are 27 such documentary passages fitted into the narrative. For example, Inge and Lolo, two little Christian girls, innocently reveal to a neighbor how their teacher has poisoned their minds against the Jews. Erna, an Aryan schoolgirl, proudly sends her prize assigned classroom essay, entitled "The Jews Are Our Misfortune," to be printed in *Der Sturmer* and I give the text of her piece. Ernest, a Jewish farmer's son, is beaten up by kids in his rural school and then expelled by the teacher. When a six-year-old Jewish boy refuses to give a passing band of Hitler Youth the Heil Hitler salute, he is stripped of his pants to show the passersby this is a circumcised dog. On Kristallnacht, when the home of 14-year-old Moses Libau is broken into by stormtroopers, he watches his parents terrorized and their belongings plundered. When the German armies roll over Poland, the Nazi killing squads collect Jews and shoot them down by the thousands, tossing them into open pits. Rivka, a young mother, describes what they did to her friends and to her baby, and how she miraculously rose from the grave, as it were, to live again, asking God what sin she committed that she was spared while all the others died. In the hell of the Vilna ghetto we watch young lovers holding hands in the evening, under the only tree still standing in that desolation. An eyewitness tells of the starving children in the streets of the Warsaw ghetto. "I once asked a little girl," he reports, "What would you like to be?" "A dog," she answers, "because the German sentries like dogs." Dr. Peretz recalls what he saw in the Kovno ghetto: "The children would play and laugh, and in their games the entire tragedy was reflected. They would play grave-digging: they would dig a pit and put a child inside and call him Hitler. And they would play at being gatekeepers of the ghetto. Some of the children played the parts of Germans; some of Jews, and the Germans were angry and would beat the other children who were Jews. And they used to play funerals."

So much for the form of a book which rests upon fact. Can such books written for young people flower into thought? Yes, if you bore into the subject with an eye sharpened by the need to see beyond fact to value and meaning. If you look for particulars that universalize experience and make it memorable. If you are concerned not with "covering a subject" as the curriculum-constructor thinks of it, but with discovering something meaningful in it and finding the language to bring the reader to the same moment of recognition.

In writing true history you are dealing not simply with the what and when of events but with the why and how. If you do not always have an easy time determining what happened and when, you are sure to have a much harder time finding out why and how it happened. For it brings you to the heart of what history is about—human behavior. This is the subject novelists deal with; it is just as much the subject for historians.

It is arguable whether history is any kind of guide, whether we have any lessons to learn from it. But even those who deny that the function of history is to be useful in a practical sense must accept the fact that it throws valuable light on human behavior—so illogical, so erratic, so unpredictable, and therefore so endlessly fascinating.

Studying the Holocaust and the behavior of human beings in that time we can detect a kind of logic in what happened. This is, of course, hindsight. Could we learn enough from it to be able to predict its repetition in the future? Not, I think, where it might happen, or when, or to whom, but only that it *could* happen again. And, I am afraid I have to say, that it is all the more likely to happen again because it has *already* happened.

Here I would like to single out one idea which runs throughout *Never to Forget*. It is that we should not see the destructive process of the Holocaust as the work of a small band of archcriminals led by a Svengali who took control of the minds of the German people and forced them to carry out an insane policy. On the contrary, the Holocaust can be better understood if we regard it as the expression of profound tendencies of modern civilization. Central among these tendencies is the bureaucratization of power. Mankind has known oppression through millennia of enforced servitude, from the ancient world down through American slavery. But it was modern methods of bureaucratization that made possible the expenditure of human life on such a scale and with such absolute ruthlessness as Auschwitz testifies to.

Bureaucratization is not, of course, uniquely Nazi nor uniquely German in its nature. It is a phenomenon of the twentieth century. Throughout my book I have made constant reference to this idea. The Jews were first defined as vermin by the German state bureaucracy. It became a matter of finding the most efficient way of disinfecting the world of Jews. As Himmler said, "Anti-Semitism is the same as delousing. Getting rid of lice is not a question of ideology; it is a matter of cleanliness." Having stripped the Jews of their humanity, the Germans saw no moral barrier to their annihilation. The first steps taken were to deprive the Jews of all property and citizenship rights. The final step was to eliminate these nonpersons altogether. And for that goal every sector of German society gave its full cooperation. The philosopher Richard Rubinstein, to whose insights we owe so much, put it this way: "The bureaucrats drew up the definitions and decrees; the churches gave evidence of Aryan descent; the postal authorities carried the messages of definition, expropriation, denaturalization, and deportation; business corporations dismissed their Jewish employees and took over 'Aryanized' properties; the railroads carried the victims to their place of execution, a place made available to the Gestapo and the SS by the Wehrmacht. . . . The operation required and received the participation of every major social, political and religious institution of the German Reich."

Nor did the Germans have to do it all alone. They found help whenever they needed it. Among the people of every nation they occupied; yes, in the ghettos and camps too. Among the Jews themselves were some who served the "master race" as police, spies, informers, and executioners.

Here, then, is the dark side of human personality, seen in action in contrast with its opposite, the faith, the dignity, the courage of those who resisted destruction in so many different ways. Civilization itself, like human character, has both sides. Again I draw on Richard Rubinstein: "Civilization," he writes, "means slavery, wars, exploitation, and death camps. It also means medical hygiene, elevated religious ideals, beautiful art, and exquisite music. It is an error to imagine that civilization and savage cruelty are antitheses. On the contrary, in every organic process, the antitheses always reflect a unified totality; and civilization is an organic process. Mankind has never emerged out of savagery into civilization. Mankind moved from one type of civilization involving its distinctive modes of both sanctity and inhumanity to another. In our times the cruelties, like most other aspects of our world, have become far more effectively administered than ever before. They have not and they will not cease to exist. Both creation and destruction are inseparable aspects of what we call civilization."

The effect of my book, I hope, is to bring the reader to think of man's nature as being neither good nor evil, but as containing both possibilities. We have the freedom to realize one or the other. "The power of choosing between good and evil is within the reach of all." If we do not allow our individual conscience to vanish in the face of "orders from above," if we persist in making our own judgments of right and wrong, if we do not let the state decide for us, if we take personal responsibility in questions of morality, then evil will be resisted.

The greatest sin is indifference. It is a sign of how dehumanized we have become. It is what can make us cogs in the machinery of destruction.

Now I come back to where I started—the possibilities of nonfiction writing for young readers. Does it have to be nothing but a pastiche of facts? Is there a function for the imagination? Is there room for ideas? for exercise of judgment? for the portrayal of character? for the illumination of human behavior? for the play of craftsmanship?

Of course there is. And teachers, librarians, reviewers, all of us simply as readers, must look for it, ask for it, point out where we find it, and where we miss it.

And, as writers, we must demand it of ourselves every time we sit down to the job.

Out in Space: A Look at Some Recent Nonfiction

Denise M. Wilms

Reviewing nonfiction books for children involves evaluation of a number of factors, the most important of which are content and readability. A reviewer begins to make judgments in these areas on the basis of his or her own knowledge of the subject and relative comparison of books already available on the topic. To illustrate how that process might work, I'm going to recount to you a reviewing experience that involved a number of books on the NASA Space Shuttle. These books were published in 1979, and one can presume by their simultaneous debut that they were meant to anticipate popular interest in the pending shuttle debut.

The first book that came to me was Charles Coombs' *Passage to Space*. I started reading it as a student might, without knowing much about space shuttles or what they're supposed to do.

The publisher's slip had said it was for fifth graders on up, and the format seemed to fit the fourth-fifth-sixth grade range: that is, the type was a bit large, but not too large; there was generous space between the lines; pages were nicely designed. As I began to read, the prose seemed a little cold, and the passive voice used in a brief history section became somewhat monotonous. But there was nothing drastic to complain about, and I kept on. Then I bumped into a phrase: *instrument payload*. Now, *payload* isn't an everyday word; I wondered if it would give pause to fifth graders. The text didn't explain it, though you could guess from the context. The glossary said "see cargo," and under *cargo* it read, "The total payload carried in the bay." There's nothing like a definition that uses the word you're trying to find out about.

And what about the word *bay*? It wasn't defined in the glossary, and by page three of the text, which is how far I'd gotten, it hadn't been defined in context either. Oh, well. I kept on reading.

There were more words, like *flightdeck, jettison, processing facility, pressurized module*. Now, you have probably heard of all these terms before, and from the context you might be able to snag their general

Reprinted from *Booklist* 76, no. 2:118–20 (Sept. 15, 1979), copyright © 1979 by the American Library Association.

meaning. But can fifth graders juggle with them? This book had a serious jargon overload, but I read on; if the jargon infestation was serious, it wasn't terminal.

Then I came to this sentence: "Two of the larger consoles are located at the rear of the flight deck, under a pair of windows facing aft into the unpressurized cargo bay amidships." I had to read that again, but I kept going. Then I read a section that told how mineral-rich blocks that have been mined on the moon could be "catapulted into space by a solar-powered electro-magnetic cannon-like acceleration device." Really? What does that mean?

By now I was reaching the end of my patience; I started to flip back through the pages just for a quick look at the pictures, diagrams, etc., and I found a series of captions describing a recovery system that is supposed to save rocket cases for future reuse. Caption number one said "nose cap deployment." OK. Fifth graders may or may not know what deployment means. If they've seen *Star Wars* or "Battlestar Galactica" there's a good chance they do. The number two caption said "drogue pack deployment." Now, *drogue* was a new word for me. The text didn't define it specifically, though from the picture you could tell it was some kind of parachute. The glossary didn't define it either. It was *Webster's* that told me it was, among other things, "a small parachute for stabilizing or decelerating something (as an astronaut's capsule) or for pulling a larger parachute out of stowage."

The third caption said "drogue shoot disreefs to full inflation." *Disreefs?* Another new word. Not in the glossary, either. And you know what? It wasn't in the dictionary! The jargon had just become terminal, and I decided not to recommend the book. There were other words here and there, and they were mostly to be found in the dictionary, but I decided most fifth and sixth graders weren't as friendly with the dictionary as I was.

I thought that was the end of it, when suddenly four more space shuttle books turned up. Since I had dealt with this first book I was the one who got to look at the new crop. Two were alleged to be for fifth graders on up; one was an adult book that looked as if junior high and high school students could get something out of it. I also found a title we had recommended for junior high students at an earlier date and decided to gather them all together and see how they compared with each other. What I found was most interesting.

Like the Coombs book, two of these titles were aimed at middle-grade audiences: *America's Space Shuttle* by Lee Priestley (Messner) and *The Space Shuttle* by Frank Ross (Lothrop). These two looked different and read differently. The Priestley book was closest to the beginner's format that marked the first title I had just turned down. Ross's space shuttle book was older looking, with smaller print and lines closer together. I began to read it.

The first thing I noticed was some attention to defining terms. For example, on the first page of text there is this sentence: "During the pre-Shuttle years of space activities, sending a cargo, or *payload,* into *orbit* aboard an unmanned launch vehicle cost approximatelly $600 to $700 per pound." In this sentence the words *payload* and *orbit* are quietly italicized; *payload* is defined in context, and the word *orbit* is defined in the glossary. As I read on, however, it was clear this book would find an older audience than the publisher's slip suggested. Sentences tended to be long; in fact, a Fry Graph testing indicated a tenth-grade reading level. There was also a style problem, with occasional windy sentences to get through, one of which follows:

> Some of the hundreds of engineering problems that needed solution before a manned spacecraft could be launched into orbit around the earth included development of practical and enormously powerful rocket motors for accelerating manned or unmanned spacecraft fast enough to counter the force of gravity and to achieve earth orbit; . . .

That's only the first clause of a three-clause sentence. Thankfully the other two aren't as unwieldy.

If you keep reading, however, you'll notice that if the writing isn't always graceful, there *is* more of an effort to steer clear of loose jargon. I decided to compare some definitions where there was overlapping coverage with the two other middle-grade books. Here is Ross's definition of the space shuttle orbiter, the part that looks like an airplane and was designed to circle the Earth in space:

> The orbiter's body is divided into three sections: a crew-passenger compartment at the forward end, a cargo bay, and a tail section housing the three main rocket engines and two orbital maneuvering rocket engines.

Coombs had said,

> From front to rear, the three primary sections of the orbiter are the forward crew and passenger compartment; the cargo bay, which occupies the mid-fuselage; and the aft-fuselage area, which carries the rocket engines and supports the wing and rudder.

This second definition is the longer and more complicated of the two thanks to syntax and the words *aft* and *fuselage,* yet it came from a book that is designed for a younger audience. Incidentally, the Coombs book tested out at a tenth-grade reading level.

A third orbiter description comes from Priestley's space shuttle book, which tested out at a sixth-grade level and was the least technical of the trio and the only one accessible to an average middle-grade reader. He says, in lengthier but simpler fashion,

> The 120 foot length of the Orbiter provides a cabin for the crew and passengers and a cargo bay for the payload [*payload* is defined in the glossary]. . . . The cabin has three decks, or sections, for working and living. The upper section is the flight deck; the mid-section contains living quarters; the lower section is filled with life support systems. Those sys-

tems supply air to breathe, power to light and heat or cool the cabin, equipment for storing wastes, preserving food, and water.

As you can see, he has made no formal mention of a specific rocket engine tail section, but on the facing page there is a cutaway view of the orbiter with a caption that reviews the sections he's just listed and also specifically notes a tail section where the engines are housed. So, he does offer the same information as the other two books, but in simpler words and sentences that compensate for extra length.

Up to this point you can see my probing has had to do with appropriate writing style and readability. This isn't always an area so specifically examined in nonfiction, but the handling of technical content in these books suggested a possible problem that turned out to be very real: of the three books allegedly for the same middle age group, there's only one that's in the grasp of the average reader. It's true that highly interested kids may well make a reading-level jump and not mind the jargon and technical nature of the explanations. But these books aren't designed for special readers. With the space shuttle a reality in the 1980s, one assumes that the appearance of five books dealing with the subject at once anticipates general interest. Boys and girls with school reports due on the shuttle need something they can read and understand. So does the browser who is not a dedicated space buff. So far only one book out of three will help the middle grader. Good junior high readers can handle Ross's tenth-grade writing level in his space shuttle book, and they won't mind the format. But the rejected book, with its young-looking format and tenth-grade reading level, is likely to be avoided by both older and younger audiences.

There are two other books, however, two *older* books, and they provide a backdrop for questions about content. The titles are *Space Shuttle* by L. B. Taylor (Crowell), and an adult book called *Shuttle* by Robert Powers (Stackpole Books). Reading through them prompts questions not only of style but also of content. For the record, the Powers adult book tested out at an eleventh-grade reading level, so did the Taylor shuttle book. Both of them made for unexpectedly interesting reading, and it wasn't simply because they were older books. Specifically it had to do with writing style and content. These books had their technical information, tempered with a bit of grace. Consider this sentence: "Like an old whaling ship of the last century, the orbiter is full of nooks and crannies in which gear and equipment are stowed." That's not a complicated sentence. It's simple and vivid, and it came from the *adult* shuttle book.

In terms of content, the Powers book in particular had a good store of colorful detail, much of which would interest children. Listen to the contrasts. Where a children's book told me "Scholarships for high school and university students interested in science are another spinoff from the shuttle flights," Powers told me, "A high school student, future undergraduate at Utah State University, will orbit an experiment dealing with bacteria growth in zero-g, in this case the bacteria which cause tooth decay." Powers also told me that a Boy Scout troop will be sending an experiment up and that a Dallas retailer who wanted to send his gerbils into orbit so he could get a better price for them at Neiman Marcus was refused space on a shuttle flight.

A children's book gave me general information. "Some of the experiments to be carried out on board the Spacelab will be in such areas as metallurgy (the creation of new alloys), medicine, and biology." Powers told me specifically that "Volkswagen has reserved shuttle cargo space to test manufacturing in weightlessness" and that "Johnson and Johnson will carry out experiments in separating chemical constituents of the human blood." These examples show that you *can* zero in on interesting specifics without getting complicated, without sacrificing basic information in other areas. It's a matter of choice shaped by an awareness of the human side of the issue.

Each of these two books also broached an issue others did not, namely, possible dangers in the shuttle flight and criticism of cost. Former astronaut Michael Collins explains in his introduction to the Powers book that there will be no unmanned test flight of the shuttle; also that the shuttle cannot pull away from its two booster rockets if something goes wrong; and that there will be no ejection seats after the first manned test flights are finished. None of the other four books mentioned these factors or hinted at risks.

Taylor's space shuttle book contains a chapter called "Costs and Critics" that addresses common complaints about the space program and answers them with NASA arguments. It's questionable how balanced that chapter really is, but its presence at least tacitly acknowledges that the space program could be open to criticism. None of the other books deals so forwardly with the question. And, in fact, a short space of time has proven all the books to be distinctly rosy-eyed on the shuttle's development and capabilities. The program has been plagued with scheduling setbacks, cost overruns, and technical problems that raise questions about its overall safety and effectiveness. These problems were present or pending at the time of the books' authorship, yet all but two remained unquestioning, and the scant negative comment that these two offered was hardly penetrating in light of concerns that persist despite a successful maiden flight.

A final area where all of the books need temperance is that of future space projects. Grandiose drawing-board schemes need to be clearly separated from what is already definitely planned. Descriptions of future space travel and colonization must dispense with rose-colored glasses. How credible is this statement on a visionary space colony from Ross's book?

> Life in this man-made space settlement would not be much different from that on earth. There would be comfortable housing, factories for work, and play facilities. Trees and grass would relieve the starkness of

the surrounding space world, along with walks and bicycle paths winding their way through the greenery.

Even if such a dream should become reality, where is the human factor here? Where is there room for individuality, fallibility? Where is the social dimension? The description is an unthinking one.

By now you can see that all of these books have shortcomings, some of them serious. The definitive space shuttle book has yet to be written. These books and their problems remind us of some simple truths in nonfiction writing. Nonfiction conveys information. Anyone producing it is bound to do so with accuracy and balance and with a measure of grace and style. Accuracy means making sure that what is written is the best version of the truth that can be found. Balance is an element of accuracy. It's sorting through facts with a wise eye and ear; it means being critically informative, pointing to weaknesses as well as strengths, the real as well as the ideal. These things are all easier said than done, but writers who weave these elements smoothly are to be applauded. It takes talent, wise judgment, knowledge, personal involvement, and integrity to do it right. When it's wrong, the writing is canned and sterile, the content distorted in varying degrees. In the case of the books here, the result was overly technical texts that assumed too much on the part of young readers. Why wasn't more of an effort made to bring the content in line with a younger audience: to interpret and popularize without sacrificing authenticity? Why does an adult book, ironically, have the kind of detail that will interest children? All but one of these books will probably be recommended by *Booklist*, not because they're especially good, but because they'll fill a need. Each has particular strengths; most have serious weaknesses. They'll provide information, but at a cost in reader tolerance. They're going to stand as reminders of what needs to be done.

Science:

The Excitement
of Discovery

A child's instinct to learn comes from his wonderings, his curiosity. The more open his mind to wonder, the more sensitive he is to the satisfactions and enjoyments our earthly life affords. If he grows insensible to these because his natural, eager curiosity has nothing to feed upon, the result is boredom; a boredom caused by the lack of those resources of the mind which find never-failing interest in the wonder of the universe.

——Lillian Smith[1]

Clarity in Science Writing

Jo Carr

The science books now being produced are impressive. They reveal the world of science in all its fascinating variety: plate tectonics, the Big Bang, carbon dating, penguins, mathematical games, baby pandas, zoo doctors, oceanography, talking chimpanzees, potatoes, Aztec counting systems, Bigfoot, microbes, supermachines, and more.

The realm of science is not only varied, it is also extremely complex. For these reasons the professional scientist, as author, needs masterly skills in simplifying and synthesizing information so that the reader, whether layperson or a child with limited knowledge and experience, can understand. Fortunately many scientists have perfected expository methods that effectively translate scientific concepts into language understandable and exciting to children and the rest of us. But first comes knowledge. The writer must be qualified to write on the subject, preferably at a professional level. Although such professionalism can almost be assumed these days, at least in books from reputable publishers, we still need to check credentials, as well as reviews. More on this later.

The writer must also be able to organize facts into a tight exposition of an idea or ideas. The organization of information or lack of it, constitutes one of the major weaknesses in science books for children, as it does for nonfiction generally, for that matter. Frequently the book may try to cover too much, thereby becoming nothing more than taxonomy. Ideally, the scope of the book should permit the writer to make a statement, and then explore it logically. In any case, it should be clear from the writing which ideas are more important than others, which facts support other facts. This can be done either inductively or deductively, either by starting with a generalization and examining particulars to determine the validity of the generalization, or by starting from particulars to see what kind of generalization may emerge from them. But some logical development of ideas is necessary, both in order to clarify the subject and to hold the reader's attention to the end.

Laurence Pringle is superb at this. Very often he so narrows the scope of his book that he can pursue one idea to a satisfactory resolution. In *Death Is Natural*, for instance, he starts with the question "Is death always a bad thing or can it have good effects?" He then demonstrates how a dead animal serves as food for other animals and eventually enriches the soil. From there he explores the role of death in evolution and ends with the answer to his original question: "The earth's elements flow on, from one living thing to another. There is beauty, variety, and change, and death helps make it all possible."[1] When you further note in this book an excellent bibliography for further reading, an index, a clear table of contents, together with good photographs appropriately placed, you recognize the work of a superior, well-organized non-fiction writer.

It is more difficult to structure material in a longer book. Yet Robert McClung keeps a firm hand on the controls as he pilots his readers on a tour of the natural world, past and present, in his book *Lost Wild Worlds*. To accomplish this, he approaches different geographical areas and, following a brief history of mankind, discusses birds and mammals that have died out over the centuries. The information in each chapter, clearly arranged chronologically, is further clarified by headings and subheadings. Across all the continents and all the centuries walks Homo sapiens, sometimes destroying the environment, sometimes preserving it. By relating quantities of information to one theme, the symbiotic partnership between humans and animals, Robert McClung has achieved a sense of unity that carries the reader to the logical conclusion:

> The passenger pigeon, the Carolina parakeet, the dodo, and most of the other recently extinct animals disappeared because they were unable to change their ways when faced with harmful conditions brought about by human beings. The sands of natural evolution grind exceedingly slow, and none of the higher animals, *except* man, can adapt quickly to extensive changes in their environment. Human beings are unique in the fact that they *can* change their ways quickly when the need arises. The important questions are: *will* we, and will we change before it is too late?[2]

Contrast the organization in the Pringle and McClung books with that of Marilyn Burns in her *Good for Me: All about Food in 32 Bites* (Little, 1978). A long book, printed in double columns, it covers everything one ever wanted to know about food, but try to find it. There is no discernible organization and no index. Many of the chapters listed in the table of contents have maddeningly vague headings: "Some Tasty Information," "Food, Food, Everywhere," "Your First Taste" are examples. Although each chapter does contain subheadings to distinguish particular aspects of a larger topic, the chapters themselves have no logical relationship to each other. And in each the reader plods from one fact to another: "Vegetables are absolutely necessary for good health." "Natural foods are foods that haven't changed in any way before you buy them." "There are about 7,000 varieties of apples." Not only does this inevitably result in confusion for the reader of such a hodgepodge of information, but the ultimate result is boredom, a natural outcome of confusion.

Once the material in a science book has been tightly organized, the author obviously needs to present it as clearly as possible. Since scientific concepts often are extremely complicated, as well as abstract, writers of science books for children must be able to use language with precision. Although this is not the place to discuss their expository methods in detail, brief examples can illustrate some of the most important techniques they use. Note how many of those techniques take the reader from what is known to what is unknown. How many involve the reader, demanding participation. How many clarify by making it possible to visualize what is being described.

Analogy
> Think of a perfectly round ball. It has no front or back, no right or left. Now imagine the ball sailing through endless space, occasionally bumping into things and bouncing off them but not going anywhere in particular. There is no up or down in such space. The ball, if it could have any experience, would live in a space without dimension or direction. There are very small animals that live in a space similar to that.
> ———Judith and Herbert Kohl, *View from the Oak* (Scribner, 1977)

Metaphor
> Microbes are nature's recyclers.
> ———Lucia Anderson, *The Smallest Life around Us* (Crown, 1978)

"You" and "I" as a way to involve the reader
> Suppose you could put yourself forward in time, into the end of the 21st century. What would your fellow citizens be like?
> ———Jeanne Bendick, *Super People: Who Will They Be?* (McGraw-Hill, 1980)
>
> I've just seen a wild mouse—smooth, sleek, darting across the sinktop. I'm going to try to sketch him.
> ———Irene Brady, *Wild Mouse* (Scribner, 1976)

Simile
> In this miniature jungle, where wars for survival are constant, this monstrous little cannibal [a fish] swings from frond to frond like a monkey.
> ———Francine Jacobs, *The Sargasso Sea: An Ocean Desert* (Morrow, 1975)

Experiment
> Here are four ways you can grow your own microbes. 1) Take a paper towel. . . .
> ———Lucia Anderson, *The Smallest Life around Us* (Crown, 1978)

Questions
> Have you ever thought about the mountain parts in your house? Not the occasional pebble you pick up in your shoe, but the rocks that hold your house together? Or the minerals that you sprinkle on your dinner? Or the rocks that you use to brush your teeth?
> ———Linda Allison, *Wild Inside: Sierra Club's Guide to the Great Indoors* (Sierra Club/Scribner, 1979)

Challenging opening sentences
> HIGH SCHOOL STUDENTS IN MICHIGAN FALL SICK WITH HEPATITIS.
> MYSTERY DISEASE FELLS DOZENS AT AMERICAN LEGION CONVENTION.
> These headlines appeared recently in newspapers. Each one

tells of an epidemic. . . . In each of these epidemics, disease detectives were called on for their help.

————Melvin Berger, *Disease Detectives* (Crowell, 1978)

Clear, catchy title

Catch the Wind: A Book of Windmills and Windpower

————Landt Dennis (Four Winds, 1976)

Telling a story

In that terrible storm no one had a clear view of what happened. . . . Only one thing was soon clear. The high girders had given way and plunged the entire train to the icy, storm-tossed waters 88 feet below.

————Scott Corbett, *Bridges* (Four Winds, 1978)

Vivid detail

Because it was the middle of winter, a wet season, water filtered down through the soil above and dripped steadily into the big room. The water fed two or three shallow pools. It glistened on the surfaces of long, slender, yellow and white stalactites and dripped from their tips.

————George Laycock, *Caves* (Four Winds, 1976)

Clear, simple sentences

But where does the popcorn come from? To find out, you have to find the flowers. Popcorn and all corn plants have two kinds of flowers; male and female. The male flowers produce pollen. They are found in the pale-brown tassels at the top of the plant. The female flowers are in the ear, which forms in the angles of the leaves on the lower part of the plant.

————Millicent Selsam, *Popcorn* (Morrow, 1976)

Glossary, or other appended matter

————David E. Fisher, *The Creation of Atoms and Stars* (Holt, 1979)

Bibliography and index

————Laurence Pringle, *Nuclear Power from Physics to Politics* (Macmillan, 1979)

A skilled writer combines these techniques in all kinds of variations. Here is an example of one clear scientific explanation that embodies many of the points just made. It will come as no surprise to note that the author is a teacher. (The italicized words are defined in the book's glossary.)

Scientists think that shortly after the Big Bang, most of the particles flying out into space hooked together into tiny *atoms*. These are so small that millions of them make up the period at the end of this sentence. But atoms are the building blocks of everything we see around us.

Almost all the atoms formed right after the Big Bang were *hydrogen*, the smallest and simplest atom in the universe. A few were slightly bigger atoms called *helium*. Scientists think these were the only kinds of atoms formed right after the Big Bang. There are more than a hundred kinds of atoms today, but in the beginning there were only two.

Why did the particles from the Big Bang hook together into atoms? Why didn't they keep flying out into space forever? The answer is that these particles respond to something called *electromagnetic force*, which pulls them together like little magnets. This force was at work from the beginning of the universe, for reasons that no one can explain.

Another mysterious force is *gravity*, which pulls groups of atoms together. As countless hydrogen and helium atoms flew out into space, they swirled in whirlpools and began to collect in larger and larger clouds. The larger an object is, the stronger its gravity becomes; each cloud was like a giant vacuum cleaner, pulling in more hydrogen and helium from space. The atoms they captured made them even more massive, which made their gravity even stronger, which pulled in still more atoms, and so on until each cloud was gigantic.

When anything is squeezed hard enough, it begins to heat up. Inside these giant balls, the gravity was so powerful and squeezed the atoms so hard that they began to burn. Scientists have calculated that this happens when there are about 1,000,000,000,000,000,000,000,000,000,000-000,000,000,000,000,000,000,000,000 (10 with 56 more zeros on the ends which scientists write 10^{57}) hydrogen and helium atoms pulled together in one place. These burning fireballs were the first stars.[3]

Although the foregoing selection from *The Story of Life: From the Big Bang to You* by Kim Marshall may not achieve literary distinction—in other words, it may not be "literature of fact," as discussed earlier in this book—the clear exposition of information satisfies the primary objective of factual writing.

Words are not the only tools used for clarification by nonfiction writers. In Millicent Selsam's *Popcorn* the definitions quoted earlier are accompanied by clear color photographs of ears of corn. Pictures in this instance reinforce the text, because they often clarify or convey meaning to children that words alone cannot. The use of illustrations is one great advantage that the children's science writer has over one whose books and articles are intended for adults. After all, writers for children are almost expected to use photographs, illustrations, maps, diagrams, cartoons, graphs, drawings, or any combination of media. Well-chosen and well-executed illustrations not only clarify science, they also seduce the child into reading what ordinarily might seem boring.

That illustration is a useful means of conveying information to children—and to adults, for that matter—can be seen in David Macaulay's book *Underground* (Houghton, 1976). If we were to descend physically into the stratum of sewers and pipes under a city street, we would probably come away less informed, and certainly less entertained, than we are after studying his detailed drawings. The botanical illustrations of Anne Ophelia Dowden in *This Noble Harvest: A Chronicle of Herbs* (Collins, 1979) not only present clear information about plants but transform that information into art; the simple drawings of Anthony Ravielli have done the same for evolution in his book *From Fins to Hands* (Viking, 1968). And the representational drawings of Jan Adkins can explain almost anything. Imagine trying to explain in words alone the technique for tying a ring hitch, or how to operate a "luff," to say nothing of a "comealong," or the best way to move a piano. His clear illustrations in *Moving Heavy Things* (Houghton, 1980) are reinforced by equally clear verbal instructions, a combination that is hard to beat in nonfiction books for children.

Although illustrations can be extremely effective in explaining or demonstrating a scientific concept, they can also confuse the reader if they are poorly executed, inaccurate, or inappropriately placed in relation to the text. Size relationships can be especially confusing. When, for instance, a drawing of an armadillo is the same size as that of a beetle on the opposite page, some child, after reading the book, might spend time looking for a beetle straight out of science fiction or a minuscule armadillo because it is an animal unfamiliar to many children. The most disturbing misuse of graphics, however, results when "cutesy" illustrations not only compromise the precision we expect in books dealing with science but insult the intelligence of children.

This brings us to the prime responsibility of a science writer for children: projecting what we recognize as scientific method and scientific attitude in the treatment of a scientific subject. Millicent Selsam has given us valuable guidelines here, not only in her comments on the subject of science writing, but also in her science books themselves. Her books always "involve" the reader in questioning, experimenting, reasoning. Her language, although simple and direct, includes technical words like "endosperm" and "plumule," always clearly defined in text and pictures. At all times she treats children with respect.

Respect is important. A reader who is assumed to be intelligent will take from an author's work the message that, although science is fun, it is fun that is disciplined, logical, and demanding. As many of the commentators in this collection have pointed out, we should be justly suspicious of the "gee-whiz" approach to science. Lack of documentation or oversimplification should never compromise the essential spirit of the scientific method. Does a child really need to be lured into reading a book about physiology, for instance, by a gimmicky title like *Blood and Guts: A Working Guide to Your Own Insides* by Linda Allison (Little, 1976)? Surely not. Then again, perhaps so. Since it is admittedly difficult to persuade some children to read anything these days, a certain amount of "hype" might be just the thing to move a science book off the shelf. If this is true, we need to ask, "How true?"

Kathryn Wolff, in her article in this book, has commented on the problem of enticing children to read about science. She admits that the built-in excitement of straight science may be only an acquired taste for those children who have already found pleasure in the 500s and 600s. We have to get them there first, obviously.

Books that lure children into the many realms of science are attractive to look at and exciting to read. Lively, informal writing is one of the ingredients that can pull a reader into the subject almost effortlessly. Humor too can be a godsend, as will be pointed out later. But one quality is probably more seductive than all the others put together. This quality is emotion. Readers who are not inordinately interested in scientific subjects, as well as those who are, need to feel deeply about something in science before they can think deeply about it. After all, many adults have developed an appreciation of science first through the writing of such romantics as Rachel Carson and Loren Eiseley and Carl Sagan. Why not children?

Many kinds of books have emotional appeal—books about dinosaurs, space, underwater exploration, archeology, unexplained phenomena, to name only a few—but those that deal with animals seem to have the greatest appeal to the widest range of readers. What child can fail to be moved when the old elephant dies soon after the death of his mate in *Zoo Year* (Lippincott, 1978) by Alice Schick and Sara Ann Friedman? Or by Carol Fenner's *Gorilla Gorilla* (Random, 1973) in which soft, charcoal drawings and poetic text pull the reader emotionally into the story of the gorilla's capture and captivity? Once books like these are introduced to a classroom of children they pass from hand to hand as quickly as comic books.

Nature books too are appealing. Victor Scheffer's *The Seeing Eye* (Scribner, 1971) is a good example. As a study of form, color, and texture in nature, its photographs and text demonstrate clearly the integral connection between art and science: "And when you look time and again at fallen leaves all powdered with frost, and at porous gray stones at the edge of the sea, and at fruits of the wild rose burning roundly and redly in the shadows, and at a thousand other images of beauty, you are on the way to appreciation both of man's art and of his science."[4] Never mind the 574 number on the spine; the emotional appeal in this book is as strong as that in poetry. Berniece Freschet has woven a similar kind of magic in her *Year on Muskrat Marsh* (Scribner, 1974) when she describes "the soft, clear call of the whippoorwill drifting across the marshland." Examples of such emotional force are to be found in many fine science books, according to Zena Sutherland in her article, "Science as Literature."

However, emotion should not be confused with emotionalism, which in science writing bears watching. Emotion can easily become sentimentality, a quality the British sometimes call "twee." Our resistance to "twee" books has fortunately stiffened over the years, as a glance at older science books will demonstrate. Yet even today we must contend with the twee adventures of "Cubby Bear" and "Ollie Otter" in the Ranger Rick books and suffer the capers of the Berenstain Bears.

After emotion comes humor, effectively used by any number of writers in delightful variety. Tomie de Paola delivers information to younger children in crazy packages labeled *The Popcorn Book* (Holiday, 1978) and *The Quicksand Book* (Holiday, 1977), among others. Jan Adkins demonstrates locomotion with pictures of a coffin being moved on marbles, a boat on bacon rind, and a tombstone on ice cubes. David Macaulay even draws an alligator in a sewer pipe, just for the fun of it. And no harm done.

When is harm done? Perhaps when an author, writing in a breezy style and treating facts with casual nonchalance, flagrantly undermines the discipline and spirit of scientific inquiry. For instance, in order to persuade children that science is fun, does an author need to write like this? "Bacteria are teeny little creatures, and they like your mouth a lot." Or is it necessary for writing to be ungrammatical to be readable? "Your brain will send the signal for saliva even if you just see or smell or even when you think of something that is real tasty." Or, in order to appeal to reluctant readers, is it necessary to draw cartoons that are not in scale, and ugly as well? All these examples are taken, once again, from *Good for Me*, a book that might have been good with heavy editing. Although the author's lively writing stresses the excitement of inquiry and experimentation, this simply is not enough to save the book. The organization of the book is so weak, the writing so inexact, the graphics so misleading, and the over-all approach so "gee-whiz" that the book does not pass muster as acceptable science writing.

But how are we to know which books do measure up? When does a light-hearted writing style, for instance, compromise a serious scientific subject? When does humor go too far? When are cartoon illustrations appropriate, if ever? When does readability undermine accuracy in what should be a reasoned approach to a subject like nuclear power? When does a sense of wonder degenerate into sentimentality?

Those of us who are not scientists by profession are seldom equipped to answer these questions, but fortunately we can rely on people who are. To the enrichment of us all, scientists themselves review children's science books. So in our fumbling efforts to separate books of solid science from those that are not, these reviewers can alert us to distortions of fact, to approaches inappropriate to proper scientific exploration, to unqualified authorship. When a book like *Wild Inside*, for instance, wins an award from the New York Academy of Sciences, we can stifle any doubts we might have had that its cartoon-like drawings are "unscientific." Or we can be reassured by a science reviewer about David E. Fisher's citation in the bibliography for *The Creation of Atoms and Stars*: "Einstein, Albert, *Die Grundlage der Allgemeinen Relativitatstheorie.* . . . ," with his note to the reader, "Go ahead, I dare you." The scientist who reviewed this book concedes that the author's style is flip at times, but this in no way modifies the over-all evaluation, "Buy the book!"[5] Such reassurance is what we need if we are troubled about the qualifications of an author who makes jokes about Albert Einstein.

Why is it that scientists themselves review books for children, while professional historians seldom review either children's history or children's biography? Is it because science seems such a technical subject to most of us that we think we need a scientist to review a science book, although we consider ourselves competent enough to evaluate history or biography? If this is our reason we could be wrong, as is pointed out in the discussion of reviewing in "What Do We Do about Bad Biographies?"

In any case, for whatever reasons, the reviews of practicing scientists do set a high standard for accuracy and clarity in science writing. And these expert reviewers may be making a significant difference in the quality of books being published. Virginia Buckley, in an *Appraisal* article called "Editing Science Books," discusses the degree to which an editor can be influenced by a reviewer's criticism. She says, for instance, that she was inclined to agree with the reaction of an *Appraisal* reviewer to a book of theirs: "My own feeling is that the drawings were aimed at an older age group and this, perhaps, was the reviewer's point."[6] Buckley is one editor who is obviously perceptive and responsive.

Since such reviews are considered to be important and apparently are making a difference in the quality of science publishing for children, it may be useful to discuss these specialized journals briefly.

Science Books and Films, published by the American Association for the Advancement of Science, comes out five times a year. Kathryn Wolff describes their highly professional approach to reviewing in her article "Reviewing Science Books for Children."

Appraisal: Science Books for Young People, published three times a year, has made a significant contribution to the reviewing of children's science books. Each book is reviewed, and rated, by both a librarian and by a science specialist. With one reviewer evaluating the book for scientific accuracy and another considering the child's reaction to the book, a different consideration altogether, we can hardly ask for better critical appraisal.

Horn Book, while not a specialized science review journal, as are the others described here, does offer a special feature of in-depth reviews to science books. The two reviewers are science teachers—Sarah Gagné, who reviews books in the biological sciences, and Harry C. Stubbs, author of two articles in this collection, who writes about books in the physical sciences.

Science and Children, published eight times a year, for science teachers in the elementary grades, and *The Science Teacher,* published nine times a year, for high school science teachers, are both published by the National Science Teachers Association. The review committee, composed of science teachers and educators and affiliated with the Science Teaching Center at the University of Maryland, turns out knowledgeable reviews. In addition to reviewing books in these two journals, the National Science Teachers Association also puts out each year a list of "the best" science books entitled "Outstanding Science Trade Books for Children." This list, which appears in one of the spring issues of *Science and Children*, is also available from the Children's Book Council.

Scientific American in its December issue presents a list of the year's best science books for children, selected and discussed by Philip and Phylis Morrison. Unlike other best-books-of-the-year lists in which descriptions either are lacking or too brief to be useful, the long, analytical annotations by the Morrisons are not only unusually thoughtful and instructive, they are a genuine pleasure to read. Philip Morrison, by the way, is a physics professor at M.I.T.

Scientists have made their influence felt, not only by reviewing books in these journals, but also by awarding prizes for outstanding science writing, illustrating, and editing. The New York Academy of Sciences deserves special praise for the yearly awards it has instituted. These, and other nonfiction awards, are listed in Appendix A.

Reviews in the six journals described earlier, as well as prizes reflecting official recognition of exemplary publishing, take on special significance when we realize that they supplement reviews in standard review sources. No wonder science books have flourished under this hawk-eye vigilance!

One example of that vigilance follows. Imagine how an editor, let alone an author, might feel after reading this review in *Appraisal:*

> [This book] does not succeed very well in any of its purposes. Its weakest point is in "principles." Some basic ones are omitted, misstated or stated in meaningless terms. For example, day-length (or more accurately, night-length) is never mentioned as important to the production of flowers and vegetables. The brown dots on the backs of fern leaves are spore cases, *not* spores. Each contains thousands of the dust-like spores. One should not summarize a list that includes ferns and mosses (which do not bloom at all) as blooming the same way. What does it mean to say that seed coat splitting is caused by "the combination of water, moisture and humidity"? It is all H_2O in my book. Dandelion seeds are *not* dust-like and *do* have parachutes, whereas ash seed wings are not usually thought of as parachutes and usually *do not* carry the ash seed great distances, relatively speaking. Unfortunately the directions are not always crystal clear or complete either, and the illustrations do not compensate. Often a confusing maneuver, such as the sequence of seed, soil and second glass slide in the seed sandwich, is bracketed but not addressed by diagrams. Diagrams are often cluttered and confusing, as in parts of a flower. Worse, they show errors of plant structure, such as giving dandelions leaves on their flower stalks and leaving seed leaves on the bean underground. The absence of *any* illustrations in the first three chapters makes it unlikely that the "pleasures" of plants will captivate a ten-year-old sufficiently to lead him or her on to chapter four. Lastly, the choice of projects often seems unsuitable for a child and, combined with the above problems, is a set-up for sure failure.[7]

Although devastating reviews like the foregoing, and others less strident but equally sharp, may have had some influence on editors, they probably have less impact on librarians who are buying science books for school libraries. The number of subscribers to *Science Books and Films* is small, incredibly small when one considers the importance of the service being offered and the number of libraries in the country. Although it is true that elementary school librarians themselves might not have budget money for this professional journal, media center administrators in school districts surely could afford to circulate it among librarians. *Appraisal* is now reaching more librarians than it did, but it still needs to reach many more. Frankly, when one realizes how poorly informed most librarians are in the sciences, it seems hardly defensible to ignore these sources for selection.

School librarians are not really to blame. Many of them have never heard of these professional reviewing sources. Schools of education, which are usually responsible for training school librarians, are often weak in promoting professional library sources. Unfortunately education professors themselves are often unaware of the rich resources familiar even to the most inexperienced graduate of an accredited library school. The same is true of media center administrators. So it goes. There may be. no easy answer to this problem.

In fact, lack of professionalism in buying science books for schools may reflect a general lack of interest in science itself on the part of most adults, both in and out of schools. Dennis Flanagan, in an article in this collection, makes a convincing analysis of the antiscientific bias in our society—or if not "antiscientific" at least "unscientific." He is probably dead right.

So it is adults we need to worry about, not children. Children, being born with curiosity, take to science like ducks to water. And, as they search in books for "facts," they may discover much beyond facts. They may find in science the stimulus to logical thinking. They may find structure and order, a kind of predictability, that can offer comfort in what seems to be an erratic world. But, most of all, they may begin to sense the emotional thrill felt by the scientist who is pursuing answers to fundamental questions. So they too may begin to ask questions, some of them deeply important, not only questions that can be answered by teachers and other books but also questions that can be answered only by the universe itself: Why? Why not? How? How much? How often? How many? When? In what order? To what degree? And, with one question following another, the world is revealed as being larger and richer than ever imagined. Eyes and ears open, every child may glimpse a universe waiting to be explored.

Reviewing Science Books for Children

Kathryn Wolff

No one living in today's world can ignore science and its products. It is also clear that, in order to use the sciences to promote human welfare—"welfare" being defined by the people affected—there must be substantial public understanding of the possible uses of science and of the potential difficulties its uses pose. Thus the need for a scientifically "literate" population. Unfortunately, just how a reasonable degree of science literacy can be developed in either adults or children remains a matter of considerable dispute, even after 30 years of study and concern.

There is little evidence that most of the adult population can be influenced to increase their general understanding of science, but children, especially those in grades 1 through 8, are usually open to new experiences and eager to acquire information on the what, how, and why of everything they see around them.[1] Yet, in spite of many new curriculum projects in elementary science and much other work in the last three decades, books from the classroom, library, or home shelves must still supply much—or all—of the science information which is acquired by the typical elementary school child. If the available science books are interesting and accurate, the young reader will be well served. If the books (and other media) are not accurate, the errors learned may never be corrected. And if the materials are dull, science may be a "closed book" for the individual for the rest of his or her life.

Book publishers have provided a flood of books for young people on a multitude of science topics. Some publishers are very careful and employ competent consultants familiar with each particular field of science. Other publishers, even some of the biggest, seem more interested in return on investment than in accuracy or intellectual quality. Conscientious librarians, educators, and parents know that the problems of selection are real, and know as well that they need critical and reliable determinants of quality, content, and appropriate age level for all those attractive and colorful science books so potentially important to every child.

None of us can be expert in all of the many fields of science, so, to

Adapted from "AAAS Science Books: A Selection Tool," by Kathryn Wolff (*Library Trends* 22, no. 4:453–62 [April 1974]). Copyright © 1974 by the Board of Trustees of the University of Illinois.

judge books, we turn to book reviews. That leads, of course, to the problem of judging the credibility of the book reviews themselves. I believe that judgment is best made by examining (1) the purposes of the organization publishing the reviews; (2) the nominal standard to which the reviewers adhere, (3) the ability and willingness of the reviewers to conform to these standards, and (4) the adequacy of the standards for making appropriate selection for a particular audience.

I can speak with personal knowledge of one such reviewing situation, that at the Association for the Advancement of Science. One of our journals is *Science Books and Films* (originally *Science Books: A Quarterly Review*), now in its sixteenth year. Prior to the publication of the first issue, its editor and an editorial board of scientists, librarians, and educators established these criteria for science book reviews:[2]

Authorship—Does the author have the scientific qualifications to write a book on a particular subject?

Subject and Content—Is the subject of fundamental interest and importance to the prospective reader? Is it handled in sufficient depth so that it will constitute worthwhile learning experience? Is the organization logical? (If the book answers the fundamental questions of "how" and "why" using appropriate technical terms, it is probably worthwhile; if it is a superficial survey covering too broad a scope, perhaps it should be avoided.)

Illustrations—Are the photographs and drawings accurate and are they accompanied by adequate explanatory legends keyed directly to the text? Mere embellishments that add nothing to the text are seldom worthwhile.

Vocabulary—Most young children can and should read any words that are the best choice for expressing scientific ideas and concepts. "Controlled vocabularies" are totally unnecessary. With pronunciation markings and definitions either in the text or in a glossary, a reader of any age can understand and learn to use correct technical terms.

Biographies—Science biographies for children and young people should be written as contributions, showing professional attainments and associations. A fictionalized biography that relies heavily on manufactured conversation and relates nonessential personal details may be interesting reading, but it has no value in science education.

Nature Study Versus Science—Animal tales and folklore have their place, particularly for preschoolers. In school, children deserve more substantial fare—no talking animals, no anthropomorphisms, no "Dick-and-Jane" reading matter. Material taught in terms of biological science (Who? How? Why?) is interesting and enables students to "get involved." Genuine biology books are preferable to superficially descriptive and sentimentally written "nature books." Look for books that give complete life histories or ecological studies.

Physical Science and Technology—Merely descriptive books about rockets, missiles, airplanes, atomic reactors will entertain but are not educationally worthwhile unless they introduce the reader to fundamental scientific laws and principles—and to the painstaking underlying research and experimentation. Such books should demonstrate to the reader how and why science and mathematics courses are basic preparation for those who want to be scientists, technologists, doctors, engineers, and space travelers.

Experiment Books—"Experiment books" designed to demonstrate scientific facts and principles should encourage the reader to do additional experimentation on his or her own initiative and should stress the values of additional background reading.

Reaching Upward and Outward—Buy books for children and young people that they will have to "grow into," books that hold their interest but that require repeated reading and study to understand and enjoy thoroughly. Books should be chosen not only to deepen the readers' major fields of interest, but also to acquaint them with other, unfamiliar areas of knowledge.

The editorial group determined that books which met all or most of these criteria would be rated "highly recommended" or "recommended," those which were somewhat deficient in one or more characteristics but which did not contain any serious errors would be rated "acceptable," and that books with serious errors or deficiencies would be explicitly "not recommended." In defining "science," primary emphasis was placed upon mathematics and the physical and biological sciences, but other areas also were included: applications in medicine; engineering sciences and technology; and various behavioral sciences, especially psychology, sociology, and cultural anthropology.

The watchword was rigor, and this meant that sentimental, anthropomorphic, merely descriptive, or overly simplified presentations were not considered to be "science." These selection standards were developed at the same time that major nationwide changes were occurring in science curricula. The scientists and educators involved in preparing new curricula for science courses for elementary and secondary students were also emphasizing rigorous presentation for science information. These curriculum developers were quite influential, and their science presentations emphasized the logic, the intellectual achievements, and the spirit of adventure and discovery which motivated the scientists themselves. It was expected that the same courses which would interest and prepare a scientist-to-be would also prepare a future citizen to "appreciate" science and to be scientifically literate.

The basic assumption underlying these new science curricula was that the study of science provided its own motivation. It is important to note that this was also a fundamental assumption in *Science Books* criteria. The quality standards for *Science Books* were thus compatible both with those of the science curricula and with the feeling of most university-based scientists, many of whom were *Science Books* reviewers.

By the early seventies, however, educators and many scientists began to realize that no single science curriculum would reach all students and that the rigorous science curricula turned off far more students than they attracted. It seemed reasonable to suppose that books selected only for accuracy or for "science for the sake of science" would also fail to attract substantial numbers of young people. So the staff at *Science Books (SB&F)* looked for additional standards for selecting science books for young people and considered some revisions of criteria already in use.

These new standards were concerned with both a book's relevance to the reader's own life and its motivational material, especially since the climate of opinion about science had then changed considerably. In 1968, for example, more than half of the public accepted science as a beneficent factor, but by 1972 that figure had dropped to one-third. In this poll, only adults were questioned, but we believed young people would surely be influenced by the climate of opinion around them. Besides, many young people seemed not to be seeking a rational understanding of the world; there was a resurgence of interest in mysticism, astrology, and the occult. Such fads come and go, but the basic problem remained. If we couldn't find some way of getting most young people interested in the sciences as a means of understanding themselves and the real world, then this civilization would be in considerable trouble.

The problem was and remains a critical one, because science, through its discoveries, its technological derivatives, and especially through its conception processes, is a major intellectual and economic force. While the theories and concepts of science may never have great esthetic appeal for most people, all responsible citizens must have some real understanding of science processes and potential science applications because, through design or through incomplete understanding, science and technology can be directed to some very destructive purposes. While some may argue that such problems can be solved by decreeing "no more science," most thoughtful people agree that our technologically based culture has progressed too far for that. More science, not less, more scientists, not fewer, are needed to cope with the technical problems we already have and to prevent much more serious problems from developing. Some young people must become scientists, but all young people must have an understanding of science.

In the schools, science must become an integral—and integrated—part of all studies. So we looked for a way to put in libraries and classrooms the kinds of science books that most young people will read willingly. I do not mean to suggest that we no longer were concerned with accuracy, logic, good design, and all the other selection criteria previously listed. Indeed, we knew we needed to be particularly careful of accuracy of both fact and implication in all science books, including those for the beginning reader, which undertake to show children the interactions of science and society. Since most children have only about ten years in which to acquire basic science information before they are eligible to vote, we will always have to view the selection of good science books *which children will read* as a matter of some urgency.

Unfortunately, it seemed that "social relevance" alone wouldn't guarantee reader interest, any more than scientific accuracy would. "Motivational" material should be included, but what kind and how much was, and is, difficult to judge adequately. Any competent scientist can say whether or not a book in his or her own field is accurate and not so oversimplified as to be misleading. But what will turn on the student not already interested? Here we move into an area of art and a maze of individual abilities and preferences. We still do not know enough about individualization of instruction to do it effectively; but we do know that we need a wide variety of different materials to satisfy different student needs. Similarly, we know that if diverse individual needs are to be satisfied by libraries, science collections must continue to expand, and books offering many different approaches to the same science areas will have to be provided. This means that additional demands will continue to be put on already limited library resources. It also means more stringent requirements for book selection, and for reviews recommending acquisitions.

We asked ourselves, what in particular should we look for in judging young people's science books? First, we certainly should look for science books in which the writing is lively and *not* too difficult. Second, we should look for a more "personalized" approach. At a minimum, characters and situations should be portrayed so that a variety of readers can identify with both. Pictures are especially important; they should have the clarity and impact of a good news photograph and they should give the reader a feeling of personal involvement in the science process in as many ways as possible. This includes such obvious factors as showing representatives of both sexes and various races *participating* in the activities illustrated.

Books should be lively, but they must avoid the "gee-whiz" presentation which tends to promote a mystic attitude toward science as magic rather than science as human investigation of natural events and forces which have explanations comprehensible to the reader. After reading a good science book, children should have the feeling that their world has become somewhat more predictable. Thus, as they gain knowledge, they also gain self-confidence and pleasure in their developing sense of personal competency.

We felt that many science books would be more interesting to children if more about the historical or social setting were included and if the author displayed some sympathy for the "ignorant" who may have opposed the use of a particular science discovery or failed to understand the significance of some newly developed concept. (After all, we also are ignorant of tomorrow's discoveries, and displaying the need for humility is not amiss.) Authors should, in addition, make a real effort to reach out to the readers who may already be frightened or alienated by a scientific culture which seems about to engulf them.

On the other hand, presentations should not be so imprecise that readers will misunderstand the implications of scientific concepts. But, for younger children especially, we felt that some abstract concepts probably *cannot* be explained properly. When reference is made to aspects of science which cannot be adequately explained, readers could be given the minimum information necessary for the story line and told to look the matter up elsewhere if they wish. Every writer should also be very faithful in pointing out that no field of science is known completely and that in most our knowledge is still scant. The scientific elitism which has plagued many children's science books in the past should be avoided at all costs.

Two other aspects of science development and discovery are interesting, important, and often insufficiently emphasized in many science books. We felt that they would make science a more approachable subject for many readers, and that they therefore should be on our list of qualities which contribute to a good science book. The first concerns the nature of the "scientific method," and the second is the part intuition plays in many, if not most, important science insights and discoveries.

The scientific method, it should be emphasized, is not some esoteric process known only to its devotees. It is rather the analytic process we all use when we are solving problems logically. We gather "data," we try to see if other people see the same things which we have seen, we sort out our information into what we are reasonably sure of and what is less likely, we try to make the best guess we can about what the "data" mean, and then we look for further evidence to see if our guess is right. This *is* the scientific method. It is a natural human mode of operation, it is carried out (more or less) by every one of us, and it is just as useful in discovering the truth behind TV commercials as it is in discovering the truth behind quasar signals. In addition, analytical thinking is withholding judgment until "enough" data are in hand. Often, science books—even those by scientists who should know better—skip the doubts, the wrong turns, the incorrect guesses which went into developing some scientific theory. Also, they may not give the reader any real basis for understanding what constituted "enough data" in a particular situation. What is "enough data"? There is no absolute answer, but certainly we need to look for books which show young readers the tentative nature of many scientific hypotheses.

The other aspect of science which we felt should be emphasized is the value of intuition. For those accustomed to the usual analytical mode and sometimes pompous certainty of science reports, the importance of intuition in science may come as a surprise. It should not. Intuitive thinking is a natural and necessary, if little understood, antecedent of scientific discoveries. Do new ideas come as a result of consciously un-resolvable conflicts in observations which are then unconsciously re-combined in new ways, leading to new insights? We do not know, but we do observe that creativity is often a product of aloneness, of appar-ent inactivity in an individual who is both knowledgable and open to new, even outrageous, notions.

Science books which point out the fact that advances have been made in all fields of science by people who did not automatically reject wild notions ought to interest young readers who are themselves trying to break out of what they see as the undue restraints of society. Let me enter a disclaimer at once lest anyone suppose that we were either fomenting revolution or proposing that young people be encouraged to believe in wind gods which blow out of the west or invisible ropes which hold the moon to the earth. We were suggesting only that we should look for books which counter an overly analytical presentation of science and the scientific method.

In summary, then, these were the additional criteria we established and that we now use for selecting good science books for children. We emphasize the need to select books which are *accurate* but which also include motivational information, lively writing, good photographs and drawings, analogies, parables, stories, uncertainties, intuition, and, yes, even humor! All are legitimate provided they add to the reader's com-prehension of the science facts or processes under discussion and pro-vided they are clearly labeled so that the young reader will understand what is going on.

The push toward rigorous science presentations was especially im-portant at a time when educators were taking first steps to ensure accuracy in teaching science principles to all students. Now it is essential to integrate science into the fabric of living. Criteria for judging science books must include standards directed to this end as well as criteria for judging scientific accuracy.

Finally, of course, the quality of any judgment depends critically on the abilities of those doing the judging and writing and editing the re-views. Nearly all *SB&F* reviewers are working scientists in the fields in which they review. They are asked to base their judgments on an ex-panded set of criteria which include but now go beyond those which I listed at the outset. They are asked to evaluate not only accuracy and completeness (scope) of the presentation in a book, but also quality and relevance of illustrations, clarity of writing, appropriateness for particu-lar groups of readers, and the value of the book when compared with other similar titles. The editorial staff is especially careful in checking reviews of children's books, and if a reviewer seems not to have fol-lowed *SB&F* guidelines, the book will be read by the staff and may be sent out to another reviewer for a second opinion. We feel that we have gained new insights into selecting books for young people who, in the early grades at least, are curious, alert, and concerned about sorting out the contradictory information that hits them from all sides. We have done this through continuous interactions with some 2,000 reviewers in our continuing effort to make *SB&F* a model selection tool—one which will help librarians and educators provide an information base so that "every citizen, every man in the street . . . [can] learn what science truly is and what risks and quandaries, as well as what magnificent gifts, the powers that grow out of scientific discovery engender."[3]

Writing about Science for Children

Millicent E. Selsam

To write about science for children an author needs to know science, to know children, and to know how to write—particularly to understand how to communicate with children on their level.

It is natural for children to be curious and to ask questions. This is also characteristic of most scientists at work. They might be said to have maintained a child's curiosity about the world in which they live, and their mode of working is to ask questions, even as children do. The form of questions asked by younger children is most often that of identity-seeking. Children pick up a caterpillar, a beetle, a shell, or the eggs of some sea animal and want to know the name of it. Having found out the name, they lose interest and usually soon forget the name. I have learned through the years not to tell them the name. Now I never know what the object is, no matter how familiar. I say "let's find out" and look it up with them in a simple guide, hoping to encourage the habit of looking up such things for themselves. As a help to remembering the name, I try to encourage them to do something with the object found. If children's interests are to be maintained and encouraged to develop it should be possible to incorporate these techniques into the writing of books.

It was in this way that I was induced to write a book called *Terry*

Reprinted from *A Critical Approach to Children's Literature* (The University of Chicago Studies in Library Science), edited by Sara Innis Fenwick, by permission of The University of Chicago Press. Copyright © 1967 by The University of Chicago.

and the Caterpillars.[1] I had known all my adult life that caterpillars spin cocoons but I had never seen them actually do it. Opposite me on the island lived a little girl who kept bringing me caterpillars. We put some huge ones in jars with some twigs and leaves of the plants on which they were found. The following week both of us saw, for the first time in our lives, the spinning of the cocoon. I saw the effect of this simple scientific observation on the child, felt the excitement myself, and realized that here science met child in a way that could produce a good book.

But how does the writer communicate the excitement of the discovery? It is not enough to say, "Here is an exciting thing. See the way a caterpillar spins a cocoon." The role of the writer is to write the book so that a child can feel he is *participating* in an observation or a discovery. It should send him out looking for his own caterpillars immediately.

A good science book is not just a collection of facts. The biology text *Life,* by George Gaylord Simpson and collaborators, asks, "Are you being a scientist when you count the sand grains on Coney Island beach? No. It is true you are gathering facts, perhaps carefully, but you are probably crazy."[2]

Scientists gather facts that are relative to some theory to be tested or extended. They have well-formed ideas of what is worth studying at any given time. All scientific work is thus approached with an hypothesis in mind. The very essence of science is the search for general rules, which when found, are summarized in laws and theories. In biology we can think of generalizations such as the cell doctrine, gene theory, the theory of evolution. For example, Darwin's concept of evolution gave us an understanding of fossils, the geologic history of rocks, comparative anatomy, embryology, and the adaptations of animals to their environment. This one concept, by linking many facts, helped to integrate the field of biology.

The purpose of science books should not be to fill a child's head with facts but to give him some idea of the great advances in science made by the linking of many observable facts into fundamental concepts.

A good science book leads to an appreciation of the methods of science. Scientists find the answers to their questions by observing and experimenting. Children are excellent observers, and if they are given a chance to look at things themselves, they will begin to appreciate the kind of patience and effort that goes into careful observation. Science books should encourage this habit of careful observation. A good book on the seashore should move the reader to go out and examine for himself the wonderful life at the edge of the sea. A good astronomy book should turn the reader's eye to the sky and make him want to buy a small telescope. A good nature book should stimulate a young person to hear, see, smell, and taste things—to use all of his senses to observe.

Observation of natural facts should lead to an interest in discovering the cause of the processes and activities observed. Questions of this kind can best be answered by experiment. The late George Sarton, the famous historian of science, had this to say about developing an appreciation of the scientific method in young people:

> One may begin [science training] with the purely descriptive parts which require only some power of observation and memory. Thus a good deal of astronomy, geology, anatomy, botany, and zoology, etc. can be explained in a very simple way. The fundamental methods of science can be illustrated by means of easy experiments, and thus will the spirit of experimental philosophy gradually inform the minds of the pupils. It is, of course, this that matters above all. It is perfectly possible—and it is not even difficult—to inculcate the scientific spirit . . . upon children in various proportions according to the age and intelligence of each. . . . No attempt should be made to teach too many facts; there is no point in that. One fact well understood, if possible by means of personal experiments, is more than a hundred learned by rote.[3]

Good science books should certainly avoid incorrect concepts such as teleology, which explains everything in nature in terms of purpose. Statements like "birds suddenly leave one locality and fly hundreds of miles to another place *so that* they will have food and a warmer climate in the new location" seem to close off all further inquiry. A great deal of serious scientific study is being devoted to the migration of birds. Experiments have led to theories about the length of day influencing the reproductive organs—and to theories about how the whole process may have originated far back in the sequence of ice-age times when birds were forced to move further south. A scientific presentation of migration gives the facts as known to date from observation and experimentation, gives the best theories available, and shows what areas are still to be explored. It avoids the easy and incorrect use of words like "so that," "nature wants or prefers," etc.

Lucretius, the great Roman poet of science of the first century B.C., in his epic poem "On the Nature of Things" had this to say on the subject of teleology almost two thousand years ago.

> . . . Avoid I beg you, teleology
> With all my heart I long that you should shun this fault of reasoning.
> Through prudent fear and foresight in advance
> This blunder miss:
> Don't ever think that eyes were made
> In order that the human race might have the power to see.
>
> .   .   .   .
>
> Ideas like these which men proclaim are false in reasoning,
> Abysmally confound effect with cause.
> Nothing at all was brought to be in all our human frame
> In order that the human race might use it.
> What is brought to be creates its use.
> Vision existed not at all.
> Before the light of eyes was brought to be.[4]

Another common and equally incorrect concept is anthropomorphism, which sees everything in nature from a human point of view. In an article entitled "The Evolution of Mind" in the June, 1957, issue of *Scientific American*, Norman L. Munn tells an ancient Chinese story which illustrates the naive human attitude in this matter, "Chuang Tzu and Hui Tzu were standing on the bridge across the Hao River. Chuang Tzu said, 'Look how the minnows are shooting to and fro! How joyful they are!' 'You are not a fish,' said Hui Tzu, 'How can you know that the fishes are joyful?' 'You are not I,' answered Chuang Tzu, 'How can you know I do not know about the joy of the fishes? . . . I know it from my own joy of the water.' "[5]

Mr. Munn then points out that modern psychology does its best to stop this kind of anthropomorphic approach and tries to find out how the animal's mind works by studying its behavior. The study of animal behavior is fascinating enough when it is based on the results of observation and experiment in the field and is not beclouded with an approach that ascribes human characteristics to animals.

The question of accuracy with regard to matters of fact in a science book is actually of much less importance than the goals above discussed. On this subject, I want to quote from an article by Eva L. Gordon of Cornell University entitled "Reviewing and Selecting Nature Books for Children." She says:

> Accuracy . . . is not simply a matter of correct factual detail. . . . Accuracy seems a much more complex matter than avoidance of vagueness or misstatement. It implies, for one thing, discrimination between proved or demonstrable truth, and hypothesis. An explanation of the origin of the universe or a description of the habits and appearance of prehistoric animals may be stated not as what we believe to be possible on the basis of evidence we have, but in terms as positive as might be used to tell how one made his garden or to describe the appearance and behavior of a pet cat. Accuracy means also, a willingness to say, "I don't know," and in general, avoidance of sweeping statements and sparing use of such words as "all," "every," and "always." It means, too, careful expression in terms not necessarily technical, but at least not in conflict with scientific language that will come into the child's later experience. . . . Good performance in this matter of careful expression, always practiced by some authors, seems to be shown increasingly in the newer books, sometimes in judicious use of scientific names, and frequently in the use of well-defined, carefully explained terms instead of awkward, written-down expressions.[6]

Good science books should communicate some of the excitement of discovery—and the triumph that goes with the solution of scientific problems. They should make a young person understand why Archimedes could jump out of his bath to rush through the streets of Syracuse shouting "Eureka" when he discovered a new physical principle.

Books about science should help young people to see that our human goals must be shaped by science and that science must be enriched by human hopes and ideals. With man's new control of the forces of nature—with atomic power and earth satellites—science books can help to develop the idea that science is not mere knowledge of things independent of our human purposes or merely a means of giving us material comforts and gadgets but is part of the fabric of our lives. The methods of science can be used to create rational attitudes free of superstition and prejudice.

By good science books, to repeat, I mean those that show the methods of science at work, that elucidate basic principles of science and are not a mere assembly of facts, that convey something of the beauty and excitement of science, and that interest young people in thinking up good questions for new young scientists to test by experiment.

Science Books for Young Children

Pamela R. Giller

The recent burgeoning of science books for young children is a multi-faceted phenomenon, reflecting increased respect for the learning capacities of young children as well as increased concern with raising all children's science consciousness. A look at science books directed at three- to six-year-olds reveals a variety of approaches, goals, and degrees of success. Before drawing any conclusions about these books it is important to trace their evolution, study several examples, and contemplate what, if any, are the special characteristics of science books for young children.

Views about the learning of young children underwent major revision amidst heated debate in the mid and late sixties. In Chicago, Benjamin S. Bloom had concluded from extensive studies that half of a person's general intelligence is formed by the age of four and as much as two-thirds by the age of six. At Harvard, Jerome Bruner, studying cogni-

Reprinted by permission of the Children's Science Book Review Committee from *Appraisal: Science Books for Children* 13, no. 1:1–6 (Winter 1980). Copyright © 1980 by Pamela R. Giller.

tive development, offered the astounding statement that, "any subject can be taught effectively in some intellectually honest form to any child at any stage of development." During the sixties, the impact of Jean Piaget's vast work on children's mental growth began receiving wide recognition in this country and significantly affecting views on children's cognitive learning. Piaget's minutely detailed observations charted the process of intellectual growth, revealing the extent of young children's capacity to learn. Burton L. White and others have incorporated Piaget's ideas in studying infants, and have demonstrated the major effects on early development of an enriched environment.

Project Head Start was born out of the concern that underprivileged children, entering school for the first time at age five or six, could never make up for their early learning deficits. Whatever its successes, failures, and shortcomings, it placed early learning firmly on the educational map.

How has current thinking about young children affected science books for this audience? Increased respect for young children's capacity to learn has certainly contributed to the growing number and variety of science books, as well as to the amount and depth of information covered in specific books. Interpretation of what interests children has broadened considerably. Science books for young children before the midsixties dealt almost exclusively with nature—plants and animals. Most often, scientific information was conveyed in picture books, in story form. Such books continue to appear, but they have been joined by books with more direct approaches as well as by books on other topics.

One author who has successfully maintained a similar style for almost twenty years is Gladys Conklin. Although the illustrations in her newest volume, *I Like Beetles* (Holiday, 1975), are more realistic and include children from a variety of ethnic backgrounds, the tone and vocabulary are very similar to those in *I Like Butterflies* (Holiday, 1960) and *We Like Bugs* (Holiday, 1962). More attention is paid to insect identification in *I Like Beetles*, but the basic information is of comparable detail. When investigating other books, it appears that Conklin was ahead of her time in the early sixties in her assumption that preschoolers would be interested in and able to absorb factual information.

A more typical contrast is between *Sun Up* by Alvin Tresselt (Lothrop, 1949) and *Sunlight* by Sally Cartwright (Coward, 1974). Tresselt's story, still appealing, speaks to the emotions as it relates to the effects of the rising sun on the surrounding farm. The emerging storm is presented in the same way.

Sunlight is a straightforward science book that successfully reaches preschoolers. By beginning with "your wakening," it immediately captures the attention of the egocentric preschooler. Through simple experiments the author directs children toward learning about properties of sunlight. Basically, the author encourages children to systematize the kinds of observation they do naturally.

Another kind of contrast is between an old and new science picture book in story form. *The Day We Saw the Sun Come Up* by Alice E. Goudey (Scribner's, 1961) relates the story of two children and their cat as they explore a day in the sun. Shadows, clouds, and the sun's warmth are all touched on in the context of the story. When their mother explains the rotation of the earth at bedtime the children demonstrate with an apple and flashlight.

The format of *A Space Story* by Karla Kuskin (Harper, 1978) allows for much more factual information. A sleepy boy named Sam wonders about the stars. The text then explains basic information about the sun and the planets, continually referring back to Sam. Again, the more recent book reflects current thinking about young children's capacity to learn.

In looking at science picture books it is useful to contrast early Tresselt with his more recent *The Beaver Pond* (Lothrop, 1970) and *The Dead Tree* (Parents', 1972). While the early books stressed ecological concerns and the interdependence of living things, his later books use these themes as the basis for deeper exploration, and include more information conveyed through richer, more complex language.

Clearly there have been changes in science books for young children—in subject matter as well as in approach to familiar material. Are there useful guidelines to what is appropriate in science books for young children?

For young children, especially, with their natural egocentricity and limited experience, science books should grow out of their interests, rather than merely introducing important scientific phenomena to children. Children's interest in animals and plants, obvious aspects of their environment, has long been recognized and met with books. But these topics only scratch the surface. The young child's environment is full of things that raise questions answerable only through scientific information. "Where is the sun at night?, Why is the moon different shapes?, Why do the lights go on?" are only a few examples. Children are curious about the world around them and are eager to make order out of it. Science books can capitalize on this interest while helping children develop a scientific approach to the world around them.

The scientific method is very compatible with the way young children learn. Piaget, White and others have recorded with what intensity, determination and orderliness children go about learning tasks and solving problems. Two successful books for children as young as three, books that emphasize careful observation, are *Look Again!* by Tana Hoban (Macmillan, 1971) and *Everything Changes* by Ruth Rea Howell (Atheneum, 1972). *Look Again!* is a wordless book in which the square centeobject is revealed first. The observer tries to guess what the whole picture will be, turns the page to find the object fully revealed, and then turns again to view the object in its proper environment.

Everything Changes encourages children both to observe their everyday world closely and to develop their sense of the yearly cycle. By focusing on the child's perspective, the book offers immediacy as well as experience in careful observation.

Emphasis on their interests as well as on the scientific method are particularly appropriate aspects of science books for young children. Peculiar to this age group are science books in picture book format, difficult to label as clearly story or science. Generally, if the purpose of the book is to convey scientific information, it belongs within the category of science books. For the most part, the overall criteria remain the same as for books for older children. Clarity and logic in the presentation of the material is important, and the material should be accurate. Oversimplification is a danger and anthropomorphism is unacceptable. The style should be fluent and the illustrations ought to illuminate the text.

These criteria present special problems in science books for young children. The tendency to oversimplify is strong when complex ideas must be presented within the confines of a restricted vocabulary. Certain difficulties arise in relation to accuracy; many scientific concepts are abstract and thus at odds with young children's reasoning powers. Piaget has shown that children under the age of seven function at a preoperational stage. During this period children respond through sensation, and need to learn to systematize their physical knowledge and construct logical structures. For instance, a youngster does not "see" that two rows of three pennies are the same as three rows of two pennies; a child must count the pennies many times and experience other, similar situations before she or he can recognize this sameness.

One of Piaget's best known experiments involves conservation, the ability to realize that certain attributes of an object are constant, even though the object changes in appearance. Children younger than seven cannot understand that two balls of clay she or he has agreed are equal are still equal when one is rolled into a fat sausage. The child focuses on a single aspect of the clay, its elongation, and cannot take into account that the sausage is thinner as well as longer. When the sausage is rolled back into a ball the child will agree that the two balls are equal. But if one is again rolled into a sausage, the child will again insist that this shape is larger. The child has not acquired reversibility, the ability to follow a series of size transformations and then reverse direction and think back to the original form, that is when the same piece of clay was a round ball. A child bound by compelling aspects of the concrete stimulus and unable to think about the earlier form of the object is considered to be in the preoperational or prethought period. At about the age of seven, children enter the period of concrete operations, in which they are able to operate in though about concrete objects.

It follows from Piaget's widely accepted theory of cognitive development that science books directed at three to six-year-olds must take into account the way children of this age function. The several classification books of Gladys Conklin and the science observation books by Sally Cartwright, *Water Is Wet* (Coward, 1973) and *Sand* (Coward, 1975), are all examples of books that are closely aligned to preschoolers' intellectual development.

Accuracy and oversimplification are legitimate problems for authors of preschool science books to wrestle with. But simplistic language and condescending tone are inexcusable. *My Snail* by Herbert H. Wong and Matthew F. Vessel (Addison-Wesley, 1976) uses very flat language and choppy sentences, reminiscent of a basal reader. Sentences such as "Go get that snail. We want to see it," are interspersed with exclamations such as "look!" and "Snail eggs!" This book is the only one in the Science Series for the Young.

The Cartwright books and many others combine simple language and a question and answer approach without a patronizing tone. *Dandelion* by Ladislav Svatos (Doubleday, 1976) begins with a question, "Do you know the dandelions?" and proceeds with easy, fluent language and beautiful illustrations to explore the life cycle of this common weed. The success of *Dandelion* is further enhanced by its focus on a narrow topic.

In contrast is *Dinosaur Mania* by Edward Radlauer (Children's Pr., 1979), one in the series called Ready, Get Set Go Books. Here, question parts such as, "Thunder lizard?" "Swim?" are used to introduce dinosaur types and characteristics. This "cute" technique, coupled with a bare minimum of arbitrary information, creates a book whose existence is difficult to understand, especially in light of more successful efforts. *Dinosaur Story* by Joanna Cole (Morrow, 1974) gives some background to the dinosaur era, offers an abundance of clear information about dinosaur types, and contains the kind of specific detail children enjoy. The author demonstrates an understanding of children's intellectual development through her emphasis. For instance, she describes the size of the dinosaurs in detail, using examples such as larger than a truck or taller than a house. However, when she mentions that "Millions and millions of years went by" she makes no attempt to explain this time span, realizing that young children cannot comprehend such abstraction.

Dinosaur Story may be too complex for young children, in such cases the book can easily be adapted to their comprehension level. Many books for primary grade children, clearly written and effectively illustrated, can be used successfully with children six and under. Children intrigued by *Dandelion* might enjoy much of the text and all of the photographs in *The Amazing Dandelion* by Millicent Selsam and Jerome Wexler (Morrow, 1977).

Apples are a food of great appeal to children. *Apples: How They Grow* by Bruce McMillan (Houghton, 1979) attempts to reach children of different ages. The large photographs tell the story to preschoolers, and the limited text can easily be adapted to them. The more detailed small picture captions are appropriate for eight- and nine-year-olds.

Although vocabulary is a consideration in science books for young children, the science picture book in story form, in common with all picture books, can include complex language when it appears in the context of a flowing storyline. Alvin Tresselt, in his recent books, and Berniece Freschet are successful practitioners of art of the science picture book story.

Freschet's *Bear Mouse* (Scribner, 1973) tells the story of a mother mouse in winter, searching desperately for food while struggling to avoid attack by her natural enemies. Skillfully woven into the suspenseful story is much information about mice.

The Web in the Grass (Scribner, 1972), also by Freschet, is a beautifully written book about the life cycle of a spider. Beginning with the weaving of her wonderful web, the spider's story continues through her life as predator and prey, her spinning of an egg sac, and the spiderlings' hatching and dispersal. Within the poetic text, the author does not flinch from the truth of the spider's predatory nature.

Science books for young children may be about plants, animals, natural phenomena, or about the practice of scientific methods. Depending on theme, they may use either straightforward or poetic language. But all successful science books for this audience respect young children—their eagerness to learn, their enormous capacity to learn, and their particular ways of learning.

Selecting Science Books for Children

Harry C. Stubbs

It is no news to a parent, teacher, or a librarian that the younger generation tends to react negatively to being told what to do, read, say, play, or like; and there seems little doubt that younger generations always have been this way. The result, or at least one result, is that the education and entertainment industries share a common problem—they want people to listen to them and be impressed—although the professionals in both groups might prefer not to put it that way.

Originally titled "The Stockpile." Reprinted by permission of the publisher from *Library Trends* 22, no. 4:477–84 (April 1974). Copyright © 1974 by the Board of Trustees of the University of Illinois.

I am aware of this from the viewpoint of both fields, having been a science teacher for more than a quarter of a century and a science fiction writer for even longer.[1] Both facts determine how much, and in what direction, the following article is slanted. I am certainly not a completely objective writer (if there is such a thing), so it seems only fair to provide some data on my more probable prejudices.

The teacher's most conscious aim is to indoctrinate his students with a reasonably large body of usable fact and a set of attitudes reasonably compatible with his culture. In the physical and biological sciences, the "facts" must include the fact that not everything is known yet, and that there are a few techniques available for learning more. The attitudes for learning these techniques should include strong curiosity, a certain dissatisfaction with any given state of knowledge or public affairs, and as complete an absence of personal arrogance as is consistent with an adequate supply of self-confidence. An imagination able to solve problems as they arise is needed, but not needed are any more of the types who feel justified in stopping everything else while the world implements their particular plan.

The science teacher and the librarian share the problem of deciding what parts of the really overwhelming supply of existing knowledge are important enough to demand student attention and consideration, or at least to be available to maturing (and to already mature) citizens. Both professions have their limits: the teacher has only so much time to monopolize the pupil's attention, and the librarian only so much space for book storage and money for book acquisition. Both, therefore, tend to dip into the entertainer's budget of techniques, and compete for that part of the public wealth and student time usually budgeted for recreation and amusement. I do not criticize this at all; to the extent that acquiring useful knowledge and attitudes can be made fun, everyone is better off. Some may regret that one important criterion for *any* book is how much fun it is to read, but that must be accepted and lived with.

Another fact, of course, is that no one has time to read everything, even if there were nothing else to do. Far too many books are published to permit this. As a teacher I am required to form opinions on between three and four hundred books a year, and certainly cannot claim that every one of them is read from cover to cover in the process. A professional librarian must, I assume, make decisions on several times as many. We need not only criteria for final choice, but criteria for where to start looking.

One criterion heavily used by librarians, but not heavily tapped by teachers, is customers' suggestions. Students do read, their bases of selection often being rather obscure to the over-thirty mind, and they sometimes like what they read. From the science teacher's viewpoint they may like some pretty silly stuff, since the human tendency to fall for fads and jump on bandwagons seems to develop rather early, but if they have read it and been impressed by it, the teacher has no choice but to know something about it. He may even find it advisable to have copies available so that more than one of his students may join in the debate. (Also, it is extremely unwise to risk giving the impression that you do not want people to read some item. The banned-in-Boston rating was eagerly sought by publishers in the days when things were still banned in Boston.)

Of course, reading the material may not be fun—although there is always a fair chance it will be. Nothing in this article is going to suggest an *easy* way to choose or advise on books. However, even the most irritating "science" books can be put to use (Velikovsky's *Worlds in Collision*, which I had to put down every few pages to recover my temper, springs to mind). Specific claims or statements make good practice exercises in scientific reasoning, demanding both thought and further reading from the student. Therefore, while I would certainly not go out of my way to acquire every science book in which a student had expressed interest, I tend to jump at any chance to get a youngster into a thoughtful argument. There is astrology, most of the flying saucer material, pyramidology, the various health food fads—I grant that these should not take up too much of one's library shelf space, since there is far more valuable material to be housed, but neither the science teacher nor the librarian should permit himself to fossilize so thoroughly that nothing of the sort is available to his customers.

The students do not see everything, though, and often are not tempted by things we think they should study, so we cannot just wait for them to make suggestions. We have to do some picking of our own, and must therefore have some criteria determined by our own objectives and hopes—and not merely by asking "should they?" but also by asking "can they?" and "will they?" *Difficulty* is therefore a factor to consider.

The science teacher has some advantage in making this decision, but cannot claim the last word. Ideally, he wants a spectrum ranging from material pleasurable to his slowest students to things which will challenge his best. However, there are several factors which combine to make up the rather broad concept of "difficulty."

A subject itself may be inherently complex, abstract, or both, like quantum mechanics or psychology; but a book on these or any other subjects may still vary widely in difficulty because of the writing. Here, the librarian may actually be able to make a better judgment than the subject matter teacher.

One kind of difficulty which also stems from the writer rather than the subject, however, must be left to the subject matter specialist; and since the type of book in question is likely to be tempting both to student and librarian, the science teacher has a responsibility in helping with the selection. This is the sort of book which bears, usually, a giveaway title of the general nature *Golf* (or *Oil Painting*, or *Calculus*, or *Cooking*) *Made Easy*. The writer of this type of book is claiming to supply shortcuts to achieving a difficult skill, or easier ways to express a difficult subject, or more familiar analogies for some abstraction. He may actually have accomplished this, and I say nothing against the attempt in any case although I am sufficiently middle-aged and corrupted by the Puritan work ethic to doubt that anything really can take the place of conscientious practice and careful thought.

The risk in the process is the loss of precision which accompanies simplification and the substitution of broad-meaning everyday words for the more specialized and precise scientific ones. My stock example is the child's (or amateur's) astronomy book which tries to explain orbital motion with the statement that "centrifugal force exactly balances gravity" so that the orbiting object neither falls nor escapes.

This statement is not exactly wrong, although many physicists would be bothered by the term "centrifugal force," which is merely one aspect of inertia, and the word "balance" is certainly ambiguous in this connection. Even though not wrong, however, the sentence has led to much misunderstanding because of its lack of precision. I have seen written expression, by literate adults, of the fear that sending spacecraft to the moon would upset this "exact" balance and send our satellite crashing to the earth or out into space. (If any of the present readers fall in this group, please read a work on astronomy which does not claim to be easy—e.g., a college freshman text.)

Simplifying or clarifying difficult scientific subjects is a tricky job, as is recognizing when the job has been well done. Even the best scientist or science teacher cannot spot all the possible ways in which a book, a paragraph, a sentence or even a word may be misunderstood. Simplification demands of the writer a good, clear understanding of the subject itself at the *professional* level, not just the level of the proposed reader. It demands a high degree of skill with language, or very close cooperation with an illustrator, or preferably both. The scientist who cannot write well and the writer who is not a scientist are both poor candidates for the job. It is quite common in present-day science books for children to put an impressive list of scientific consultants somewhere near the title page, but one sometimes wonders how much these people actually influence the final choice of words and illustrations. I tend to be somewhat more impressed when the scientist is listed as "coauthor," although this is not a really firm criterion.

I fear that a science book must be judged at least three ways: for accuracy by a scientist, for clarity by a nonscientist, and for effectiveness on the basis of ideas and understanding that it actually engenders in students. The last, I grant, does make things a little hard on author and publisher.

A widespread tendency exists to equate "simplified" with "nonmathematical." Indeed, I have seen the latter term used in textbook advertising as though it were a virtue. Using *advanced* mathematics in a science book intended for students untrained in the field is, of course, as pointless as employing any other language they have not yet studied. However, the physical sciences are essentially quantitative, and all students have had *some* mathematics. Mathematical notation is the clearest and most concise method of explaining any point which involves questions of "how much?" or "how many?" or "how big?"

The notation may merely involve written numbers for the child, who has just learned to count, or numerical examples for the one just learning arithmetic, but it can and should also involve basic algebra, trigonometry, logarithms, or calculus if the intended reader can reasonably be expected to have any training in the use of these tools. I know about, and resent, the widespread antimathematical bias in the U.S. population, and feel strongly that something should be done to counter it. If the science writer makes it obvious that mathematical terminology is the easiest way to express and solve quantitative problems, we may hope that an occasional student will be stimulated to learn its use. I suggest that to the science teacher selecting books, the phrase "completely nonmathematical" on the jacket or in the sales literature is *not* a point in a book's favor.

The preceding criterion tended to overflow somewhat into the question of accuracy, which is also a point for independent consideration. I get the impression that librarians worry more about this aspect of a science book than do most science teachers, not because the latter care less, but because they feel more sure of themselves in judging the matter. I can offer the librarians some comfort.

Without belittling the importance of accuracy, please remember that no book has ever been written with *no* scientific mistakes—at least, there is no way to say that one has been, because we do not really know how many mistakes remain in our picture of the universe. Furthermore, if one ever is written it will be dated very quickly. As a science teacher I am not seriously bothered by an occasional misstatement of fact in a book, although I admit that some books go much too far in this direction.

There is, in fact, a variety of mistake which rather pleases me, however much it embarrasses the author. This is the slip in internal consistency. I will name no names, but when a book says on one page that the year of Mars is more than twice as long as that of the Earth, and on another page that the year of Mars is 687 Earth days in length, I sit happily back and wait for my more alert students to spot the inconsistency and start finding out for themselves which of the statements (if either) is correct.

When two books intended for the same level of reader disagree on some point, I am equally happy. I regard it as extremely important that students learn, as early as possible, that scientific "knowledge" is constantly changing as new information comes in, and that unlike chess or baseball, there is no human authority in a position to state absolutely the rules of the universe we live in.

I realize and regret that this knowledge can lead to insecurity in some people. I consider this danger as much smaller than the one arising from *lack* of this bit of truth. A person who has grown up under the impression that everything he has learned (or even that *anything* he has learned) is unassailably correct is on thin ice. He is likely to suffer far more from his collision with a nonconforming fact than is his classmate from an inability to make decisions (I realize that this view is disputable). I feel that much of humanity's social and political troubles stem from people's misplaced confidence in the validity of their own beliefs and viewpoints.

Librarians should not be overly concerned about spotting all the scientific errors in a newly acquired book. If a young reader comes up indignantly to point a new one out to you, would you really want to deprive him of the pleasure? And science teachers should delight in the useful classroom situation where two students cannot agree on whether a certain book statement is correct. I am not proposing that a whole library, or even a whole shelf, should be devoted to horrible examples. But those too stuffy about accuracy and updating will not have a library.

There is, however, one other general criterion which should be mentioned—that of subject matter. I mentioned above that there should be a wide range of difficulty available to the student, which naturally demands shelf space. This demand is greatly increased by the enormous variety of subjects calling themselves sciences. Someone must decide on a balance between the traditional subjects on one hand and the borderline and bandwagon ones on the other. It might seem at first that this responsibility belongs chiefly to the science teacher, but there is a danger here. Some of my esteemed colleagues, including myself, have trouble controlling the urge to dismiss a book as nonsense when it does not fit the conventional pattern. This may be the conservatism of age, or a considered opinion that basics should come first. In either case, we risk omitting books that many students will feel should be on hand; and student trust in and respect for the library as a source of information is very, very important.

I happen to be on the basic side myself; I felt that *Silent Spring* was much too emotional, and still resent the instant ecologist who does not seem to realize that the first blow at the "balance of nature" was not the flit gun but the garden.

Nevertheless, students become interested in such things, and professionally I have no choice but to qualify myself to discuss them. I cannot afford to exclude all this from the library, if only because I cannot afford to have students thinking that I am trying to censor their reading.

What I can do, and all I can do, with student food faddists is to have books on scientific nutrition available, backed up by basic chemistry and biology texts. For astrologers there are the astronomy texts, plus mathematical works on the analysis of observational errors and cause-

and-effect criteria. For ecologists who disapprove of the Alaska pipeline there are books on ecology by professionals, again with chemistry, biology and meteorology backups.

I teach at the high school level, but make it a point to have at least a few college and graduate school books available in the library; I feel fortunate at being close enough to Boston to be able to use a number of local university libraries for backup. Teachers should attempt to make the library's scope as wide as possible, and think twice before rejecting a book because it is palpable nonsense.

I have emphasized chemistry, biology, and the like in the foregoing paragraphs, and have emphasized belief in the importance of basic studies in depth. I do not mean by that to discount the interdisciplinary fields which keep springing up. We need them, however negatively I may react to the bandwagon syndrome. We need people who can come as close as humanly possible to viewing the whole picture at once. We also need, however, people who are aware of the vast body of detailed fact which must be uncovered and the appalling amount of work which has to be done before we can *ever* decently utter a sentence beginning with the words "I know."

There is the person who makes public pronouncements on ecological matters without knowing the difference between a microtome and a chromosome, or being able to balance a simple chemical equation. There is also the person who writes a tale of nautical adventure without knowing the difference between a sloop and a lugger, and believes that splicing the main brace is something done with rope.

The important difference between these two idiots is that the first is less likely to be found out (many readers of sea tales know something about ships) and more likely to do irreparable damage (we are irrevocably part of this planet's ecology ourselves) if he is a persuasive talker. Even if we do not produce an entire generation of scientists, it is up to us—writers, teachers, librarians, parents—at least to produce citizens competent to recognize the scientific faddist when he starts to talk. After all, it is now about two centuries since we committed ourselves to the technology-or-starve branch of history's roads. Maybe we should not have done it, but it is much too late to complain now.

Libraries have limited space and funds, and teachers have limited time, but both should do their best to provide reading collections of broad scope in both difficulty and subject matter. They must keep their ears, eyes, and minds open. They should remember that any book which can start debate has some potential use in communication bridges.

Science and the Literary Imagination

Dennis Flanagan

Richard Adams's epic novel about rabbits, *Watership Down,* has received a remarkable amount of critical attention in Britain and in this country. On the whole the verdict has been favorable, with almost universal admiration being expressed for the book's unexpected narrative power. In my own view *Watership Down* is even more interesting for what it represents than what it says. It is a significant expression of the current state of relations between the literary culture and the scientific one.

"The two cultures" is now well-established as a figure of speech. As a concept, however, it has had its vicissitudes. When C.P. Snow gave his Rede Lecture titled *The Two Cultures and the Scientific Revolution* in 1959,[1] the literary culture was, so to speak, laying for the scientific culture. It also seems as if it had been laying for Snow. He was riding high as a popular novelist, on the strength of his coping with "real" worlds of modern life; science, the government, academia and so on. He was nonetheless out of literary style in a time when most serious novels were more introspective. He was not much praised by literary critics, and there even seemed to be a certain amount of resentment that this somewhat old-fashioned approach was going over so well with serious readers—even though it was fortified by inside knowledge and considerable storytelling skill.

In this critical environment Snow's metaphor of the two cultures was assaulted with remarkable violence. The best-known attack was delivered by the distinguished Cambridge critic F.R. Leavis.[2] At least some of these commentaries were based on a curious misconception: that in placing science on the same cultural footing as literature Snow was trying to upgrade science and downgrade literature. Others assumed that Snow was somehow advocating a division of the two cultures. Even the redoubtable Aldous Huxley wrote: "Snow or Leavis? The bland scientism of *The Two Cultures* or, violent and ill-mannered, the one-track, moralistic literarism of the Richard Lecture [by Leavis]? If there were no other choice, we should indeed be badly off."[3]

Actually, of course, Snow was simply calling attention to the deepening fissure between the two cultures and fretting over it. What was really

Originally titled "To Each Generation Its Own Rabbits." Reprinted by permission of the publisher from the *Wilson Library Bulletin* 49, no. 2:152–156. Copyright © 1974 by the H. W. Wilson Company.

happening, in my view, was that many people in literary circles had become resentful of the rising influence of science, particularly in the universities, and Snow's fame as a novelist of the other culture gave them an uncommonly handy target. Such critics might have been doubtful of their ability to meet science head-on, since they knew so little about it, but Snow, after all, wrote novels, and that was something they did know about. Something had to be done to stop the intellectual juggernaut of science from overwhelming all the finer things of life: literature, painting, music, the dance and so on.

It is a pity that the idea of the two cultures should have been the locus of such a volcanic eruption of intellectual passions. It all came out as a scrimmage between the tribal institutions of literature and science, whereas the original intent had been to take a step in the direction of reconciling the two. Snow's original formulation is correct, and hardly anyone really doubts it; there are people who have considerable knowledge of the arts and very little knowledge of the sciences, and there are people for whom the reverse is true. This bifurcation is one of the main weaknesses in modern man's ability to improve his personal and social lot. The proper recognition of that fact, and efforts to do something about it, must surely rank high on the agenda of the perfectibility of man.

Merging the cultures with rabbits

What does all this have to do with *Watership Down*? A good deal more than one might think. *Watership Down* is a book about rabbits. It is soundly based on modern knowledge of the rabbit. Who gathered this knowledge? Biologists. What is a biologist and what does he do? He is a scientist and he does science. (Adams, who is not a member of the scientific culture, generously acknowledges his debt to *The Private Life of the Rabbit,* by the naturalist R. M. Lockley.) In other words, *Watership Down* is a scientific novel, a work that embraces the two cultures.

What happens in the creation of such a book, it seems to me, is that a thoughtful and imaginative nonscientist masters a certain body of scientific knowledge and begins to think on it. What would it be like, he might say to himself, to be a rabbit? How might I convey in human terms what it is like to be a rabbit? What could being a rabbit tell us about what it is like to be human? We are all the beneficiaries of such efforts to inform our factual knowledge with its potentialities. One can even argue that the main social function of art is to encompass factual knowledge and then to imaginatively dilate on it, to consider not only what is but also what might be.

Watership Down, of course, is about what it is like to be a rabbit. It is a gripping tale, full of adventure, deadly combat, blood, sadness and triumph (not much sex, in spite of what most of us are led to expect of rabbits). It is refreshing that the rabbits in the book are not cute little humans; these rabbits are tough, brave and resourceful. They are also ecological, that is, they are treated not simply as individuals but as members of an animal population interacting with its environment. They are a far cry from Peter Rabbit, a homunculus who would not pay the proper heed to his mother. The difference is probably no accident; it may be that each generation has to have its own rabbit legend.

One may be grateful for *Watership Down*, but if Adams's main purpose is to tell us what it is like to be a rabbit (in the light of modern knowledge about what a rabbit's life is like), the book has some major flaws. For one thing, the rabbit characters in *Watership Down* talk, which automatically introduces a feature of human life that rabbits do not share. Adams even goes so far as to introduce a rabbit vocabulary called Lapine; for example *silflay*, to browse, *tharn*, paralyzed with fright and *hraka*, fecal pellets. He has a mouse character who speaks pidgin English with an Italian accent, and a heroic seagull who speaks with what I take to be a Norwegian accent. The choice here was clear: either use the more descriptive third person or the more dramatic first person.

The odor is the message

There can be no doubt that human speech is the most highly developed form of communication in the biological world (at least on this planet). Speech, however, is only one of a great many different forms of communication. It is well known, for example, that many other mammals communicate intensively by means of odors. In *Watership Down* Adams refers to the fact that rabbits rub their chin on objects around their home burrow. He does not say, although he probably knows, that they do this because they have glands in their chin that secrete odorous substances. When a rabbit rubs its chin on a log near its burrow, it is leaving a message something like: "This is Joe's place. Keep out!"

Experiments conducted by Dr. Roman Mykytowycz in Australia indicate that for rabbits odors are a veritable symphony of messages.[4] Rabbits frequently urinate on each other for communication purposes. If a rabbit smelling of strange urine enters a warren other than its own, the other rabbits will attack it violently. The rabbit also has a well-developed set of glands around its anus that secrete odorous substances; these substances give each rabbit's fecal pellets a unique smell. When rabbits pass *hraka*, as Adams would say, they often park the pellets in a place where they will be encountered and sniffed at by other rabbits. Rabbits have a social hierarchy, or "peck order," and Dr. Mykytowycz has shown that the odor of the fecal pellets can convey a message rather like: "Joe, No. 1 rabbit in the warren, goes along here."

Adams may know these things too, but the point is that the social life of the rabbit may be even stranger, richer and more intriguing than his book makes out. If such notions as rabbits communicating with each other by the smell of urine and fecal pellets are offensive to us, that is not the fault of the rabbits. If we seek to understand another animal and its role in the same natural system to which we belong, we must allow it the dignity of its own way of life.

Whatever became of Renaissance Man?

Of course, when nonscientists think of science, they do not usually think of biology. Everybody loves plants and animals, and it is easy to forget that most of what we know about these organisms is the result of the patient labor of recent generations of scientists. "Science" is usually taken to mean hard science, the technical stuff that nobody can understand. The fact is that there is no technical stuff; there is only lack of knowledge and failure of communication. None of the findings of modern science is inherently more difficult to understand than the anal glands of the rabbit, given a remarkably modest amount of background information. Advances in scientific knowledge do not make nature more complicated and more remote from common understanding; they make it simpler and more accessible. For an intellectual to assume that an entire realm of knowledge is beyond his comprehension is for him to cut himself off from a part of his shared humanity.

For a person who has solved this problem there is a descriptive figure of speech much older than "the two cultures." It is "Renaissance man." What ever became of the Renaissance man, the Leonardoesque figure who was supposed to encompass all aspects of culture? He is not much mentioned today as a model for personal striving. The exceptions, however, are instructive. One is Thomas Pynchon, whose novels abound in flights into quantum mechanics and relativity. Another is Vladimir Nabokov, who was once, to be sure, almost as much a biologist as a writer.

Nabokov himself apparently has a rather stern view of the two-cultures problem. Alan Friedman of the University of California at Berkeley recently called my attention to some remarks Nabokov had made about it to Alfred Appel:

> I would have compared myself to a Colossus of Rhodes bestriding the gulf between the thermodynamics of Snow and the Laurentomania [referring to D. H. Lawrence] of Leavis, had that gulf not been a mere dimple of a ditch that a small frog could straddle. . . . One of those 'two cultures' is really nothing but utilitarian technology; the other in B-grade novels, ideological fiction, popular art. Who cares if there exists a gap between *such* 'physics' and *such* 'humanities'. . . .
> Science means to me above all natural science. Not the ability to re-

pair a radio set; quite stubby fingers can do that. Apart from this basic consideration I certainly welcome the free interchange of terminology between any branch of science and any raceme of art. There is no science without fancy, and no art without facts.

There is something admirable about this aristocratic view, but the fact remains that many cultivated people are unable or unwilling to straddle the ditch. Let me tell you a little story about an encounter I once had with Pauline Kael, *New Yorker*'s excellent film critic. Miss Kael and I had not met before, and she asked me what I did. I said I was the editor of *Scientific American*. She remarked: "That's nice. I know nothing about science." I said, perhaps a little too aggressively, "Whatever became of the idea that an educated person should know a little something about everything?" Her eyes snapping a bit, she said: "Ah, a Renaissance hack."

My feelings were not hurt. That, I think, is what it is all about. It is not enough for a few gifted Renaissance men to write things we can enjoy (assuming we can follow the fun). We all have much to gain from a more unified culture, not only for intellectual reasons but also for reasons of survival. It is widely believed that science and technology are somehow at the root of our trouble, and that if we could only "get back to nature" the trouble would go away. For better or worse our entire culture has been based on technology since men first learned how to make stone tools, and technology is always based on knowledge, that is, scientific knowledge. It is genuinely impossible to turn back. There is plenty of room for a more humane science and technology, but if we are to have it, a much larger component of society will have to understand and love the stuff.

To reweave the rainbow

How does the scientific culture get separated from the literary one, anyway? One reason is fear and loathing of mathematics, and here many teachers of science willingly help to dig their own grave. It is widely believed that mathematics is the essence of science, whereas it is not the essence at all. It is a tool, a language, a way of expressing relations and laws. Anyone who has taken the pains to learn this language wants to speak it to others, even if it is not essential to their general understanding of the subject. To be sure, mathematics has its own fascination for many people, and no one would suggest that it is not essential to the work of science. It may be, however, that the scientist who is a teacher has to choose between teaching the student what he has learned and teaching the student to do what he does.

The trouble probably lies, however, at a deeper level. Fear and loathing of scientific knowledge has a long history. John Keats put it best:

> Do not all charms fly
> At the mere touch of cold philosophy?
> There was an awful rainbow once in heaven:
> We know her woof, her texture; She is given
> In the dull catalogue of common things.
> Philosophy will clip an Angel's wings,
> Conquer all mysteries with rule and line,
> Empty the haunted air, and gnomed mine—
> Unweave a rainbow.

Keats was keening over Newton's explanation of the rainbow, but he was of course expressing an even older split in human conceptions: the dualities of feelings and thoughts, emotions and reason, body and mind, heart and head. Such dualities are probably the best explanation we have of the dualism of the two cultures. The bifurcation of culture is established early in our lives by a pervasive pattern of myth-making in which schools, teachers, parents and literature benevolently and unwittingly participate. The role of children's literature is particularly interesting. We live in a golden age of children's literature. The great classics endure, but the sheer weight of first-class children's books being published today dwarfs anything that has gone before. The best children's books are written by members of the literary culture, and under present circumstances that is inevitable and even right. The imagination of a child is not going to be stretched by books that merely recite facts. The present state of affairs does, however, reinforce the duality of culture. Here is where the case of *Watership Down* is particularly instructive. Even though Adams has not escaped the bonds of anthropomorphism, his epic of the rabbit does more to encompass the facts than anything that has gone before it.

Animals bulk very large as characters in children's literature. For the most part they have not caught up with the splendor of real animals. When we see a leopard in the zoo, we admire its beauty and grace. That, of course, is only a small part of what a leopard is about. A leopard is the result of an evolutionary symphony, a counterpoint between predator and prey, animal and plant, and animate and inanimate nature. If we are to understand the leopard and allow him to live, we need to see him not as an object but as a part of a seamless web of life with a past, a present and a future. It is this symphonic view that is usually missing in the treatment of animals in children's literature.

Where is fancy bred?

If *Watership Down* is the rabbit epic of our generation, the next generation's animal epics will probably be informed by the evolutionary view. It is a remarkable fact that it has only been about 150 years since men began to have some real notion of the past and the future. When it came to estimating the age of the world, an educated Englishman in Victoria's time had only Archbishop Ussher's calculation that it had been created in 4004 B.C. Today we know that the universe began between 20 billion and 10 billion years ago, that the earth was formed five billion years ago, that terrestrial life arose two billion years ago, the modern man (there were earlier members of the genus *Homo*) appeared 40,000 years ago. Our modern knowledge of the past tends to put things in perspective, and yet the evolutionary mode of thought has not yet been much integrated into our daily philosophy.

To choose only one example, consider the prevailing view of death. Most people regard death as a tragedy, and in a limited sense it is. In the larger biological sense, however, it is otherwise. Death is a progressive evolutionary invention. Every living species is a population; every member of the population is a fleeting experiment in the crucible of the environment. The same is true of man, even though much of his environment is created by himself. More primitive organisms were immortal and evolved slowly; more advanced organisms incorporated the mechanism of death and evolved rapidly. Without death there is little change. I find it hard to believe that a wider acceptance of the evolutionary view of death would not have a benevolent effect on life in our death-obsessed society.

If such views are to be encompassed by children's literature, the writers and illustrators of children's books will need to pay closer heed to Nabokov's "There is no art without facts." The facts in this case are not nuts and bolts but the larger view of man and nature that has been gained by modern science. The other part of Nabokov's dictum is no less important: "There is no science without fancy." Here we are listening to an echo of Shakespeare's "Tell me where is fancy bred, Or in the heart or in the head?" As Nabokov suggests, it is bred in both places.

Science as Literature

Zena Sutherland

When experts in the field of children's literature speak or write about their field and comment on "great" literature or classics, they are usually referring to fiction. Why? Why can't an informational book—a science book—be considered in this category?

Most of the criteria by which books for children are evaluated apply to nonfiction as well as to fiction: good format, clarity, accuracy, communication of the author's attitudes, adroit use of language, and concepts and vocabulary appropriate for the age of the intended audience; no jargon or writing down; no teleology or anthropomorphism; respect for the integrity and adaptability of the reader; humor where it is appropriate; logical structure or organization; a writing style that is distinctive for its originality in the use of words and word patterns.

There are additional standards by which one may measure each kind of book. Some of the requisites of good books are: for fiction, the ways in which an author uses dialogue, develops characters, reinforces theme; for nonfiction, the ways in which the author demonstrates a scientific attitude, accuracy, currency, and sequential arrangement of material.

But are good books literature? In one sense, yes. Everything published for children is part of their literature. In the sense of great literature, no, not necessarily. What is the criterion for greatness? While the lasting pleasure a book may give to generations of children may endow it with greatness, it is primarily in the style of writing that greatness is inherent. It must be acknowledged that the books commonly accepted as children's classics are primarily fictional, although informational books do win some awards, awards not designated to be awards primarily for nonfiction or science, and many do endure. But does this not reflect, perhaps, more our traditional attitudes about what literature is than the intrinsic merit of the best in nonfiction? If the nature of the literacy experience per se is to involve the reader in the author's creative (or created) world, to communicate excitement, to encourage the reader to go farther than the book, can it not be said that great science books do these things?

The purpose of a science book is to give information, that of a work of fiction to entertain, but it is not rare to find a story that gives informa-

Reprinted by permission of the publisher from *Library Trends* 22, no. 4:485–89 (April 1974). Copyright © 1974 by the Board of Trustees of the University of Illinois.

tion or an informational book that entertains or stimulates the imagination. A stellar example is Victor Scheffer's *Little Calf*, the description of the first year in the life of a sperm whale, written by an authority on marine biology. It begins, "It is early September when for the first time the Little Calf sees light . . .,"[1] and continues, "On a morning in early October the sea is glass, without a ripple or sound. A feather falls from the breast of an albatross winging its lonely way northwestward to the Leeward Islands and home. The plume drifts lightly to the sea and comes to rest on a mirror image. It is a day when time itself is still."[2]

The narrative style and story framework are used by many authors in writing about animal life; Robert McClung, Alice Goudey, and Bernice Kohn Hunt use them regularly and capably without anthropomorphism. Comparatively few animal books are written with the combination of authoritative knowledge and elegant prose that Scheffer contributes. Aileen Fisher achieves it in *Valley of the Smallest*, the story of a shrew:

> Undisturbed by the road of the wind, she was snatching a bit of sleep in a sheltered place away from her nest before hunger drove her to hunt again. For hunger ruled her life. No one in the valley searched for something to eat with such continual frenzy. . . . She never sat just doing nothing, like the Snowshoe Rabbit who lived under the spruces at the edge of the old beaver flat. She never lazily sunned herself on a rock while she surveyed the world, like the Ground Squirrel who lived near the old pine. She never slept quietly all day, like the Deer Mouse. She kept on the run day and night, winter and summer, searching for something to give her the energy to keep on running and searching.[3]

If one of the purposes of a good science book is to communicate the author's curiosity and enthusiasm (rather than to flatly state, "This is exciting"), and one of its tests, the ability to arouse a similar curiosity, Fisher does both in her poetry. From *Feathered Ones and Furry*, "How?"

> How do they know
> the sparrows and larks
> when it's time to return
> to the meadows and parks?
>
> How do they know
> when fall is still here
> it's the "thing" to go south
> that time of the year?
>
> Do you think that a bird
> is just smart, or, instead,
> that he carries a calendar
> 'round in his head?[4]

Jean Craighead George, whose Newbery Award book, *Julie of the Wolves*, is the story of a feral child whose patient cultivation of wolf behavior is solidly based on observation and research, has written outstanding science books for quite diverse age groups. In *All Upon A Stone,* a provocative vignette that surveys the complex community of flora and fauna on a single stone, the text is for the primary grades reader. In *Spring Comes to the Ocean,* for ages eleven up, the author conveys a sense of wonder in dignified prose that verges—but just verges—on the lyric.

> On the surface, the light ticked off the inner clock of a diatom. Sea foods flowed inside its tiny cell, and the diatom used the nitrogen and phosphorus and grew a wall which divided it in two. And each half was the same as the other. Violently they split apart and there were two glassy plants, with green spots of chlorophyl shimmering inside them. The two sections drifted apart, and the nutrients of the sea seeped through their porous walls. A delicate wall grew down the middle of each, they split and separated, and then there were four. There were eight—sixteen! And all over the ocean from Georgia south each plant that bright sunny morning took in food and split in half until there were tons of plant life by the one billion, two billions, four billions.[5]

While it is true that most of the science books that are distinguished for their style seem to be in the various biological sciences (from books for the very young, like Alvin Tresselt's *Hide and Seek Fog* and Golden MacDonald's *The Little Island,* to Rachel Carson's *The Sea Around Us* and *The World of the Ocean Depths* by Robert Silverberg) there are outstanding science books on almost every subject. Some of these are: Franklyn Branley's *The Christmas Sky,* based on the Christmas lecture at the Hayden Planetarium, where the author directs the educational program; Millicent Selsam's *Birth of an Island,* lucidly written as are all her books, describing the evolution of a volcanic island; Lancelot Hogben's *The Wonderful World of Mathematics* or the provocative *Beginnings and Blunders: Before Science Began;* Isaac Asimov's *The Clock We Live On* or *Building Blocks of the Universe* and dozens of other titles as witty as they are erudite; Corinne Jacker's *Window on the Unknown;* Alan Anderson's *The Drifting Continents;* Joan Lexau's *Archimedes Takes a Bath;* and Leonard Cottrell's *Digs and Diggers.*

All of these are lively books that can stimulate curiosity and satisfy it at the same time, books written with distinction and sometimes with humor or poetic vision, books illustrated with care: pictures placed correctly in relation to the text, accurate in their captions or labels, true to scale, and often beautiful. The precision and restraint of the drawings by Edwin Tunis in his *Chipmunks on the Doorstep,* the meticulous accuracy of Anthony Ravielli in his book *From Fins to Hands,* and the brilliant colors of the paintings in Colette Portal's *Life of a Queen* all add immeasurably to both the beauty and the informational value of the texts they illustrate.

There are values in the best science books beyond the fact that they instruct or even that they excite the reader's imagination. Even such a wordless picture book as Iela Mari's *The Apple and the Moth* can stimulate a child's awareness of discovery through observation. All of the books in the Crowell's "Young Math Books" series (distinguished for the discretion with which the scope of the text is limited for the young audience) focus on basic concepts. *Chemistry of a Lemon,* by A. Harris Stone, was one of the first trade books to reflect the use, in science education, of the process approach. From books like these the reader can learn the pleasure; the objectivity; the need for patience in sifting, matching, comparing, deducting, and testing needed; the pooling and diffusion of knowledge; and the fact that there are no national boundaries in scientific knowledge.

Much of what is published for children each year is pedestrian or ephemeral. Some of it is good, some very good. Very little is great, and this is true of nonfiction and fiction. But *if* there is more fiction that is good or great; it is still true that some informational books—science books among them—stand out as distinguished exceptions to the mass of what is now in print. Perhaps we have not fully appreciated what we have. Certainly in the comparative paucity of books from abroad (a paucity, for example, compared to the British fiction that appears in American editions) and in the slighting of nonfiction in our major awards, we may be accused of partiality. Perphaps we tend to forget that children not only need both fiction and nonfiction, but that, as Lillian Smith says in *The Unreluctant Years*, "A child's instinct to learn comes from his wonderings, his curiosity. The more his mind opens to wonder, the more sensitive he is to the satisfactions and enjoyments our earthly life affords. . . . As soon as he can read, a child is attracted to books which give tangible form to the vague shape of his imaginings about his world."[6]

History:

The Past Realized, Remembered, and Enjoyed

If history has any value beyond providing a livelihood for historians, it is to enlarge the imagination, to provide more acres for the mind to grow in. The humblest household plant, as it grows, needs to be transplanted into larger and larger vessels. With the shrinkage of space to live in, individual freedom becomes much more an inward affair. Though we may scarcely swing a cat in our cities, we may still swing a dinosaur in our minds.

——Leon Garfield[1]

History: Factual Fiction or Fictional Fact?

Jo Carr

Remember *Northanger Abbey*? Remember Catherine Morland chatting with her friend Miss Tilney about her opinion of historians?

> to be at so much trouble in filling great volumes, which, as I used to think, nobody would willingly ever look into, to be labouring only for the torments of little boys and girls always struck me as a hard fate; and though I know it is all very right and necessary, I have often wondered at the person's courage that could sit down on purpose to do it.[1]

Most children would probably agree with Catherine. They usually assume that history, being factual, is therefore dull. Because they feel this way they never really give history a chance, never reading enough to discover that history books can be every bit as engrossing as the historical fiction books they usually read instead.

It is because they are mistaken about history that many children miss the pleasure, and enlightenment, of reading an account of life in a thirteenth-century monastery or the experience of a pioneer family moving west, true tales that have real potency mainly because they are true —fact, as opposed to fiction. Fact is different from fiction; not necessarily better, but different. Children should have the privilege of knowing both.

What makes history—fact—important? In what way does it differ from historical fiction? In what way is historical fiction important? In what way is it different? Isn't there, after all, a place for both? To consider the distinctive quality of each, we might do well to turn to Jill Paton Walsh, who has written both historical fiction and history. She stoutly maintains that there is no difference between them: "What I am saying amounts, in effect, to saying that to be a historical novelist you have to be as good at history as any historian."[2]

Walsh, of course, is speaking of the rigors of solid research, and nobody would argue with her about that. A writer of historical fiction must be so steeped in history that, according to Molly Hunter, you'd know as you read the book just what clothes the hero would be wearing, what kind of bed he'd be sleeping in, even what coins would be jingling in his pocket. Rosemary Sutcliff, Erik Haugaard, Hester Burton, and many others, all agree. They have all testified to the painful labor of digging through volumes and volumes of history before they could get on with the story.

And with good reason. Were they inclined to take shortcuts in their research, these writers might have to face, as did Geoffrey Trease, the admonitory charges of a consummate history buff, age 10. Trease has described a letter he received from such a boy, a pint-sized reader of one of his books about the Anglo-Saxons. The boy pointed out that Trease must have been misinformed when he described his characters as eating rabbit stew in Gloucester, since rabbits didn't appear in England until the Normans. Considering that he had pored over an Ordnance Survey map of Roman Britain in order to check out every single detail of the journey on the old Fosse Way, Geoffrey Trease may have been less than delighted to be briefed on the ancestry of rabbits in the British Isles.

Jill Paton Walsh, then, is correct in stressing that historical fiction must be as authentic as history. But she would also contend that more than careful research binds the two. She has suggested that history is *fict* (Latin, meaning "something made") as much as *fact* (meaning "something done"). History does not really exist, she says. Evidence of it exists, but history itself is a "construct of the mind. The evidence has been selected, and patterned, and arranged; it has been masterminded into significance by the writer of the history book."[3] In other words, since the historian in creating history has given structure and meaning to raw data, his or her function is the same as that of the novelist. "Both novelist and historian—merely in recounting a sequence of events—reveal the orientation of their most profound beliefs."[4]

The foregoing discussion of *fact* and *fict* brings to mind the current word "faction," with all the controversy surrounding "the New Journalism." Fact and fiction, as we all know, have lately become muddled in disturbing ways. Stories with real people are being called fiction; stories with fictional characters are being sold as nonfiction; and books like *Ragtime* have mixed the two with such wild abandon that nobody seems to know what to call them. Alex Hailey is not the only author who could accurately describe his writing as "faction."

Michiko Kakutani has come close to making sense of this cross-fertilization in an article called "Do Facts and Fiction Mix?" in the *New York Times*. He suggests that it is not the existence of factual fiction, or fictional fact, that is alarming, but the proliferation of it in recent years. After all, the two have always been mixed to some extent, as Herodotus and Shakespeare have rather effectively demonstrated, but the confusion of forms has now reached proportions that raise real problems of veracity. New questions of interpretation, he says, "touch on the very nature of truth, objective or subjective, literal or figurative."[5] In view of these serious problems of veracity, it is important to be clear—especially clear when the reader is a child—about the difference between what is known to have happened and what somebody thinks might have happened.

It is undoubtedly true, as both Jill Paton Walsh and Milton Meltzer have pointed out, that no historian can be totally objective. History is not science, after all. Facts will indeed be chosen in accordance with "the orientation of profound beliefs," but the discipline and scholarly tradition of historiography place a limit on the degree of subjectivity in the historian's interpretation of these facts. Although subjective in selecting which facts to include and how to structure them, the historian is forced to extrapolate from facts and from facts alone. The "trappings" of history books—footnotes, bibliographies, and other forms of documentation—are not to be dismissed. They are extremely important in permitting the reader to interpret the significance of the historian's point of view, as Milton Meltzer so ably indicates in his articles in this collection.

In contrast, the historical novelist has considerably more freedom to interpret the facts of history without being held to account. The interpretation can be far more subjective—figurative rather than literal. All of this is a question of degree, of course, but the balance between "subjective" and "objective" must be recognized as significant.

The central characters in historical novels, for instance, are usually not actual figures from history. They tend to be fictional characters, usually children, placed in settings and situations that reveal the issues, as well as the atmosphere and ideas, that are peculiar to a particular period of history. The plot unfolds, not according to what history tells us happened but according to what the author conceives might have happened. Although the reader, eagerly following the plot, is absorbing the ideas of that historic period as naturally as details of clothes and currency to which Molly Hunter has referred, the "truth" of the story is figurative rather than literal, more subjective than objective.

In other words, the figurative truth of fiction should be understood as being distinct from the verifiable truth of history. Quintessential history should, by its very nature, strive toward exactitude and objectivity. Thus it is especially important for children to understand the difference between figurative truth and verifiable truth. When children read straight history, they are being exposed to a process as well as to information. As in the case of straightforward science writing, they are learning how to think about a subject as well as what to think about it. A historian's account of how the information was tracked down in the first place may turn out to be the crucial spark that ignites a child's curiosity. This leads the child to more books, which in turn may result in a letter scrawled in a childish hand that begins "Dear Mr. Trease. . . ."

The distinction between fiction and fact does not mean, however, that one is necessarily "truer" than the other. Not in the sense of underlying truth. Jill Paton Walsh is correct in this. The truth, in the deeper sense, can certainly be revealed by imaginative fictionalization as well as by documented history. Without question, her book *A Chance Child* (Farrar, 1978) comes just as close to giving children the truth about the Industrial Revolution as any historian with an arsenal of facts could ever do. Facts in this instance could not make us feel any more poignantly the hunger and exhaustion of the children in the mills and mines. Creep's story haunts the reader as doggedly as the ghost of Creep haunted his brother.

But there are other roads to the past. History, well written, deserves to be one. To travel this road, along with such companions as Milton Meltzer or Olivia Coolidge, is a trip worth taking. Furthermore, the verifiable truth of history, as opposed to the figurative truth of fiction, need not "torment" boys and girls, as Jane Austen's Catherine Morland seemed to think. Compare the following excerpts, one fiction and the other nonfiction, to see how far history has come since the old days when battles and dates vied with each other to reduce the reader to catatonic boredom:

> So here they were, fewer than eight hundred people including women and children. With their own hands they built houses along the fjords. There was not only grass for their cows and sheep. There was food for their tables: milk, cheese, fish—and butter to spread on the fish. (Fish was their substitute for bread; there was no grain to make bread.) More fish dangled on every drying rack, soon to be sorted for winter eating. At different seasons there would be reindeer and seals, sometimes a big white bear (not to mention wolves), and small wild creatures still unafraid of man. Every Norseman knew how to flight an arrow. Come spring, there would be birds' eggs and tender dandelion greens. There was wood enough from the stunted trees and huge shaggy stacks of driftwood to warm their homes and cook their meals for years to come.[6]

From a book called *Strange Footprints on the Land: Vikings in America* by Constance Irwin, the foregoing is nonfiction. The next is from another book about the Vikings called *Blood Feud* by Rosemary Sutcliff. It is fiction.

> Spring in the land of the Rus proved to be a wet and muddy time. The blocks of broken ice piled up and dammed the Dnieper, so that soon there were floods all across the marshes; and for a while, the world that had been frozen under white snow seemed foundering in black mud. . . . The long-ships were run out from the high-crested keelsheds down on to the slipways. And the ship-building that had begun with timber felling in the autumn got into full swing, so that all day long the waterside of Kiev rang with shipyard sounds: adze on timber, hammer on anvil, the shovelling of great fires that steamed the light planks into shape for the sides of the new vessels. And everywhere was the smell of pitch and new timber and the sharp tang of burning cattle-dung, and the green freshness of spring.[7]

Both books, each in its own way, permit us to view the world much as the Vikings saw it. And since all the selections quoted in "Writing the Literature of Fact" also were taken from history books, it should be fairly obvious that children can find good reading, and plenty of it, on the history shelves.

The commentators on the following pages, although few in number compared to commentators in other disciplines, will confirm the value of history. We need to hear from them, as well as from all the other historians who have yet to share their ideas. We need to understand how historians go about interpreting evidence from the past.

Above all, we need their enthusiasm to promote interest in history itself, both for children and for adults working with children. If Jill Paton Walsh thinks that historical fiction has been treated with "amused dismissiveness," she should be aware that straight history has been and is still considered by too many as hardly worth dismissing. The fictional Catherine Morland is not the only reader who has never willingly "looked into" history books. If all the tormented readers who now hurry past the 900s on their way to the fiction shelves would only open these "great volumes," they might encounter as much pleasure, although quite different in kind, as Catherine Morland did in reading *Udolpho*.

History Books for Children

Frances Clarke Sayers

For the student of history at his beginnings it is accordingly imperative that his appetite be hearty and catholic to the verge of indiscriminate. Just as abundant production is requisite for the happy occurrence of outstanding work, so abundant reading develops the original mind. It does so by forcing the student himself to frame a synthesis—his particular fusion—out of the diversity of other historical minds and the second sight of the events themselves.[1]

Anyone who is fortunate enough to be a true lover of history is probably so endowed because, early in life, he felt himself involved in the past. Those schooled in the texts of the first decade of this country found history a matter of dates and kings, wars and revolutions, conquests and defeats, broken up into short paragraphs and summarized in outline form at the end of the chapter. History was not for such as these unless they were fortunate enough to have a text which somehow, at some point, flowed like a story, climax following climax; or came upon a teacher who made the past live as part of their own present, and contrived to concern the children he taught in the whole fate of the human race.

Modern education interrupts the "stream of history" by making it a part of Social Studies; but in so doing, the role of the common man, the fascination of daily life through the centuries, and the connection between past and present become intimate and full of human meaning. The emphasis upon the social interpretation of history for children has resulted in a body of historical writing which is inspiriting, imaginative, and dynamic.

Books such as *The History of Everyday Things in England* by the Quennells and *Colonial Living* by Edwin Tunis succeed in using a specific subject or topic as a clue to the greater concept of the history and progress of man. They offer opportunity, also, for a full exploration of a period, and this pattern follows the natural interests of children. Certain periods have a strong appeal for children; the life of primitive man, the feudal period, the age of the great discoverers—these are subjects upon which many children are intent in the span of reading years between the ages of nine to twelve and thirteen. Children find exhilaration in reading history when it is based on sound, even minute scholarship, and has in addition that edge of distinctive writing which brings it into the area of literature.

The judicious use of source material strengthens the appeal of history for children. The journals, letters, and diaries of men and women and their contemporaries give immediacy to historic accounts of their accomplishments. The words of Columbus, the diaries of Jefferson, the letters that passed between father and son or husband and wife at the time of the War of the Revolution or the War Between the States—these serve to wear away the lackluster acceptance of reiterated fact piled upon fact, year after year. Suddenly, through his own words, a man is revealed, and the magnitude of his accomplishment is freshly realized. Much of the present-day child's interest in history is due to a new recognition of the appeal of source material. To read the Elizabethan prose from Hakluyt's Voyages is to know the flavor of the age, to freshen the perception, and to arouse the imagination of the reader. It was thus. And here are the very words, spoken at the time.

Certain writers show themselves steeped in and colored by the reading they have done. James Daugherty, in his books of biography and history, reveals his fervent contact with historic sources, and his books are moving and memorable as a result. In 1938, a book of unusual character appeared: *Never to Die: The Egyptians in Their Own Words* by Josephine Mayer and Tom Prideaux. Here the Egyptian civilization was presented by excerpts from the sacred writings and illustrated with reproductions of Egyptian art. This book set the pace for much that was to come.

But it was the distinguished historian Hendrik Willem Van Loon who risked the heights of maturity in his interpretation of history for children. His *Story of Mankind* is a philosophical approach. He invites the judgment of children upon their past, showing them the necessity of weighing evidence in disputes, and giving them the material with which to work. His bias is toward tolerance and compassion, an opening of minds, a sharpening of perception. His humor and wit enliven the text as does the play of his rich individuality. It is significant that this book won the first Newbery award in 1922, setting a standard of achievement for all the titles which were to follow. The book put an end to the authoritarian, the bigoted, and the prejudiced points of view which so often in the past had been acceptable where children were concerned. It put an end to dullness, and gave to the generations of children caught between two World Wars a spiritual balance wheel. It is a book for children, but, like several other classics of childhood, it has leaped over boundaries of age to be acclaimed by readers of all ages who seek to know their own place in the long and enduring story of humanity.

With all inventive, fresh ways of presenting history to children, the chronological approach still holds an appeal for young readers. Genevieve Foster, gifted writer and artist, has experimented with time in her unusual books which combine history and biography. Her *George Washington's World* and *Augustus Caesar's World* present the contemporary world as background for the life span of the subject of her biography, and include accounts of the arts, science, and politics of the time in which her subjects lived. These richly documented, horizontal views of history are infinitely varied and interesting. This approach adds a new dimension of reality to facts which had not been formerly related to each other, and it comprises a singularly original presentation of history for children.

The outstanding tenet of writing for children in the second quarter of this century is an insistence on first-hand authenticity in science, the arts, history, biography, and travel. A renewed and vigorous research in history and biography is called for, a sound knowledge of the sciences, a lively and genuine interest on the part of the author in his subject, and the ability to inform his writing with a measure of his knowledge and his feeling. These touchstones have been substituted for a previous acceptance of much that was diluted, rewritten, and many times removed from original sources of knowledge and research.

Even the field of travel has received a new vitality from this emphasis upon direct experience, with the result that several books of marked distinction have come into being. Gone are the boring compilations of facts, wearing a weak disguise of fiction, in which an all-knowing aunt and uncle—one wonders why the parents were never able to travel—accompanied two children to a foreign land, apparently for the express purpose of giving guide-book answers to the unnatural questions the children were made to ask. Now men and women whose knowledge of the land they describe is intimate or native give accounts of the life led there, as well as the descriptive details, beloved of tourists. . . .

A new sense of responsibility informs the outstanding books which seek to acquaint children with the wider world. The immense and immediate necessity of our living together on a shrunken planet is responsible for a search for understanding and sympathy, and for the realization that the dignity of man is a term that applies to all peoples everywhere.

But though in many respects we live in an enlightened period, as far as children's literature in these areas is concerned, the need to apply critical judgment becomes increasingly acute. The truth is that the whole field of nonfiction is being somewhat exploited. Titles roll from the presses in quantities which may be far in excess of the normal and natural demands of the children themselves. The harvest is abundant, but much of the bulk is chaff. The supply may well reflect the abundance of the sources, rather than the genuine interests of the children. The very plethora of books makes it more difficult to recognize the individual, deeply felt, and well-realized expression of an author than it was when the major problem was scarcity. The judicious selection of books for children must be attained in the shadow of the great threat of our time to the inviolability of individual reaction and individual taste: namely, a mass conformity induced by mass pressures and mass markets.

The Ten Bad Things about History

F. N. Monjo

I am often asked why, in dealing with men such as Thomas Jefferson, Benjamin Franklin, Abraham Lincoln or Theodore Roosevelt, I permit myself to invent, occasionally, scenes that may never have occurred and to introduce dialogue that was, assuredly, never spoken. In other words, why do I fictionalize biography in writing for young children?

The answer is that I always try to use, as narrator, a child associated with the great figure in question: Ellen Randolph, Jefferson's favorite granddaughter, in *Grand Papa and Ellen Aroon;* TR's son, Quentin, in *The One Bad Thing About Father;* Franklin's grandson, Benny Bache, in *Poor Richard in France;* Lincoln's favorite son, Tad, in *Me and Willie and Pa;* and U. S. Grant's young son, Fred, in *The Vicksburg Veteran.* The use of a child as narrator, a child intimately associated with the person under scrutiny, makes possible a casual intimacy which, I believe, young readers find congenial.

But it presents the writer with unusual difficulties, too. For history takes a slapdash approach to what it chooses to record. And history can often be most unobliging. It can inundate us with trunksful of trivia on subjects hardly worth discussing, while remaining obstinately silent about all manner of crucial issues. It will tell us precisely what Mrs. Lincoln wrote to her bonnet-maker about the shade of lavender ribbon she wanted on her hat. But it will tell us not one word about whether or not Lincoln's young son, Tad, ever talked with his father about the Emancipation Proclamation. It will tell us that Jefferson's grandchildren ran footraces on the lawn of Monticello, and that their Grand Papa gave the winner prizes of ripe cherries gathered with his own hand. But it won't give us a single hint as to whether or not he ever said anything to them about Alexander Hamilton, or Napoleon, or Aaron Burr, or the Louisiana Purchase.

No, history goes its wayward, uncooperative way; dumps its jumble of facts at our feet; and forces the writer to sift the meaningful from the nonsensical, the amusing from the dull.

If one is committed to writing nothing but out-and-out nonfiction, and if one is left with huge gaps of vital information, one must be brave and stoic about it, confess the hiatus and get on with the facts that the documents supply.

But if one is writing fiction, one is surely not committing any crime to give in to the temptation of stuffing these awkward gaps with bits of plausible conjecture.

Thus, in writing *Grand Papa and Ellen Aroon*, I couldn't bear to omit all mention of the vast extent of the Louisiana Purchase, which more than doubled the size of our nation in 1803—even though history had nothing to say about how Ellen took the news of that great acquisition. All it told me was that Ellen's mother, Patsy Jefferson Randolph, used to teach her daughters mathematics, English, French and history, at home. So, I invented a little scene in which Mrs. Randolph has Ellen figure out, by long division, just how much money her Grand Papa paid for one square mile of the Louisiana Territory. Something like that *may* have happened—though I make no claim that it did.

In the same manner, fiction can be used to amuse and instruct simultaneously. In writing *Me and Willie and Pa*, a story told from Tad Lincoln's point of view, I earnestly wanted Tad to be able to ask his father what Emancipation was all about. But history was provokingly close-mouthed on the subject. So I resorted to the device of having Tad ask the question anyhow, and allowing Lincoln to explain the principle of Emancipation in the very words of a contemporary humorist, Petroleum V. Nasby—a writer whose works Lincoln was known to chuckle over and admire.

Both these fictional scenes are plausible, I believe, though I certainly do not put them forth as fact.

But history disappoints us in many, many more ways than in merely withholding information we wish it had supplied. I should like to discuss ten of these disappointments here, briefly, though I feel sure that it could supply us with many more than ten if we were to delve closely into the matter. So let me simply list them, then: The Ten Bad Things about History.

1. Men and events refuse to hold still in a single pose while we try to sketch their picture. It doesn't matter how far back they are in time or how long they've been dead. The moment we shift our point of view, the whole picture looks different. When I was studying biology, as a sophomore in college, I was supposed to draw the picture of a microscopic animal called the *rotifer*. Now the rotifer lives in water, and he moves faster than the speed of light. It is impossible to focus a microscope on him, because he swims away too fast to be caught up with. To try to draw him, therefore, is simply laughable, but that is what you're up against when you want to draw a sketch of, say, Thomas Jefferson. Every time you think you have him in focus, he swims out of the field; and when you catch up with him

again, you are looking at an entirely different facet of the man. Now you glimpse him as he must have appeared to Aaron Burr. Or to Hamilton. Or to Franklin. Or to his daughters. Or to his old teacher, George Wythe. Or to John Adams. Which is the real Jefferson? History is most uncooperative. It doesn't say a word. It just leaves you with your microscope—or your kaleidoscope—while somebody stands over your shoulder, impatiently murmuring: "Haven't you finished sketching that rotifer yet?"

2. History almost never contents itself with a single straight answer to our questions. It much prefers to give us three or four sets of possible answers. We want history to be a simple arithmetic problem. We want it to tell us. "Five plus six makes eleven." Instead it faces us with an awful set of quadratic equations: 3X plus 4Y minus 8Z equals 1/8, bracketed with 19X minus 7/11Y plus Z over 3 equals 419, and so on; where X, Y and Z turn out to have several plus and minus solutions, and both sets of answers are the "right" ones. If you happen to be Theodore Roosevelt, or John Hay (his Secretary of State), you think the U.S. was right to allow the Republic of Panama to come into being. If you are Woodrow Wilson, you think that Colombia was bitterly wronged, and is entitled to $25,000,000 compensation. And history seems to be saying that both sides are "right." It offers us no help whatever in our attempts to simplify our moral problems and choices. And it gives us double and triple sets of answers to far too many of our urgent questions.

3. History hates to tell the truth, but would much prefer to suppress it and to conceal whatever hard facts it does possess. Once you have read a good deal of history you begin to realize that most of its momentous decisions occur behind closed doors, among people sworn to secrecy, people who will go to great lengths to keep all the rest of us from knowing precisely what happened. Did President Abraham Lincoln know that he was forcing the start of the Civil War when he sent supply ships to the Union troops in Fort Sumter in Charleston? Did Franklin Roosevelt and Cordell Hull have positive knowledge, in advance, that Pearl Harbor was about to be bombed? Some of us suspect that the answer is yes, in both cases; but we shall never know for sure. Those decisions were so important that no records were allowed to exist.

4. The fourth bad thing about history is that—despite what you may have heard to the contrary—it categorically refuses to repeat itself. Events and men come together once and only once in just the same way, in actions that can never be duplicated. Events flash by at top speed and they cannot ever be replayed in slow motion, just because we missed something or would like to have a closer look at what really happened.

5. History is elusive and evasive. It wou't tell us which came first, the chicken or the egg. It won't tell us whether great men make

great events, or whether great events make great men. If you question it too closely it will probably tell you that both are true. Or neither—because accident plays its part, too. And ignorance. And discovery. And calamity. And chance.

6. History supplies us with facts we won't ever be able to use again. Now that we know that Queen Marie Antoinette was a foolish spendthrift, it is much too late to alter the course of the French Revolution. Nor can we go back and warn the nineteenth century to keep an eye on that dangerously warlike Corsican, Napoleon. It keeps teaching us things we no longer need to know. It's like that joke they were telling when Goldwater ran for President, the one that went: "What shall we do, Barry, if the Russians attack us?" And his answer was, "Well, first thing we gotta do is get all our covered wagons together in a circle. . . ."

7. History refuses to yield up its secrets, as an exact science will do . . . it refuses to teach us things the way a chemical experiment will. Every time we combine two parts of hydrogen and one of oxygen, we know we shall have a molecule of water. It never fails. Chemistry gives us hundreds of thousands of formulas we can depend upon. They never vary. History refuses to give us even *one* formula we can put our faith in. Not one infallible rule that will work every time.

8. History doesn't know the meaning of a happy ending. Every ending it has ever written is a tragedy. And very often it laces this melancholy scene with a dash of cheap cynicism. It is not enough that the great French chemist Lavoisier, the discoverer of oxygen, must lose his head on the guillotine. No, somebody must add: "La république n'a pas besoin de savants" ("The French republic has no need of learned men"). Why does history tell us that? What sort of moral uplift is that supposed to provide? It is mean-spirited and barbaric. But it happened.

9. The ninth bad thing about history is that—like the old priestesses at Delphi, in ancient Greece—it gives us nothing but two-faced, oracular answers, answers that say both yes and no when we ask why there has had to be so much suffering through all the ages of the past. What have they all meant—all those millions killed in wars; all those dead of the plague; all those human sacrifices to evil gods; all those chained slave laborers, building the pyramids, rowing Roman galleys, tilling someone else's fields? We ask it to sum up the meaning of the past for us, but we don't get our answer. We ask it to give us a clue to the everwidening mystery of life. It remains silent.

10. And the tenth bad thing about history is that it is just as useless in predicting the future as it is in helping us understand and accept the outrages it has recorded in the past. But, if it can't give us any reliable or useful answers for the present, if its lessons be-

come obsolete before we have had time to learn them, if it can't justify the past or predict the future, why do we bother with it? What good is it? Why should we countenance its presence any more in our midst? What will it ever do for us? What will it ever do for our children?

Well, it will tell us that once there was a man named Shakespeare. That once there was a woman named Sappho. There was a Mozart, a Lincoln, a Galileo, a Joan of Arc. There was an Aesculapius. There was an Archimedes. There was a Martin Luther King. No, it refuses, and will always refuse, to give us the crisp, easy, fast answers we keep hoping for. But it will tell our children of great human beings and great accomplishments, if we help them to learn to listen to its voices.

Even more than astronomy, a sense of history can help give our children a sense of this mysterious human existence we all share, with its endless, inexplicable linkings, from generation to generation . . . an infinity of beings, moving through an endless stretch of time.

And best of all, a broad knowledge of history can give a child an unparalleled sense of the wide, wide spectrum of humanity that he or she is part of—a sense of its teeming variety, its throbbing multiplicity. And that child may conclude that, in so much diversity, surely there can be an honored place for him, no matter how daring and outrageous his dream may be. And how exhilarating it will be for him to know—for that child to know—that history has never mapped, and never will be able to map, the final limits of human possibility.

Who's Neutral?

Milton Meltzer

While doing research for a history of the Jews of Eastern Europe, I was struck by how often they spoke of a book that had come as a revelation to them when they were growing up. Again and again the angry young men of Czarist Russia mention Chernishevsky's *What Is to Be Done?* The novel's utopian vision of a socialist society became Holy Scripture for the radical intelligentsia of the 1860s and '70s.

Adapted by the author from a talk given in 1973 at Exeter, England. Reprinted from *Children's Literature in Education*, no.14:24–35 (1974) by permission of the publisher, Agathon Press, Inc., New York.

Such books make their greatest mark when they reach the reader in his adolescent years. That is the time when each young person, as Erik Erikson put it, must forge for himself "some working unity out of the effective remnants of his childhood and the hopes of his anticipated adulthood." Of course it isn't books alone that play a part in the young person's quest for self-actualization. There is his upbringing in family and community, his schooling, the films, television. He looks everywhere for that ground of truth on which he can stand before he commits the power of his body and his mind to the world as it is, or as he may wish to remake it.

What about the writer whose work is meant for these young readers? He too is trying to find some pattern or meaning in the struggle to realize his own humanity. He starts his work with what he is. The direction his work takes comes out of the values he is committed to. He is never disinterested, no matter how much he may claim to be. It is a matter of what interests he will serve, quite openly. Peace, racial equality, economic security, freedom of expression: if he believes in such values, then he will want his work to contribute to the ending of war, of poverty, of racism. At the least, if his writing encourages a spirit of cooperation and concern in the generation growing up, then his effort has not gone for nothing.

The writer cannot be neutral, even if he wants to be. Whatever he writes has some effect. Writing of one kind may make the young reader feel cynical, passive, hopeless. Another kind of writing may turn him in a new direction and give him courage, pride, and confidence. How this happens it is very hard to determine.

Each of us is different, and what moves us to change is incredibly complex. It can be the most casual remark of a teacher. A negative instance is recalled by Ed Bullins, the black American playwright. At college, years ago, he worked for a long time on a dramatic sketch of life in the black ghetto. Thinking it was the best thing he had done up to that moment, he gave it to a teacher he respected very much, asking him to read it over the weekend:

> When I went to class next Monday, I waited through the whole lecture for him to say something about it. He didn't say a word. So after class I went up and asked him if he had read it. "Yes," he said. "I read it. And if I had my way, someone like you would never be in college." He handed it back to me and walked away. I dropped out of school for about a year. It took me that long to get over it. . . . When I went back I decided I was going to write, do, and think anything that *I* felt was right—and it wouldn't matter again what *any* critic thought of it.

It is not always such a direct, personal experience that reshapes us. Many whites who had never been South became persuaded simply by what they read that slavery was wrong, and that they must help to overthrow it. The life of Lydia Maria Child furnishes examples of the power of both the personal and the literary experience. She was a successful young American novelist of the early eighteenth century. One day she heard William Lloyd Garrison, the abolitionist, make a speech in Boston. That speech changed the whole pattern of her life. "He got hold of the strings of my conscience and pulled me into reforms," she said. "It is of no use to imagine what might have been, if I had never met him. Old dreams vanished, old associates departed, and all things became new."

She decided to study slavery, to trace its roots and causes, to understand its consequences. She wrote a book about it, making an attack upon race prejudice her central theme. The book, which came out in 1833, was called *An Appeal in Favor of That Class of Americans Called Africans*. It was the first book attacking slavery to be published in the United States. It is equally distinguished as one of the early arguments against racism. It proved to be the most influential book of its kind until the arrival twenty years later of *Uncle Tom's Cabin*. It had a profound effect upon many individual readers, whose lives were changed by the power of her thought and feeling. William Ellery Channing, Wendell Phillips, Thomas Higginson—such giants of the antislavery cause publicly declared that it was Lydia Maria Child's book which converted them to abolitionism. Channing said reading it woke his conscience and made him end his silence on the great issue. Phillips said her book "obliged" him to become an abolitionist.

Reading *An Appeal* made people ask questions about themselves and their world. Writing a book can make you do that, too. Sometimes I think I know the answers before I start work on a book. The act of writing it often teaches me better. If I am lucky, I may find out what the true questions are. And while I'm at it, if the book is any good, it may suggest some useful questions to the reader and help him find his own answers.

What is most important for us to learn is the art of asking questions. It's what we've long said we hoped the schools would teach—not facts, not dates, not formulas—but the art and *necessity* of asking questions. Real questions, questions about things children care about, questions that can often embarrass or threaten us. Why are things this way? Do they have to be this way? Can't they be changed? How do we go about making change? If institutions have become rigidly resistant to change, is violence justifiable to bring it about?

I don't know to what extent we can expect school or teachers to answer such subversive questions. Our American society, like all societies, represses dissent at some point the authorities consider dangerous. For Richard M. Nixon that point seemed to have been the end of his nose. Watergate revealed that we failed lamentably to impart any moral sense or any critical spirit to some of those whom our schools and colleges have instructed. "A profoundly sinister event," the *New York Times* said of Watergate, "because in so many of its aspects it reflects an authoritarian turn of mind and a ready willingness on the part of those at the highest levels of Government to subvert democratic values and practices." The Watergate scandal alerted us to the dangers of a society whose leaders lie because they do not want the people to know, and whose people fear to ask questions or have forgotten how.

Here is where a radical approach to history might have helped. It does not go in for the myth-making which so many books for young readers are ridden with. It confronts contemporary issues. It doesn't pile up the "objective" trivia which many academics delight in. Rather, it follows what the historian Carl Becker said is "the imperative command that knowledge shall serve purpose, and learning be applied to a solution of the problem of human life." What the concerned historian chooses to investigate in the past, as Croce put it, is determined by "an interest in the life of the present." Past facts must answer "to a present interest."

If commitment to human values guides a writer's questions, it does not follow that it distorts the answers. There is no need to tamper with the truth. We will know the historian selects only some of the facts out of the vast mass which may be available to him. In my case, I am interested in stressing certain facts which have been buried or bent, because recalling them may help serve human needs now.

To show what I mean, perhaps the easiest thing to do will be to talk briefly about some of my own books. Only as examples of intention and method. It's up to reader and critic to decide how good or bad the work is. I know that books written with the best intentions can be terrible. Even those which have had a recognizably profound effect upon masses of readers can be adjudged a literary mess. Chernishevsky's *What Is To Be Done?* has been called an "unbelievably bad didactic novel." The same was said of *Uncle Tom's Cabin* until Edmund Wilson rediscovered merits in it which generations of critics had ignored.

Many of my books have had something to say about minorities in American life. They deal with that question which is at the heart of our history—racism. More and more of us are now coming to see the centrality of racism in the United States. The black experience is what it is because of white racism. The same could be said of the Asian Americans, the Native Americans, the Hispanic Americans. . . . For more than 300 years the white majority has systematically subordinated black people. Consciously or not, white America has acted as though it believes there is a superiority in its whiteness which justifies actions that harm black people. Why has racism lasted this long? Largely because we whites profit by it. Millions of us gain economic, political, and psychological benefits from racism. Others—and far more of us—profit from institutional racism. By that I mean the actions of institutions we are part of—school boards, businesses, churches, trade unions, newspapers, city councils, hospitals, welfare agencies, the courts—the institutions of our society which always have and still do place White over Black.

Well-meaning though we may be, unknowingly and unthinkably we whites operate in and through institutions which oppress life in the black community. The question of intention isn't as important as the effects these institutions have. Their policies, procedures, and decisions do in fact subordinate blacks and permit whites to maintain control over them.

Only recently has any attention been paid to those institutional practices which give advantage to the white and penalize the black. Few of these institutions in America are openly racist any longer. Civil rights measures have deprived much institutional racism of any status in law. But institutional practices remain covertly racist nevertheless. Built into them are attitudes, traditions, habits, assumptions which have great power to reward and penalize.

As a white writer concerned with racism, I think one's main job is to combat racism within the white community. It should be obvious that you cannot deal with the black experience without talking about the white experience. And vice versa. Each has shaped the course of the other. The quickest glance at American history illustrates the point. Our constitution and our political parties were molded by issues concerning blacks. The new nation's commerce and industrial growth rested on the South's slave economy. Our territorial expansion South and West were a direct product of slavery. The Civil War and the politics and economics out of which it exploded were linked to slavery. Our imperialist expansion in the nineteenth and twentieth centuries—down through the war in Vietnam—has been conditioned by racism. From the 1950s to the present, American history has been marked by repeated struggles for full freedom and equality. And not only for the black American, but for the native American, the Hispanic American, the Asian American.

In thinking of how to write about racism, I decided not to use the traditional approach of historians. They usually look at past societies from the top. This, they tell us, is what the King, the President, the General did, the men who ruled. But what about the people on the bottom? How did the strange new land look to kidnapped Africans carried in chains across the Atlantic? What was life like for the slave picking cotton or cutting cane? For the despised free black living on the fringe of a slave society? For the preacher plotting an uprising in the piney woods? For the mother standing with her child on the auction block? For the fugitive hiding in the swamps?

I dug into letters, speeches, memoirs, diaries, journals, slave narratives, newspapers, court records, public hearings, interviews, affidavits, eyewitness accounts. In them I found more than enough traces of the past to edit a documentary history of black Americans. Called *In Their Own Words*, it appeared in three volumes. My aim was twofold: to help the reader understand what blacks felt, thought, and did, and to make whites see themselves in the light blacks had seen them, down through the centuries of racism. Such a history is no panacea for racism, but it is a necessary medicine, a kind of truth serum, that is indispensable if we are to make any progress toward building a healthy society.

Racism and slavery were at the heart of the American Civil War, of course. But they were also crucial elements of other American wars. Young people have been told little about them. Our war with Mexico in the 1840s was called by one of our presidents, who soldiered in it as a young lieutenant, the most disgraceful war America had ever fought. Some time ago I had occasion to examine a dozen books about that war, written for young readers. They were all long on battles and short on morals. They asked none of the significant questions about the past that could help young people think more clearly about the present.

Realizing what parallels there were between the war in Vietnam and that Mexican war, I wrote a book about the earlier conflict. In it you see the war from the standpoint of the men who joined up in a patriotic fever to do the fighting. You hear about the handful of people back home who opposed the war as a ruthless land grab, as a means to expand slave territory and strengthen the power of the slaveholders in the national government. And you look at the war through the eyes of the Mexicans, too. How does an American war feel to the victims on the other side? What do they think when invaders come killing and burning their way into their homeland, piously declaring they are doing it for the enemy's own sake, to introduce an inferior people, largely Indian, to a higher, Anglo-Saxon civilization?

You see too how a president manipulates a congress into war. How congressmen twist and turn between what their conscience tells them is right and what political ambition tells them is "necessary." How politicians influence military decisions no matter what the terrible consequences for the other side or for their own soldiers. And how when people come to see a war as unnecessary, unjust, and evil, they can mount a tidal wave of opposition to end it.

To do this I used letters, diaries, journals, news accounts, legislative hearings, eyewitness reports, joined by a sustaining narrative to illuminate the connections and contradictions, the parallels and opposition, the truth and the lies.

The other war whose issues I thought are significant for today was the Seminole War of 1835–42. It was the longest, bloodiest and most costly of all the Indian wars in our history. It was fought in Florida by two minorities—the Seminole Indians and the blacks—joined as allies—against the dominant white majority. The whites were greedy for the Indians' land and wanted to recapture the escaped black slaves who were being hidden by the Indians. The Indians fought to protect their homeland and the runaway slaves they had given shelter. The blacks were fighting for their freedom. A ragged, starving guerrilla force, the Indians and blacks defied the power of an invading army ten times their number. In the end, four thousand Seminole were driven into exile by a mighty nation that boasted of its justice, its honor, and its love of liberty. But America paid a heavy price for its racism, a price we still pay in many ways. What conquering the Indians did to us as a people and a nation we are only beginning to understand. "That process of fraud, corruption, trickery, violence, spread like a sickness through all the American body politic, and those methods are often the methods still used in settling political, social and international problems," one historian has pointed out.

What the young will learn from reading about historical experience, I hope, is that citizens—then and now—must act for themselves. They cannot rely on government alone to satisfy their needs or give them justice and equality.

But coming to understand what is wrong does not necessarily move us to action. We have to believe that something else is possible, that what we do, each of us, can make a difference. Otherwise, the young may decide to live only for themselves, to retreat into drugs or despair, or cynically to ride with things as they are and to get a little piece of the action for themselves. This is where biography can be so important. As a white writer, I am especially concerned that children learn there have been white people, as well as black, who have refused to accept racism, who have challenged it at great risk. Men and women such as John Brown, William Lloyd Garrison, Wendell Phillips, Prudence Crandall, Theodore Weld, Lucretia Mott, to name only a few. I thought it useful to write the biographies of three such whites—Lydia Maria Child, Samuel Gridley Howe, and Thaddeus Stevens—for young readers. Telling the stories of such brave men and women is important. We are not just showing young people what is wrong with American life when we do this. We are introducing men and women who found that out for themselves, who struggled to overcome white racism in themselves, and who joined in the social and political fight against it. The young reader sees that history isn't made up only of the great and powerful who oppressed others, or of those who didn't care. We have had heroes and heroines who were frontline fighters against racism and injustice. And we will always need their kind.

History Books: Making America's History Come Alive

Carol Gay

"Books that remain faithful to the very essence of art . . . offer to children an intuitive and direct way of knowledge, a simple beauty capable of being perceived immediately, arousing in their souls a vibration which will endure all their lives."[1] These words of Paul Hazard in *Books, Children and Men* offer us a key into an area that we neglect with peril—our nation's past—and emphasize the role that children's literature can play better perhaps than any other learning resource. History books can help us, texts can too; but we should bear in mind that children often don't relate to names of battles, to dates of treaties, to statistics. Like us, they relate to individuals, to emotions they can feel within themselves, to stories that arouse their curiosity. That is why teachers of literature are in a unique position.

But why the note of urgency in the phrase that it is with peril that we neglect our past? After a rather rude awakening in the fifties to the fact that much of what we had cherished about our past was based on meaningless clichés, and worse, distortions of history, we are just emerging from a period of rather desolate rootlessness when anything smacking of patriotism was suspect, and schools and teachers were urged to avoid anything that came close to empty "flag-waving" and when the 4th of July became something of an embarrassment. Historians and scholars have since taken another look at our past and after careful scholarship and serious reevaluation, we have, for the most part, placed in our children's hands texts that recognize the many-hued cultural and racial threads contributing to both our country's weaknesses and its strengths. Many history books, for instance, start now, not with the traditional narrative of the Mayflower, but with our strong Chicano beginnings in the Southwest. Emphasis on "our country's heritage" is now broadened to our country's "multi-ethnic roots." Even more important, perhaps, it is no longer necessary for us to pretend that there is no shame in our past, and most of our texts include the racial conflicts that have marred our history from its beginnings.

Adapted from "Children's Literature and the Bicentenniel" by Carol Gay in *Language Arts* 53:11–16 (Jan. 1976). Copyright © 1976 by the National Council of Teachers of English. Reprinted by permission of the publisher and the author.

Now that we have reached this point, it is time again to stress the importance of learning about that past. In a society already suffering from so-called "future shock," when a "golden oldie" is a song of a few years previous to the present, when ancient history is frequently the First World War, we need to stretch our children's minds and imaginations further back than "Happy Days." This becomes even more imperative as we realize that most children today do not have the close association with their grandparents that children once had. "Tell me a story about when you were young," used to evoke memories of at least three generations, but no more. In a society in which it is becoming increasingly difficult even to define "value," a society which is almost completely devoid of a sense of the past, we must give our children a past to remember, a past to build on.

There are numerous arguments to be made for putting the past before our children, of course, but why the emphasis on children's *literature?*

Because we must keep a firm grasp on the principles of literary quality if we are going to arouse any "lasting vibrations" in the souls of our students. Not just any book can "offer to children an intuitive and direct way of knowledge, a simple beauty capable of being perceived immediately. . . ." Sometimes it is easy to forget this. That is why we all too often allow in our classrooms the brief excerpt, the easy-to-read adaptation, the retelling of a classic. But literary quality is not something that is automatic with putting words on a page. Literary quality is a combination of style, theme, and characterization that builds into an integral, unified work of art that is easily destroyed with too much tampering. Too frequently we give our students only words on a page and then blame them for not liking to read, when it is we who are to blame. We do not want words for children that they will ignore. Only the words of a true literary artist or the words transmitted through true folk art can help students to an understanding of their heritage that can extend beyond the pages of a textbook and become part of their lives.

But how do we get those words to work for us?

One way to enable students to develop closer ties with the past is by sharing with them the poems and tales loved by children of times past. The suggestions made here are based on colonial times, an era that received much attention during our Bicentennial, but an era perhaps hardest to reach in ordinary times because it seems so far removed from us not only in time, but in attitudes and mores. This barrier can be overcome by reading students the same stories that were read by Puritan children who lived through the years of the birth of our country. A hasty glance at a history of children's literature might seem to indicate that the only fare that our forefathers had when they were children was the redoubtable *Spiritual Milk for Boston Babes in either England, drawn from the Breasts of Both Testaments for their Souls' Nourishment,* but this is to overlook the fact that the Puritans were direct descendants of the lively Elizabethans and inheritors of the same oral traditions as their English brethren. That this tradition persisted in America is borne out by such evidence as an entry in Cotton Mather's diary which complains, on September 27, 1713: "I am informed that the Minds and Manners of many people about the Countrey are much corrupted by foolish Songs and Ballads, which the Hawkers and Peddlars carry into all ports of the Countrey. By way of antidote, I would procure poetical Compositions full of Piety, to be published, and scattered into all Corners of the Land." It ignores also the fact that not all Puritan productions lack interest and charm, that they often were no more didactic than their Church of England counterparts (and many of our own current tracts on drugs and homosexuality decked out as realistic novels). What elementary school child could resist the appeal of the tiny hornbook that colonial children carried about with them and learned from?[2] One of the most widely published books that almost every American child for over a century and a half was familiar with was, of course, the now pedagogically, theologically, and literarily disdained *New England Primer*. But in almost every edition was included the most widely known hymn in colonial America, Isaac Watts's "Cradle Hymn." How many American children, Puritan or not, were lulled to sleep by its comforting words:

> Hush, my dear, lie still and slumber,
>   Holy angels guard thy bed,
> Heavenly blessings without number
>   Gently falling on thy head.

Why not let your students get a little closer to American history and traditions by teaching it to them?

The suggestions made here have been chosen because they are in editions easily available and because they include tales that can be presented to the modern child. Children today are far more protected than their colonial counterparts, who all too early were introduced to death and pain, not necessarily by the Puritan preacher, but by the high infant mortality rate and the rigors of colonial living. I have not included, for instance, such juicy productions as "The Reprobate's Reward, or a Looking-Glass for Disobedient Children, being a full and true Account of the barbarous and bloody Murder of one Elizabeth Wood, living in the city of Cork, by her own Son, as she was riding, upon the 28th day of July, to Kinsale market. How he cut her throat from ear to ear; as also how the murder was found out by her apparition or ghost; the manner of his being taken; his dying words at the place of execution; with a true copy of verses written with his own hand in Cork jail, being a warning to all disobient Children to repent, and obey their parents," a child's book published in Philadelphia in 1798.[3] The teacher would be sure to receive a few calls from parents on this one, although it obviously inculcates some of those down-home virtues we so often are decried for ignoring.

As a matter of fact, most of the children's stories mentioned here are probably already familiar. The point is to present them in the perspective of history. Make clear to even the smallest child that "The House That Jack Built" was a poem that seventeenth- and eighteenth-century children loved and chanted long before it was printed in America in 1806. The older child who might consider himself too sophisticated to be caught up in the rhythms of this cumulative tale might enjoy hearing it if he were told that this is what his colonial counterpart once chanted to his younger brothers and sisters and probably secretly or openly loved himself.

This raises the question of grade levels. The answer, except in a few cases, is that this kind of material can be offered to any grade level from kindergarten to sixth grade through slight variations in presentation. The reason for this is that most of the material stems from the long oral tradition before children's literature became differentiated from so-called "adult literature" (an event that took place in the eighteenth century at the precise time period we are interested in here) or has such high literary quality that it transcends these superficial boundaries and joins with those classics, *Alice in Wonderland, The Hobbit,* and *Wind in the Willows,* that are for all ages and all times.

What were American children preceding the Revolution reading and enjoying besides the abovementioned works? Almost the same things that their English cousins were. In 1770, Thomas Fleet of Boston printed a work that has a long printing history and was probably popular for centuries before it was printed: *Children in the Woods,* more commonly known as *"Babes in the Woods."*[4] In 1774, Hugh Gaine published the first American edition of *Robinson Crusoe,* an abridgment for children. American children have been enjoying it ever since. Even the youngest can enjoy Crusoe's exploits if their teacher will read them aloud (not from an abridgment). A popular book which all ages can still enjoy and which was early published in America and went through edition after edition was *Little Goody Two Shoes,* still readily available in several recent editions. This, of course, was one of the many pirated Newbery editions. After the Revolution there were some attempts to "Americanize" the British tales. For instance, a footnote to a 1796 edition of *Little Goody Two Shoes* comments on the "tyranny" of the English landlord in the tale: "Such is the state of things in Britain. AMERICANS prize your liberty, guard your rights and be happy."[5] *The Life and Death of Robin Hood* became available in an American edition in 1792, but American children were probably already familiar with the first printed version that appeared in England in 1663. In 1794 Isaiah Thomas published *Mother Goose's Melody,* or *Sonnets for the Cradle.* (As anyone who has even the slightest knowledge of children's literature is aware, the originator of the Mother Goose rhymes was not a gossip of Boston, though her grave will undoubtedly continue to be a tourist attraction.) These were the same rhymes that children had been singing for centuries. In bringing these rhymes to first graders and sixth graders, we can point out the long literary tradition they are sharing. We can read some of the *Arabian Nights* tales to children and assure them that children in the eighteenth century enjoyed them too, probably in very cheap editions. No child should be deprived of the fun of *Peter Piper's Practical Principles of Plain and Perfect Pronunciation,* which came along in the 1830s.[6] Its purpose is proudly put forth in its preface: "Peter Piper, without Pretension to Precocity or Profoundness, Puts Pen to Paper to Produce these Puzzling Pages, Purposely to Please the Palates of Pretty Prattling Playfellows, Proudly Presuming that with Proper Penetration it will Probably, and Perhaps Positively, Prove a Peculiarly Pleasant and Profitable Path to Proper, Plain, and Precise Pronunciation. He Prays Parents to Purchase this Playful Performance, Partly to Pay him for his Patience and Pains, Partly to Provide for the Profit of the Printers and Publishers, but Principally to Prevent the Pernicious Prevalence of Perverse Pronunciation." Peter prances through the alphabet with a verse for each letter:

> Lanky Lawrence lost his Lass and Lobster:
> Did Lanky Lawrence lose his Lass and Lobster?
> If Lanky Lawrence lost his Lass and Lobster,
> Where are the Lass and Lobster Lanky Lawrence lost?

Who can resist Lanky Lawrence or Davy Doldrom or Kimbo Kemble or Villiam Veedom? Who can resist trying to parallel Peter's performance perchance? The older child might enjoy Benjamin Franklin's "The Story of the Whistle," written by Franklin for children and available to the teacher in any complete edition of Franklin's works. It is didactic and pompous, but fun.

These are a few of the tales that can help the child gain an insight into the past by sharing the literary joys of the past. These are tales and poems to be read aloud and shared, a part of a living tradition of literature that will not fade.

A second way to make the past come alive through literature is to encourage children to take a penetrating look at a historical figure, as does a biographer or historian. Through journals, letters, contemporary newspapers, biographies, geographies, and additional source materials the child can recreate, not a typical day, but as far as possible an *actual* day of Thomas Jefferson, Alexander Hamilton, George Washington, Benjamin Franklin, or perhaps even a minor figure.

Gathering the materials together might necessitate several trips to the public library, to a university library if one is nearby, or to the historical society in the area; but the result would be an exercise in research that would teach the fourth, fifth, or sixth grader much about America's past, as well as the process of scholarly research. This, after all, is what education is all about—teaching children how to find meaningful answers to interesting questions by means of a disciplined, knowledgeable method.

The first step would be choosing a figure, one on which much source material was readily available—Thomas Jefferson, for example. Then focus on one date, or several. The class, divided into three groups, might each work around a date in a specific period of Jefferson's life: his early years, for instance, or his peak political years, or his old age. Then assemble materials in the classroom (rather than sending the students off to the library to surprise the unsuspecting librarian). Leonard Wibberley's magnificent four-volume biography of Jefferson would be an excellent source.[7] Another source might be a book about Monticello, one such as Gene and Clare Gurney's *Monticello* or Edwin M. Getts's *Thomas Jefferson's Flower Garden at Monticello*. Edmund Morgan's authoritative and readable *Virginians at Home: Family Life in the Eighteenth Century*, although not designed for children, offers much information and many illustrations. A book which describes Virginia geographically, one that is illustrated profusely and well—as well as a few valuable sources, although not directly related to a day in Jefferson's life—might broaden and deepen the picture the students are developing: for instance, the *Memoirs of a Monticello Slave* by Isaac Jefferson or a journal of a young college student from Virginia, Philip F. Vickers, *Journals and Letters: 1767–1774*. Some volumes of Jefferson's papers, journals, and letters would document the dates the class is researching. *The Union List of Serials*, available in most libraries, would indicate which newspapers might have been available to Jefferson on the dates in question; newspapers such as the *Virginia Gazette*, for instance. A librarian can photostat copies of the first page. Students could also find out about the weather during a specific period from a current *Farmer's Almanac*. Climate has changed a bit, but not enough to distort your composite picture. Or, better yet, find out exactly when the sun was shining in Jefferson's life by consulting a contemporary almanac. Oscar Brand's *A Folksinger's History of the Revolution* can indicate the sort of songs that Jefferson might have heard around him and that he might have sung himself.

The possibilities are endless. Be sure to scour Wibberley's bibliographies and bring in as many primary sources as possible. At first glance these might not seem suitable for a fifth- or sixth-grade class, and they will present difficulties, but their historical appeal and their sense of immediacy should outweigh their surface disadvantages. Of course, all this will call for careful preparation; students will need help in finding their way around.

After the material is assembled, each child in each group could cover a specific small area, as near to the chosen date as possible. When finished, each group should have a composite picture of what Jefferson did on a specific day, what letters he wrote, what papers he read, what the weather was like, how the room looked where he wrote his letters, what he was worried about, what he ate, who visited him, and the like.

The child should gain two things: such a close intimate look at a day from the past that the day and the person and the place will come alive for him; and an awareness of how we go about discovering the past. At this time, when we are bombarded with so many stimuli that it is difficult to see beyond the immediate, it is more and more necessary to strive for a sense of the past, to create in our students a realization of the ties that bind us to the men and women who have suffered and loved and hungered and hoped before us. One of the ways that this can be done most effectively is to become aware of past suffering, past loving, past hungering, past hoping, those human qualities that persevere through each century and bind together the past and the present. The assignment should be climaxed with some of the words of Jefferson, or whatever figure you choose. Most of these men were highly articulate and have left us their dreams in their own words for us to build on: the Declaration, for instance, the Hamilton papers, the *Autobiography* of Franklin, and others. In this way children can see how words, artfully and precisely recorded, can speak to them through the centuries, setting up "a vibration which will endure all their lives."

Biography:

Facts Warmed by Imagination

Good biographies are not common. Great biographies are rare. But a good biography is a worthy companion, guide, and friend; and a great biography represents the most difficult and finest achievement of literary art.

——Helen Haines[1]

What Do We Do about Bad Biographies?

Jo Carr

According to Philip Guedalla, biography is "a region that is bounded on the north by history, on the south by fiction, on the east by obituary, and on the west by tedium."[1]

If this is true, then in the region of children's biography we must add more points to our compass. On the northwest, hagiography: George with his little hatchet and Honest Abe gazing into the coals. On the northeast, didacticism: Helen Keller obscured by "mists of adulation." On the southwest, oversimplification: Einstein and his theory of relativity reduced to the third-grade reading level. On the southeast, propaganda: Crispus Attucks, a black hero of convenience. And, from all directions, sentimentality, unwarranted fictionalization, lack of solid documentation, and distortion of history.

Are these views of children's biography too deprecatory? Not according to most of those who have written articles on this subject, including the writers in this collection. As Margery Fisher puts it: "It is in the sadly drab shelves of so-called biographical material for the middle years that a change is long overdue. Between the ages of eight and twelve, how much energy, curiosity, and good will is going to waste!"[2]

What can we do about bad biographies? First, we can cultivate nimble dexterity to skirt the dreadful biographies already on the shelves. Then, we can cultivate equally nimble wits to keep such books off the shelves in the future.

Before we engage in any of this, however, we must decide what we expect biography to do for children. Patrick Groff, in two articles he has written on the subject,[3] demolishes biography-as-inspiration-to-the-young. For one thing, as he points out, biography rarely works that way. And, most unforgivably and all too often, books of that sort are boring. Nobody likes to be preached at, children no more than the rest of us.

In only one particular might we modify what Groff has said about biography as personal inspiration to the young. Although there is certainly no defense for presenting public figures as "human saints," there is a place for "identification" as a child reads about a kindred spirit. Any child who stores dead birds in the refrigerator, for instance, might delight in reading Barbara Brenner's biography of Audubon, but this is an instance of one "odd-ball" of ten joyfully discovering another odd-ball of forty. Identification, yes; emulation, no.

There is no question that identification can be a real attraction to reading biography. Realizing that someone else has faced the same problems, a child may identify instantly with the hardships of the hero. As an example, Elizabeth Segel has ably demonstrated in her analysis of two biographies of Beatrix Potter that pain can result from social injustices over which we have no control. A child similarly victimized might be grateful to Margaret Lane's biography for the honest treatment of rigid social pressure—much the same now as then—instead of being falsely reassured that "nothing is impossible."

The power of biography to encourage the identification of one kindred spirit with another does appeal to children, but no less so than does the vivid dramatization of history. Good biographies, like all good history, reveal exactly what it was like to have lived long ago—"in olden times." It is only when biographies are irresponsibly written and history distorted that we face a problem of considerable significance. All too many biography collections for children fail to measure up to decent professional standards. In deciding what to do about these unfortunate books, since in most cases we are unable to replace them without inordinate expense, we might devise, in desperation, a fresh approach to the problem. Perhaps librarians who can manage to look at weak collections as a challenge might consider the suggestions that follow.

Encourage children to read more autobiography and less biography. In discovering the past, either for school work or for pleasure, a child reading an autobiography will be walking around in the skin of someone who lived in another place at another time. For example:

Johanna Reiss compels the reader to come with her when she enters *The Upstairs Room* (Crowell, 1972), where she and her sister spent two years in hiding during World War II.

Hiroko Nakamoto, in her autobiography called *My Japan, 1930–1951* (McGraw-Hill, 1970), shares with the reader her anguish after the bombing of Hiroshima.

Eloise Greenfield, her mother, and her grandmother all remember, in *Childtimes* (Crowell, 1979), what it was like when they were children. It is almost as if they were reminiscing together on the front porch, "Did I ever tell you about the time . . . ?" Since we all want to give children an enriching exposure to minorities, what a privilege to share these memories, to feel the love and solidarity that carries from one generation to another. The truth about this fine black family is ten times more inspiring than the fabricated idealization of Crispus Attucks, about whom we actually know next to nothing.

Margery Fisher maintains that the use of authentic social detail is the biographer's most important tool. In these three autobiographies, *The*

Upstairs Room, My Japan, and *Childtimes,* social detail, by the very nature of the first-person account, makes past life as real as today to the reader.

Promote books that focus on a short, but significant, period in someone's life. Often a chronological account, from childhood to death, must omit social details that children love. At least this is true if the book is not to be as long as *War and Peace.*

In illustrating and writing *The Boy Who Loved Music* (Viking, 1979), for instance, David and Joe Lasker have revealed intriguing bathing rituals in the Austrian castle of Esterhaza, along with the musical protest of Haydn in his "Farewell" Symphony of 1772. This is a short book, covering only a few weeks in Haydn's life. In a cradle-to-the grave biography, such delightful detail would have been out of the question.

There are now quite a few of these sharply focused, miniature excursions into biography: Lindbergh flying solo across the Atlantic, Benjamin West learning from the Indians how to mix colors for his paints, Robert E. Lee struggling against defeat at Gettysburg in *Three Days* by Paxton Davis (Atheneum, 1980).

Avoid watered-down, talking-down biographies for younger children. In simplifying the life of a public figure, biographers are often forced to leave out facts that are essential for a balanced portrait. The result is distortion by omission, which is just as unfortunate as distortion by commission. It should come as no surprise, for instance, that history will inevitably be distorted when a biographer labors to give third-graders some understanding of FDR's efforts to pull the United States out of the Depression or to explain Jefferson's wisdom in drafting the Declaration of Independence. Should a child of that age even be expected to understand such complex ideas and issues?

But even the less complicated exploits of Benjamin Franklin can be distorted in oversimplified accounts. One author rattles off Ben's accomplishments, including the famous stove, without any explanation of how they worked or why they were important. Even Franklin's "Rules of Behavior" have been drastically abridged. Still another author covers sixty years of his life in six pages! Ben Franklin himself would turn over in his grave if he, or his ghost, could read these books.

Unfortunately there is really only one way to determine how flagrantly omissions have distorted a biographical portrait. This is to read many accounts of the same life, including an adult biography, as Margery Fisher has done so effectively in *Matters of Fact.* This exercise is so revealing that third- and fourth-grade teachers who presently assign biographies should be persuaded to try it.

Apart from distorting history, writers of simplified biographies frequently "talk down" to children in sentences that sound like the most boring of all easy readers: "Let's start libraries and hospitals. Let's clear the streets and put up lights. Let's work together to fight fires. . . ." Such choppy writing, combined with the adulatory tone that characterizes biographies for beginning readers, does an injustice to the person who is the subject of the book. For that matter, it also does an injustice to the reader.

The point is that there is no necessity for young children to read biography at all. Why not let them wait until they have enough historical background to understand the true significance of past events and the men who inspired them?

Seek out biographical material in subject areas. This may be the most productive way to resist misbegotten biographies. Admittedly, discovering these books may be a slippery process, since books are classified quite differently in various libraries. (*The Upstairs Room*, for instance, can be found in the 940s in some libraries, in fiction in others, and in biography in still others.) But the accuracy of these biographies, concerned as they are more with the person's working life than with childhood "stories" about curing a pet dog or buying a bun in Philadelphia, justifies extra effort. Besides, hunting for them can be intriguing, as children might agree if they were set loose on a biographical treasure hunt.

Consider the following examples:

Michael Collins, in *Flying to the Moon and Other Strange Places*, describes his extraordinary journey through space:

The feeling was less like flying than like being alone in a boat on the ocean at night. Stars above, pure black below. At dawn, light filled my windows so quickly that my eyes hurt. Almost immediately, the stars disappeared and the moon reappeared. I knew from my clock that the earth was about to reappear, and right on schedule it popped into view, rising like a blue and white jewel over the desolate lunar horizon.[4]

His book is classified in the 629s.

Polly Brooks and Nancy Walworth in their fine histories of Rome, the Middle Ages, and the Renaissance, have also placed public figures as the dramatic center of events. In *The World Awakes* (Lippincott, 1962), for instance, we find Lorenzo de Medici and Leonardo da Vinci "awakening" the Renaissance world of Italy. The classification number is 940.21.

William Kurelek, in *A Prairie Boy's Winter*, tells a great deal about himself as he describes life in Manitoba when he was a boy. In addition, he gives us a book of outstanding graphic beauty. The classification number is 917.1.

Lennart Rudstrom also has created three books of graphic distinction by presenting the artwork of Carl Larsson in *A Home*, and *A Farm*, and *A Family* (Putnam, 1974, 1976, 1980). These books are classified and shelved, logically enough, in 759.85, but, despite some unevenly written text, they are enriching as biographies in addition to being "art" books.

As a matter of fact, we can reap some special benefits by engaging in this kind of biographical treasure hunt. Many nonfiction books, not purporting to be biographies at all, may inadvertently give us a valuable glimpse into the lives of extraordinary "ordinary" people. Marilyn Jurich, commenting on the lamentable quality of biographies for children,[5] pleads for more biographies of not-so-famous people who have led interesting lives in one way or another. Fortunately we can find some of these people at home in the various areas of nonfiction. *As I Saw It: Women Who Lived the American Adventure* (Dial, 1978), by Cheryl Hoople, is a notable example; so are *Museum People* (Prentice-Hall, 1977), by Peggy Thomson and *Plane Talk: Aviators and Astronauts' Own Stories* (Houghton, 1980), edited by Carl Oliver. And certainly many of us have been moved by the searing accounts of the slaves in Julius Lester's *To Be a Slave* (Dial, 1968). Anyone exploring the nonfiction shelves might be surprised at how many ordinary people, just as interesting as these, are waiting to be discovered.

Yet another bonus to be derived from reading biography from the nonfiction shelves is the privilege of experiencing the unfolding of events, just as they happened, recorded in the journals and diaries and eyewitness accounts of people who "were there." Eric Sloane, after finding a diary of a farm boy named Noah Blake from the year 1805, has illustrated, in scrupulous detail, the events described in words. The book, called *Diary of an Early American Boy* (Crowell, 1974), can be found shelved with the 630s in many libraries. This classification, perhaps logical but nevertheless absurd, effectively removes the book from circulation.

George Sanderlin has allowed Francis Drake and his shipmates to tell in their own words the story of their journeys. This account, in a book called *The Sea Dragon* (Harper, 1969), is one of several eyewitness histories compiled by Sanderlin. Other historians have done the same: Joseph Martin, Phillip Viereck, Cheryl Hoople, Henry S. Commager and Richard B. Morris, Robert Meredith and E. Brooks Smith, to name a few. John Anthony Scott once edited the "Living History Library," now unfortunately defunct, to which Milton Meltzer was a contributor. Honest books like these can be a most refreshing antidote to the sickly fictionalization that characterizes story biographies.

Do not lean on biography. Once we have reminded ourselves that the purpose of biography is not to edify children, we can find other, less troublesome, ways to discover the past. For one, we can move most directly to biographical fiction, of course, as Denise Wilms has pointed out in her article on biography. Happily oblivious to the scholarly restrictions shackling a biographer, we can share a cloud with Eleanor of Aquitaine as she waits in heaven for Henry to arrive from "down below"

. . . or "kibbitz" a chess game between Ben Franklin and a French lady in her bath!

But if, as we have determined, our goal is simply to explain and enliven history, we can joyfully promote, not just biographical fiction, but all historical fiction. Here the writer intent upon satisfying the child's natural desire for a good story need not twist historical fact as so often occurs when a biographer puts imaginary dialogue into the mouths of real people. Fortunately, historical fiction needs no promotion. It has always been deservedly popular with children and adults alike.

What about straight history? Here we run into difficulties. As selections on history writing in this collection have suggested, we in the schools have been guilty of not-so-benign neglect. C. Walter Hodges, Gerald Johnson, Alfred Duggan, and all the other fine writers of history, deserve to be read more than they are. Without any question a lively history book can be a stimulating and honest alternative to undocumented biography.

These, then, have been some suggestions for working around problems already sitting on biography shelves.

What about buying better biographies in the future? Is it possible to find biographies that are both well documented and still a pleasure to read? Before deciding, we need to examine fairly critically, not only the reviewing of children's biographies, but also the intellectual climate surrounding their writing and publishing.

Trade publishers seem to be emulating textbook publishers of history, discussed elsewhere in this work, by working backwards, and inside out, as they manufacture new biographies. They have been quick to recognize the need for biographies about blacks, about women, about the Founding Fathers on the occasion of the Bicentennial, about sports figures appealing to reluctant readers, about. . . . Since the bandwagon is rolling, we can hardly blame the publishers for jumping on board. They are in business to make money, after all.

Patrick Groff in his article "Biography: The Bad or the Bountiful?" documents the extent to which biographers have responded to the lure of the market. He describes a practice that many of us have long suspected—the "borrowing" of material from an adult biography to construct one for children. Armed with scissors and rubber cement, almost anybody, according to Groff, can produce a juvenile version of an adult biography. His evidence reveals that some have already done so.

Reputable biographers, of course, would be aghast at this practice of "cutting and pasting" what is supposed to be original work. Original work is the result of a far different, and more arduous, process. The best biographers start, not with concern for what will or will not sell, but with a compelling interest in a particular public figure. Jane Yolen, in her book on writing nonfiction,[6] describes this fascination as a "tap on the shoulder." She says she wrote the biography Friend because she was convinced that she had been tapped on the shoulder by the fiery mystic

George Fox, just as Elizabeth Gray Vining had felt the same compulsion when she wrote the biography of William Penn. From this "summons" comes a serious commitment to the subject. Biographers then read all they can find by and about William Penn, or George Fox, or whoever has captured their imagination to begin with. There must be, of course, a limit to the amount of original research that can reasonably be expected, and Olivia Coolidge considers these limitations in her article, "My Struggle with Facts."

In addition to dogged and sometimes tedious research, the biographer often walks in the footsteps of the person whose life is being recorded, visiting houses and schools and anywhere else where traces of that person might remain. Mary Haverstock, for instance, went herself to all the places that George Catlin had traveled on his painting trips to record the lives of Indians in the West. In addition, the biographer usually interviews anyone who might be able to supply unpublished information.

Once the facts have been assembled, the writer of biography must face what may be the most difficult task of all: to organize the material and select from it those details that will create an accurate and illuminating portrait. Naturally the portrait that emerges will reflect the biographer's perception of why that public figure is great. Any writer presuming to interpret someone's life must be particularly sensitive to the choices that person has made at crucial periods, choices that inevitably resulted in a decisive change of direction. By shaping the material to make it reveal the background behind these choices, the biographer has, in essence, explained why and how a human being eventually becomes important. In fact, the biographer has gambled on what might ultimately be the judgment of history.

Biographies crafted with this combination of hard work and imagination should be the ones, and the only ones, that we buy for our libraries. But how do we identify honest and inspired books among all the made-to-order stuff that floods the market? Unfortunately discriminating selection is not always as simple as it should be.

Reviews are the obvious selection tools, but reviewers have failed in the past to be sufficiently hard-boiled in their evaluation of biography. Either ignorance or compromise has seemed to dictate the same uncritical standards in reviewing as it has in publishing. As a consequence, it is instructive to contrast the reviewing of science books with the reviewing of biography; to recognize the impact of specialized reviewing, not only in what is bought for libraries, but also in what publishers think they can get away with. As has been pointed out in the article on science writing, children's book editors have become sensitive to the reviews of professional scientists in *Appraisal* and *Science Books and Films*. This is not surprising. How can any editor afford to risk having a science book disembowelled by a hawk-eyed, predatory scientist?

Perhaps we need hawkeyed, predatory historians. Perhaps we need more reviews of biographies like the recent review of a history book about the making of the Constitution. Garry Wills, a historian who has won an award for an adult book on Jefferson and the Declaration of Independence, reviewed a children's history for the *Washington Post Book World* and censured it unmercifully. Two reviews of the same book in library journals, written of course by nonhistorians, picked up neither the "warmed-over scholarship" nor the abundance of errors pointed out by the historian. The book may not actually be as weak as Garry Wills maintains, but his professional judgment obviously adds valuable perspective in considering this book for purchase. The *New York Times* often uses specialists in the adult field to review children's books—Tom Wicker reviewing the book by Paxton Davis on Robert E. Lee, for instance—but unfortunately there are very few books reviewed in the *Times* during the course of the year.

So what would happen, one wonders not altogether facetiously, if Barbara Tuchman or Leon Edel were to review children's biographies? What would Catherine Drinker Bowen have said had she read *Abigail Adams: Girl of Colonial Days* (Bobbs-Merrill, 1962), a "life-story" for children in grades two to four? But this kind of speculation is nonproductive. Until historians give us the benefit of their knowledge, we must depend on standard review sources. What we need from these is more painstaking reviewing, more time and thought spent before arriving at a judgment. And we need more literary criticism of biography, especially criticism as analytical as that of Elizabeth Segel's evaluation of the biographies of Beatrix Potter in this collection. At the very least, we have a right to expect that a reviewer will check the facts in a juvenile biography against those in a reputable adult source, as well as to compare that book to other children's biographies. Unfortunately evidence suggests that not all reviewers do this. It can be especially revealing, as well as discouraging, to read a review of a particular biography after you have read three or four different versions of that same person's life.

Following is an example of one inaccuracy, among many unnoticed by the reviewer, in a biography of Benjamin Banneker. The biographer gives highly romantic significance to the fact that Banneker never married because the girl he loved killed herself. The adult biography, with impressive documentation, states simply that he was a bachelor all his life and that there is no evidence of a love interest at all. Not only does the biographer of this book for children invent scenes on the basis of what must be flimsy evidence—and of course there is no bibliography or list of sources to check the evidence—he also omits other facts and significant events. Yet a review in one of the most reputable library journals said of this biography that it was "well-researched" and admirable in every way.

Quite apart from the distressing fact that children may be swallowing misinformation in the biographies written for them, this kind of inadequate reviewing inevitably sends a message to publishers that accuracy is not important. Editors do respond to demands that are made on them. If reviewers would dig in their heels, they would probably stimulate the publication of good biographies, just as science reviewers have successfully set a higher standard of expectation in science books.

The first step toward a higher standard in biographies could be taken fairly easily. Surely it would not be too difficult for publishers to include a list of sources at the end of every biography, even those written for younger children. Then reviewers and librarians, as well as readers, would be able to tell how reliable the information is. In the case of contradictory evidence surrounding some details in a person's life, a common dilemma for biographers, perhaps the author could explain in a short note why one source was chosen instead of another. This sort of information can be intriguing, even for children. It may give them a fascinating glimpse of the challenge to the writer who had to decide what to include, which facts to choose in order to create the most accurate portrait. And some may even understand that truth is elusive and subject to interpretation. Being able to handle the mutability of truth, in fact, could be the first step toward a healthy, active skepticism. But, quite apart from any salutary effects on children, honest bibliographic information would be a godsend to reviewers. With a complete knowledge of scholarly sources, reviewers would be able to appraise a biography realistically and fairly. And those who buy the books and those who read them would all benefit.

Under the present circumstances, however, librarians have no choice but to read, critically, as many reviews as possible in order to determine which reviewers and which journals are most reliable, or, rather, least unreliable. In deciding whether to buy a particular biography they should probably be guided by the most negative comments. If, for instance, a review suggests that a book about Socrates might be stimulating reading for eight-year-olds, or if the words "fictionalized" or "story-biography" appear even parenthetically, or if no mention is made of the qualifications of the author or sources of information, then why not reject the book? Librarians do have the power of the purse, after all. Only by exercising that power can they, and reviewers, convince publishers that good books mean good business.

Denise Wilms in her article on biography says that we should "take stock" and demand the best. Yes, we should take stock, thoroughly and realistically, but at the same time we should recognize hopeful signs when we see them. Although it is true that most of the current biographies would appall Barbara Tuchman, enough fine books are also appearing to brighten the prospects for the future. For instance:

Selected illustrators have been drawing and painting their autobiographies. Erik Blegvad and Margot Zemach, as a start, have given us a taste of pleasures in store as other illustrators continue to interpret their lives with paint and brush.

Some biographies focus on scientists and their work in the laboratory and in the field. Although these simply written accounts give the reader little feeling for what the scientists were like as people, the importance and excitement of their discoveries come through without distortion.

Some new collective biographies, much neglected in school libraries, portray individuals—musicians, civil rights leaders, reformers, spies, whoever—in accounts so short that there is no need for unwarranted fictionalization. An abbreviated biography might also appeal to a child who would be discouraged by one hundred or two hundred pages of solid print in a longer book.

Another refreshing approach to biography is a play called *Escape to Freedom* (Viking, 1978) written by Ossie Davis about Frederick Douglas. Why hasn't this been done more often, one wonders?

Above all, there is Jean Fritz. Her lively biographical writing has blown like a fresh breeze across the children's book world. She sticks to the facts, but she ignites them with such a spark that they illuminate ordinary events. She especially loves to include little-known but authentic details to enhance the day-to-day life of the past: Paul Revere writing in his Day Book, "This is my book for me to _____" and never finishing the sentence because he was, as always, in too much of a hurry; John Hancock practicing his signature over and over again to make it as imposing as possible; Patrick Henry imitating a mockingbird imitating a jay. An example of her writing revealing her light, sure touch follows. It is taken from *Where Was Patrick Henry on the 29th of May?*

Patrick Henry stood up and pushed his glasses back on his head which was what he did when he was ready to use his fighting words. . . .

"I know not what course others may take but as for me . . ." Patrick dropped his arms, threw back his body and strained against his imaginary chains until the tendons of his neck stood out like whipcords and the chains seemed to break. Then he raised his right hand in which he held an ivory letter opener. "As for me," he cried, "give me liberty or give me death!" And he plunged the letter opener in such a way it looked as if he were plunging it into his heart.

The crowd went wild with excitement. One man, leaning over the balcony, was so aroused that he forgot where he was and spit tobacco juice into the audience below. Another man jumped down from the window ledge and declared that when he died, he wanted to be buried on the very spot that Patrick Henry had delivered those words. (And so he was, 25 years later.)[7]

As the foregoing selection vividly illustrates, fabricated dialogue and inaccurate fictionalization are not at all necessary for a lively interpretation of history.

So, all in all, the future for children's biography looks less hopeless than we might have feared. In terms of Philip Guedalla's dreary geography with which we began this exploration, Jean Fritz has changed the face of the map. Other writers are doing the same. In the future, boundaries of the new biography could be quite different from those described by Guedalla: to the north, scholarship; to the south, humor; to the west, well-documented detail; and to the east, pleasure.

Biography

Margery Fisher

Few terms of literary criticism need definition more than biography. *The Shorter Oxford Dictionary* provides a broad definition: "The history of the lives of individual men, as a branch of literature. A written record of the life of an individual." In the sphere of children's books, such a definition could be made to cover many kinds of book, from picture-books to historical studies.

Very few lives written for children are biographies, in fact, as we normally use the term. Some other word is needed—but what? "Junior biography" is convenient but grammatically ambiguous. "Story biography" is a true description, but only of studies which take a narrative form. "Lives" can be a useful term if it is qualified by some series title of intention. But a "Life" for children is more often an account of deeds than an interpretation of character, and this latter element is surely essential to true biography. It seems inevitable that we shall continue to use the term "biography" loosely, but that it can never be relied upon to define a book which could be a picture-story book, a selected episode, a dramatised study, a monograph or an historical novel in disguise.

A biographer must be prepared to be simple and confident in his statements in order to bring a personality within the comprehension of a young reader. In a review of new biographies for adults, Dennis Potter sharply indicated the basic problem of the biographer:

> As soon as they pick up their pens to pin another person on to the page biographers take a license which is so enormous that it far transcends the humble virtues of mere impertinence. It helps to make sense out of

Adapted from chapter 4, pages 300–308 of *Matters of Fact: Aspects of Non-fiction for Children* by Margery Fisher. Copyright © 1972 by Margery Fisher. By permission of Thomas Y. Crowell, Publishers, and Hodder & Stoughton.

your subject (hero or victim) when you can dare to assume that the child is father to the man, that thought is prior to the deed, that what we do is what we are, and a score of other such familiar little tags designed to diminish the irreducible mysteries of the human personality into prosaic order.[1]

To explore that "tangle of contradictory motives, warring emotions, habit ridden responses, fearful apprehensions and improbable longings" beneath a man's "outer front" (as Dennis Potter puts it in his review) the biographer needs the imagination of a novelist; even when he uses imagination to go behind fact and interpret character, he is faced, in the end, with mystery. How can a biographer, with all the resources of contemporary record, yet put into a true relation Abraham Lincoln's innate melancholy and his particular kind of rustic ribaldry? Yet these seemingly contradictory sides of his nature are crucial to any proper account of his life. Myth and reality are constantly at war in the biographer's enterprise. And even if he could have been present at any of the scenes he describes at second hand, he would be little nearer to understanding his subject. Boswell's life of Johnson is in some way the most *immediate* biography ever written; but this is Boswell's Johnson. No biographer can leave himself behind when he goes to meet his subject.

A recent new series for the young, Harrap's As They Saw Them, is designed to draw on eye-witness accounts, diaries and other contemporary documents to show how a man fits his century and how he was then regarded. This would seem to give the biographer the chance to withdraw and let other people speak for him—as, for example, two Sellonite nurses offer a sharply personal view of the Lady with a Lamp in the Crimea, as it were on behalf of Alan Delgado, author of *Florence Nightingale* (1970). This method of writing a "Life" is a logical extension of the quotation which any biographer has at his command, but even here the author himself decides, from his personal prejudices and preoccupations, the particular aspect of the subject that will be presented. The volume on *Charles Dickens* (1970) by Michael and Mollie Hardwick in this same series abounds in vignettes, caustic comments, sentimental reminiscence from a host of contemporaries of Dickens, eminent or obscure. Yet in the long run the authors have really directed us to a conclusion, to the interpretation which shows us a sociable man tormented by the need to be private. This disparate method of constructing "biography," so-called, is nearer to suggesting diversity of personality than more regular studies, but this is not necessarily the method that will best suit children if they are meeting a man or woman for the first time; and at all events it is a method which exposes a writer to the same difficulty of reconciling myth with reality.

Biography is an illusion, a fiction in the guise of fact. In Desmond McCarthy's phrase, the biographer is "an artist upon oath." He is working with facts and calling upon imagination—his own and the reader's—

to warm those facts, as Paul Murray Kendall suggests in picturesque terms:

> At best, fact is harsh, recalcitrant matter, as tangible as the hunk of rusty iron one trips over and yet as shapeless as a paper hat in the rain. Fact is a cold stone, an inarticulate thing, dumb until something happens to it; and there is no use the biographer waiting for spontaneous combustion or miraculous alchemy. Fact must be rubbed up in the mind, placed in magnetic juxtaposition with other facts, until it begins to glow, to give off that radiance we call meaning. Fast is a biographer's only friend, and worst enemy.[2]

Here is a clue to the paramount duty of the biographer who writes for the young. If he cannot guarantee to show a man as he really was, he can try to draw from his readers the admission "This is a living human being." If the man or woman he writes about does not live in his pages, the child would do better to turn to an historical treatise or to fiction. Biography can, and occasionally does, give him the best of both worlds in a form he can understand. A story biography like Elfrida Vipont's *Weaver of Dreams* (1966) could wake an interest in Charlotte Brontë because the writer has fused facts and invention in the fire of her own enthusiasm. Elizabeth Grey in *Winged Victory* (1966), another biography that takes narrative form, shows the perception of a novelist in her discussion of Amy Johnson's restricted girlhood and the skill of an historian in the way she illuminates events with accurate technical detail and by feeling herself into the social pressures and ideas of the 'twenties.

Social detail—an important tool of the biographer—plays a dominant part in lives for children. Many such lives are in fact social histories in which facts are grouped round a central figure. The title of Josephine Kamm's story biography, *Joseph Paxton and the Crystal Palace* (1967), suggests the way her material has been organised; the man comes to life but in particular circumstances. A very lively book, *Invincible Miss* (1968) by Jean Hughes, provides a panorama of Africa in the last century through a study of Mary Kingsley's scientific work and her attitude to science, and to the native tribesmen who helped her researches. Betty Schecter's book on *The Dreyfus Affair* (1965) employs the resources of history to explain the tragic dilemma of an individual. The purpose of books like these is as much to help a young reader to develop a sense of period as it is to give him a view of a particular man or woman. Details of personality which would be out of place in a direct study of a period or an event can be accommodated in a story biography about a man or woman who played a significant part in that period.

I do not believe that authors of books like these consider themselves biographers in the strict sense. They have written about real people through the means of a story, establishing them by means of techniques used in fiction. One obvious indication of this is the use of deduced or in-

vented conversation to enliven an episode. In a true biography this kind
of licence would, or should, be out of place. The orthodox view is out-
lined by André Maurois in "The ethics of biography":

> Under no account has the biographer a right to invent a single fact. He
> is writing history, not fiction, and witnessing under oath. He cannot
> even say that the weather, on such and such a day, was good or bad, if
> he has no evidence for it. He should not put into his hero's mouth, nor
> attribute to any character, sentences they have not spoken. In *Ariel*,
> I took the liberty, not to attribute to Shelley things he had never said,
> but to turn into dialogue conversations that we possessed, in indirect
> form, in his letters. I have never done it since, nor do I approve of that
> method. It undermines the confidence of the reader, and also there is
> always a risk, even with the best of good will, of mutilating or deform-
> ing a thought. If you have a letter, quote it, or part of it; if a conversa-
> tion has been preserved by a reliable witness, make use of it. But never
> indulge in imagination. Once you cross the line between biography and
> fiction, you will never be able to retrace your steps.[3]

Such austerity would be difficult to achieve when writing for children
whose historical knowledge and experience of life were limited. To draw
a line too sharply between known fact and reasonable deduction would
be to deny them a great deal of persuasive detail. Story biography must
claim a degree of flexibility if it is to remain a viable and necessary alternative to historical fiction.

The distinction between the two literary forms is not a purely artificial one. It is not merely a technical difference that the writer of a story
biography will sometimes introduce a dramatised scene by a piece of direct explanation of historical background or will add to such a scene an
appropriate comment or summary of a general kind, whereas a novelist
interrupts his narrative with a change of style at his peril. A biography
is overly didactic in a way that a novel is not. In a story biography a judicious mixture of narrative and exposition helps the writer to make the
points round which his interpretation of character is built. Equally, the
invented episode can often clarify as well as invigorate a general idea.
The writer of a life of Dickens might choose to describe in direct terms
the kind of people and places that lie behind his novels. He might, on
the other hand, take certain liberties with his material to make fact more
interesting for the young. In *The Boy Who Asked for More* (1966), Elis-
abeth Kyle presents certain events in Dickens's life in a form so dramatic
and active that a child could readily guess how an ostler might have suggested the character of Sam Weller, how Bowes Academy was translated
into Dotheboys Hall, how evenings with Maria Beadnell and her harp
helped to shape his conception of domestic felicity. This is "how it might
have been" based on recorded fact of a general kind. This is, I believe,
a necessary licence, but one which is highly susceptible to abuse.

When a writer attributes certain words or actions to a person when
he cannot be sure of their authenticity, he is certainly departing from

the strict truth—if such a thing exists at all in relation to a man's life. But truth can be dealt more serious blows than this. Biography for children is basically didactic. It sets out to instruct them in certain sets of facts and, very often, to convey a certain message as well. The subject of a biography is usually chosen as an example—in most cases of a virtue though, as the *Oxford Junior Encyclopedia* puts it. "Occasionally . . . a man is included because, like Adolf Hitler, his evil character and ill-doing have convulsed the world and changed history."

This purposive attitude to biography is by no means confined to children's books. Down the centuries the argument has gone back and forth —how should an example be given? To many it has seemed that a hero must remain a hero in every respect; the attitude is only too familiar in the compendiums that find their way into school libraries, whose titles, *Great Men, Famous Men and Women*, and so on, are a warning of the pomposity and stiffness so often to be found within. As Edmund Gosse pointed out, the effort to preserve "the dignity of the subject" can lead to presenting a man "as though he spent his whole life standing, pressed in a tight frockcoat, with a glass of water at his hand and one elbow on a desk, in the act of preparing to say: 'Ladies and Gentlemen?' "[4] Dryden's view, that domestic detail could add rather than detract from a man's stature, would find support among the young. In defending "a descent into minute circumstances, and trivial passages of life," he suggests:

> You may behold a Scipio and a Lelius gathering cockle-shells on the shore, Augustus playing at bounding-stones with boys; and Agesilaus riding on a hobby-horse among his children. The pageantry of life is taken away; you see the poor reasonable animal, as naked as ever nature made him; are made acquainted with his passions and his follies, and find the Demy-God a man.[5]

You may behold a human being. But, if you are a child, you may behold this human being most often in his active moments—Shackleton on the *Endurance* expedition rather than frustrated in England, Churchill in Parliament rather than in committee, generals on the field of battle rather than retired in Cheltenham. Children respond to action, and most biographies written for them emphasise deeds rather than words and thoughts. The biographer who selects the events of a man's life to emphasise his achievement may be guilty of *suppressio veri* though not of *suggestio falsi*. But selection can give a child a false idea. How carefully Lady Hamilton must be dealt with, in a life of Nelson for the young; how tactfully the vicissitudes of Dickens's domestic life must be treated. Geoffrey Trease's sane and forthright life of Byron (1969), Elfrida Vipont's life of George Eliot, *From a High Attic* (1970), might not have found the acceptance fifteen years ago which they have found in the past two years.

Hero-worship is natural to young people: so is cynicism. The biographer faces a fact inherent in most types of non-fiction. It seems to be generally assumed that if a subject is treated at all, it must be treated from the lowest level upwards; if a life of Shackleton or Churchill or Drake is to be offered to a reader of fifteen, there must also be one available for a reader of ten, of eight, even of six.

In the case of biography this is tiresome and hampering. Formulas can be found for offering great figures to very young readers. In the case of most "great men," though, too much of the man has to go if the relative experience of young and very young be considered. Certain subjects seem unsuited to biography for all but older boys and girls, who may be expected to make reasonable judgments of their own on irregular or unusual or puzzling behaviour.

Few biographies have yet caught up with the changes in a school-child's attitude to public figures of present or past. In the family and the classroom, discussion has become freer and more open between the generations, but books are still too often mealy-mouthed and evasive. Nearly forty years ago, John Drinkwater voiced a prevalent attitude when he wrote:

> . . . documents can be made to support anything if you have enough of them to choose from. Nelson possibly was a coward, and someone may have evidence up his sleeve to prove it. But the important thing is not the assurance that sooner or later truth will out, but that there comes a time when certain convictions are so firmly established that they become proof against any spectacular revelations, become, that is, the potent truth itself. If a select committee of the High Courts of the world were to decide on an impartial examination of the evidence that Nelson was a coward, we should laugh in their faces.[6]

No such easy excuse should be available to the biographer today; his choice in the matter should be free. Yet only recently Mary Eakin could write critically:

> It is true that histories change from time to time, but the changes are, more often than not, instituted for the purpose of justifying a present action or attitude of the government rather than to stimulate a young mind to seek out more accurate information about events of the past. Even when new information is available regarding events and famous figures of the past, such information is usually made available to children only in so far as it enhances those events or figures; seldom is it included when it reveals a weakness or error of judgement. No country has ever had a history of perfection; always there has been good balance against evil; failure against success; yet, in all too many books for children the evil and failures are selected out, leaving only a dull and wholly unbelievable account of continuous success and well-being.[7]

It is not enough to present selected facts correctly; an honest attitude to all available facts is just as important—probably more important when one is addressing young people whose power to check an author's use of his material is limited.

An Evaluation of Biography

Denise M. Wilms

In theory, biography has much to offer children, but in practice its potential is too often undermined by unskilled execution. Moreover, the persistent weaknesses that mark these faulty life stories are perpetuated by the uncritical acceptance of teachers, librarians, and others who continue to put them into the hands of children.

This disregard for quality stems partly from pressure to look at biographies in functional terms—from being caught up in filling a need, whether it's for one child or a whole class with an assignment on Abraham Lincoln—when it's easy to forget about literary or artistic values. More seriously, though, the neglect stems from not knowing just what biography is about. I think there has to be more concern with substance in biography; there has to be more attention paid to its crafting and to its full value as a rich, entertaining, educational tool.

A review of what biography is supposed to do will help give some context to what I'm saying. Ideally, a biographer's aim is to bring a person to life in a way that is true to the reality of that person's life. Facts alone aren't enough; an encyclopedia can give the dry, bare-bones facts; and what is fact anyway? Did Margaret Fuller marry her impoverished Italian Count Ossoli or didn't she? One recent biography said she did; another says there's confusion and leaves the matter open.

Then there is the matter of context. No person operates independently of time, or society, or the world at large. A sound biography relates the subject to his or her time. John Anthony Scott does this well in *Woman Against Slavery*, the life of Harriet Beecher Stowe.

He writes:

Harriet's work was extraordinary not only because it was a new and pioneer type of novel but because it was written by a woman. Until 1852 few American women had broken the barriers of convention that forbade women to write about anything so real and brutal as slavery. Angelina and Sarah Grimke had written about slavery and had agitated against it. Lydia Maria Child had edited an antislavery newspaper and published her own antislavery tracts. But the most popular women writers wrote polite or conventional novels in which discussion of the topic of slavery was taboo. . . . For a woman to depart so boldly from custom took both

Reprinted from *Booklist* 75, no. 2:218–20 (Sept. 15, 1978), copyright © 1978 by the American Library Association.

courage and conviction. It is part of Harriet's supreme achievement that she dared to give a bold and scorching expression to her feelings as a woman and a mother when she saw innocent and often defenseless human beings ground up or torn to pieces by the workings of slavery.

His last emotion-laden sentence gets its credibility from earlier portions in which Scott describes Harriet's experiences in Cincinnati, Ohio, where she came to know the stories of many escaped slaves.

Another consideration is the writer's own attitude, interest, and enthusiasm for his or her subject. You have to sense an author's pleasure in the subject, whether that involvement is highly visible, or subtle, or somewhere in between. Think of the humorous overtones in Jean Fritz's biographies, and then think of Virginia Hamilton's portrait of Paul Robeson. These are two very different books, but each one projects an authorial sympathy that pulls strongly at the reader's interest.

When biography is working, it sparks your interest—even if you thought you had none in the first place. It's a human encounter, it's literary people watching, and that's what makes it many people's favorite reading. When it comes to this basic fascination, children are no different from adults.

In a working biography you watch the person grow, learn, achieve, or even fail; you might identify with the person, or be inspired, or you might not. But in each case there's a vital human connection; a life experience in all its richness has been transmitted. And because what you're dealing with is real, there's a special weight to it. This immediacy is at the heart of biography's potential as a teaching tool—it's a perfect accompaniment to the humanities and the sciences because it gives the chance to reflect on events from one individual viewpoint, to step off the beaten track and into fresh territory.

Biographies for children too often get bogged down by questionable notions of what is suitable for children to know and how it should be told. In this aversion to dealing head on with a subject, biography can be faulted for lagging behind the main body of children's literature. Look at fiction: we've watched, over the last ten to fifteen years, one breakthrough after another in what was thought to be suitable reading for children. Topics that were once taboo are now acceptable, as contemporary realism so pointedly shows. Nonfiction, too, has grown. Think of your science collections, your history collections. You find books on logic, on nuclear physics, on lasers, on the intricacies of ecology, on the histories of women and minorities. There are books on death, divorce, drugs. The enduring ones among these books are well written, straightforward, honest, and definitely informative. They show that in the hands of a skillful, sensitive writer, almost any subject can be responsibly explained. These books were written under the assumption that children are capable of understanding and appreciating the world around them. Why, then, does biography so often veer away from dealing more fully with the subject at hand?

Why, for example, is biography often looked on as the *story* of a life, rather than the *history* of a life, which in fact it is. Why is fictionalization so acceptable? Why are character and personality sidestepped in favor of a recitation of events and accomplishments? Why do we have biographies that leave out the negative or unfortunate aspects of a life? In short, where is the depth, the dimension, the richness?

At this point it's interesting to take a quick look at how biography developed. For one thing, it hasn't been around all that long; scholars say biography as we know it first appeared around 1640. Before that were so called lives of saints or kings, which set in motion the role of biography to set an example and/or glorify the subject. Unfavorable things were not considered proper form—the whole point was to show how special and different the subject was from ordinary humans. Invention was freely used to help the image along. There's a wonderful example of this in James Clifford's *Biography as an Art*. He tells of Agnellus, a ninth-century bishop of Ravenna, who was writing a series of lives of his predecessors. Agnellus had been unable to find any detailed information on some of them, either from oral tradition or any authentic source, and writes, "In order that there might not be a break in the series, I have composed the life myself, with the help of God and the prayers of brethren."

Then in the eighteenth century came Boswell's life of Dr. Samuel Johnson, which scholars mark as the beginning of modern biography. Boswell was interested in completeness; he said:

> Indeed I cannot conceive of a more perfect mode of writing any man's life, than not only relating all the most important events of it in their order, but interweaving what he privately wrote, and said, and thought; by which mankind are enabled as it were to see him live, and to live over each scene with him, as he actually advanced through the several stages of his life. Had his other friends been as diligent and ardent as I was, he might have been almost entirely preserved. As it is, I will venture to say that he will be seen in this work more completely than any man who has ever yet lived.

Boswell's Life of Johnson set an enduring standard that didn't change measurably until the twentieth century and is still considered one of the masterworks of English-language biography.

These broad developments in adult biography offer an interesting backdrop for looking at juvenile biography, for in some ways biography for young people has gone through similar stages. As with much of early children's literature, there was the wish to teach and set examples: Lives of saints and cautionary stories are on record; Parson Weems gave us the image of honest George Washington, who couldn't lie about chopping down the cherry tree. In modern children's biography that pure intent is considerably diluted but it still crops up: In the D'Aulaires' *George Washington* you can read that George sat quietly around the fireplace in the living room with his brothers and sisters listening to Bible stories, that George "learned to be good and honest and never tell a lie."

To be fair, though, children's biography has come a long way from the old days. With the '60s and '70s in particular there was a burst of life stories that paralleled information breakthroughs in other areas. Names like Malcolm X, Fanny Kemble, and Sojourner Truth reflected the new awareness of history, of women, of radical social movements, of information that had never seen the light in children's books. These books set precedent for looking at people from all walks of life and gave juvenile biography some necessary breadth. Now we need to deepen the genre.

Of course no one will argue that the mammoth works by dedicated scholars of biography need be replicated in children's literature. But the ideals they aimed for can't be forgotten: we must expect them, but it seems too often we don't. Compromises like fictionalization, lack of documentation, or a failure to examine personality and character or lend an appropriate examining eye need to be questioned. I think librarians need to pause and think about these things and ask whether "compromise biographies" are, in fact, useful and serve the purpose of a good reading experience. Does a strictly linear account of events that happened to or because of the person really constitute a biography? Is a biography that allows only one dimension of a person to show through really an educational reading experience? Where are the boundaries between artful simplicity and the overgeneralization that is distortion? Was it justifiable for the D'Aulaires not to include Lincoln's assassination in their account of his life or for Patricia Miles Martin not to identify the Emancipation Proclamation in her biography of Lincoln? And what about the truth of absolute statements like this one in May McNeer's generally strong biography of George Washington: "No one could ride a horse or hunt as well as George Washington." Or, to take an extreme, this enthusiastic endorsement in F. M. Milverstead's *Henry Aaron:* "He is the sum total of the best part of 200 years of American history."

And fictionalizing; is it really necessary? Take this passage from a biography of Elizabeth Fry by Spencer Johnson:

Once upon a time there was a girl named Elizabeth who lived in a great house in England. . . . She should have been very happy, but she wasn't.

"I like being kind to people," she said, "because it makes people happy."

"I wish I could go out and be kind to those people who no one else thinks about."

There were days when Elizabeth was sad. It was on one of these days that a butterfly came flitting into her garden.

"Why are you so sad, pretty lady?" asked the butterfly. Elizabeth was surprised to meet a talking butterfly, but she was a very kind person and didn't want to be rude. So she pretended that it was quite usual to chat with butterflies.

"I am sad because I am not being kind enough to people," said Elizabeth.

What child can happily relate to such a didactic pitch?

Much more common is the problem a child would face had he or she to do some comparing—as indeed some classroom assignments require. Here is how fictionalization might raise questions for the thinking reader: Take the case of a child who has to do a report on Mary McLeod Bethune and needs several sources. Here are two passages that might be found. One, Eloise Greenfield's *Mary McLeod Bethune* reads:

> The sun had just come up when Mary McLeod left the house with her mother and father and brothers and sisters to go to the fields. Every morning, the whole family had to get up very early to work on the farm. *But they didn't mind* [italics mine].

The other, in Beth P. Wilson's *Giants for Justice:*

> The family was constantly hoeing to keep the crab grass away from the young, tender plants. Mary Jane always sang as she worked. Sometimes she would stop to pray right in the field. "Please God," she would say. "Help me get away from this crabgrass."

In fact each of the books from which I pulled these lines do a reasonably good job of introducing Mary McLeod Bethune to children; but the background details don't match, and so a reader might wonder what the facts of Mary's characterization really are. This third passage from Ruby Radford's *Mary McLeod Bethune* offers the most balance; listen to its simple, reasonable tone:

> The whole family worked on the farm. Even the smallest children helped plant cotton and grow vegetables and rice. It was hard work but the McLeods were thankful for their freedom.

No implied heroics here, or victimization; just a clean statement of what is known to be true.

Another situation that often comes with fictionalization is switching back and forth between story and straight narrative. What is the logic of using an artificial novellike opening that's followed or interwoven with straight narrative? If you expect the reader to cope with facts, why not present them straight away? It's devious not to; and it doesn't have to be boring. What is a reader to make of the jolting and misleading stylistic switches like this one in Lillie Patterson's recent biography of Benjamin Banneker. Opening, it reads like a novel:

> "Tell me that story again. Please!"
> "What story, Benjamin?"
> "You know the one I mean. Tell me about how you came across the big ocean on a ship. Tell me how you came to this place."

Then, a page and a half later, there is smooth, straightforward narrative. In explaining indentured servitude the author writes:

> Hundreds of such prisoners were coming to the colonies during the seventeenth century. This was a way of bringing much-needed workers

to the newly settled lands. Any businessman or landowner could sign a contract, called an indenture, to pay for prisoner's passage. In return, the prisoner worked free for this "master" for a number of years, usually seven.

Fictionalization seems too often an easy way out in suggesting color and character. The rationale is that you want to spark the child's interest, and imagined scenes are an effective way to do this. But biography is, in fact, the history of a life, and histories deal in fact, not fiction. A writer must decide if he or she is writing biography or historical fiction. For many figures, especially contemporary ones, there is sufficient material for the writer to merge the interesting *and* the factual.

When a writer feels invention is a necessity, perhaps the answer lies in the term biographical fiction—which is not to be confused with biography. Alex Haley, in discussing *Roots,* coined the term "faction"—a responsible merger of fact and fiction. Both these terms might rightfully fall under the umbrella of historical fiction. But referring as they do to real-life people and families, they are naturally associated with biography.

Biographical fiction offers a way to merge careful research with novel perspective or a strong sense of story that doesn't compromise the standards of biography. In juvenile literature the star practitioner in this area is Ferdinand Monjo, who also takes the time in his books to point out where the line between fact and fiction lies.

But biographical fiction is not biography, in the way that historical fiction is not history. Each has its rightful place and follows its own set of rules; and each one informs and entertains accordingly.

Clearly, writing biography is complicated business; Boswell said: "Biography occasions a degree of trouble far beyond that of any other species of literary composition." It demands both art and scholarship; neither can be compromised with good results. The best children's biographies we have show us the task isn't impossible. They set the standard for judging other works. So, what is a reviewer faced with? Very simply, compromise. Many of the examples I touched on came from books that *Booklist* reviewed. In fact there aren't many biographies around that successfully combine everything you'd hope would be in a biography. Some are stronger than others. Most are useful in some way, particularly when they cover a subject who is little written about. It's vital though, to pause, and take stock, to remind ourselves what's good and why, and demand more of it. If we don't, who will?

My Struggle with Facts

Olivia Coolidge

Facts are the bricks with which a biographer builds. The more facts I have to work with, the freer I am to design my own book. Biography, however, is not just a mass of facts, and the perfect biographer is not a tape recorder. If this were so, and thus the more detailed a biography the better, there would be no place for young-adult biographies. Furthermore, an autobiography would be, potentially at least, a greater work than any biography. Who knows the facts of a life as well as the man who has lived it? Yet actually an autobiography can be as misleading as a poor book by somebody else. When I was writing the life of Edith Wharton, I read her autobiography and accepted without question a great many details which came from her personal knowledge. When I compared the book, however, with what Edith said in her letters, with what other people said about her, and even with what she put into her fiction, one conclusion was inescapable. Edith Wharton was a shy woman who led an intense and not always happy emotional life. Her autobiography was written as much to prevent the public's really knowing her as to give the basic facts of her career. The suggestion has even been made that her main purpose was to put off the evil hour when a biographer would try to understand her inner secrets.

Actually, a biographer has a different task from a man who is writing his memoirs. These last contain invaluable material, but a good biography is also concerned with the effect its hero has on other people, with environment and background, with the nature of the great man's achievements and their value. I find that I examine facts in all these and many other spheres before I form judgments and that it needs great care to do what sounds quite easy, namely to distinguish a fact from a judgment. For instance, a contemporary's opinion of my subject is a fact. Its reliability and importance are estimated by my judgment, which is shown by my decision to quote or not to quote it, and even by the tone in which I refer to it or the context in which I introduce it.

Reprinted by permission of the publisher from the *Wilson Library Bulletin* 49, no. 2:146–50 (Oct. 1974). Copyright © 1974 by the H. W. Wilson Company.

A Lincoln fact, a Conrad contradiction

My struggle with facts starts, then, at the elementary stage of recognizing what they are and why they are important. Let us look, for example, at a plain fact. Abraham Lincoln was born on February 12, 1809; anyone who denies this is wrong. By itself this fact seems one of those insignificant details which are hard to keep straight in the memory and about which accuracy does not matter very much. The 11th or 13th would presumably have made no difference to Lincoln's later career. Even a year or two one way or the other might not have mattered. Yet the date does have importance because it places Lincoln in history. If he had been born ten years earlier, for instance, he might have been too old to grow with the immense changes that were sweeping over the midwestern prairies in the Forties and Fifties. He might have become set in his ways and never risen to be presidential candidate in 1860, though he certainly would not have been considered too old for the job. Alternatively, he might have become President, but proved unable to cope with unfamiliar situations or to endure extraordinary emotional and physical strain. In other words, a good deal depends on the simple fact when we put it in combination with other facts of environment or background. Because it has this kind of importance, we must give some recognition to its shape. February 12, 1809, is the correct date. There is no other.

So far, so good. But what if the facts are in dispute? Joseph Conrad, escaping from effective supervision at seventeen, was in serious trouble in Marseilles at twenty. His uncle, summoned from the Polish Ukraine by an ominous telegram—CONRAD WOUNDED. SEND MONEY. COME—arrived to find his nephew recovering from a bullet wound in the chest. Conrad gives two accounts of his escapade, one in a book of reminiscences about his adventure at sea, which covers his smuggling arms into Spain on behalf of Don Carlos, pretender to the Spanish throne; the other in a novel written many years later about his affair with the mistress of Don Carlos and his wound in a duel fought on her behalf. Since Conrad assured his friends that the novel was true to life and told his wife that the scar on his chest was a wound from a duel, his own account of the incident is fairly plain. Unfortunately, Don Carlos had given up the fight and left Spain a year before Conrad—by his own account—was smuggling arms to him. One of Conrad's companions on the venture was, according to ship's records, at the time on a voyage to the East Indies. A boy who Conrad says was drowned turns up many years later as captain of a coasting vessel. Don Carlos' mistress did not speak French at this time, was almost certainly not in Marseilles, and would not yet have been capable of playing the role of chief conspirator which he assigned to her. Conrad's uncle in a letter to a friend says nothing of a duel and puts down Conrad's wound to attempted suicide. Must we conclude that Conrad was a big liar? This would contradict a great deal of what we know of him from other sources. Can the records which conflict with his story be explained? In detail they can, but it is at least remarkable that so many of them need an explanation. In some ways I found this an easy problem to tackle because it is so fundamental to the relationship between fact and fiction in Conrad's writings that we can consider our verdict in the light of other stories he wrote concerning adventures which paralleled events in his own life. Furthermore, what we conclude is so important to an understanding of the man that even in a short biography I can marshal the evidence and give the reader some chance to judge independently.

The Goose-Nest Prairie dilemma

More difficult for me as a writer of short biographies are the contradictions which are not important enough to warrant discussion. In these cases, I often have to make up my mind, while yet the obligation to be right on matters of fact is just as binding on me as on those who have more space to argue about details. Let me take an admittedly small point by way of illustration because its simplicity makes it easy to see what is at issue. The most exhaustive book on Lincoln's pre-presidential years is the monumental work of Beveridge, published in 1928. In it he records that Lincoln's father died in 1851 at a place he describes as "Goose Nest Prairie." Nearly thirty years after Beveridge, Charles H. Coleman, professor at a state college only seven miles from the spot where Thomas Lincoln died, published a book on Lincoln's contacts with his relations in that area. In this he describes Thomas Lincoln's death at "Goose-nest Prairie." Both spellings are contradicted by a county history originally published in 1879 and recently revised, which calls the place "Goose-Nest Prairie." Which spelling shall I adopt? The spelling of the name today proves nothing about 1851. Lincoln's father was illiterate and had no version of his own. Legal documents may vary because spelling at the time was generally imperfect. Perhaps a biographer may be forgiven if he makes up his mind on this small matter on evidence which satisfies him but is not conclusive, like that for instance of a local paper. Nevertheless, it is just this kind of thing which represents one of the most serious difficulties which I face as a biographer for young adults. I do not always have room to explain why I take the position I do. I try to be careful and even find myself asking questions to which I do not absolutely need to know the answer, since I do not plan to include the disputed detail in what I am going to write. It simply seems that I need to know everything possible—because knowledge may affect judgment or because I am not yet really certain what I shall use or omit. In other words, I find it necessary to have a habit of worrying about facts, small or large, because my buildings are made up of these bricks, stones, or even pebbles.

Can a woman judge Napoleon?

Perfect accuracy on simple facts may not seem important to those who deal in generalizations, but at least a date or a spelling is presumably right or wrong. Many facts, however, are not easy to disentangle from judgments. Everyone who studies the career of Napoleon with an understanding of military tactics seems to have come to the conclusion that he was a great master of artillery on the battlefield. May I then regard this as a fact? In some contexts it would be fair to do so. If, for instance, in writing a biography of Lee I wished to emphasize his skill in handling artillery, I might do so by comparing him with Napoleon, even though I had made no study of the latter's career. If, on the other hand, I were writing a biography of Napoleon himself, I would have to treat this statement as a judgment. I would not be doing Napoleon justice if I did not examine his battles in detail and come to this conclusion for myself. So important is the distinction between a fact and a judgment or opinion that I would not even like to embark on a life of Napoleon, simply because as a woman I have no experience of battle. I fear my conclusions about his tactics might not have enough basis to have any value.

Fact or judgment?

It is clear that if the same statement may be used in one context as a fact and in another as an opinion, it will not always be easy to distinguish between judgment and fact. Most people are quite careless about doing so in ordinary life, just as their speech tends to be sloppier than their formal writing. Juvenile biographers often set a bad example also. The shorter and more elementary a biography is, the more likely its author will be to take other people's opinions and repeat them in positive tones as if they required no examination. To my mind this is exactly what people should never do if they are writing for those who have not finished their education. The distinction between a fact and a judgment is one of great importance, but we do not make it instinctively. We have to learn how. If we have not done so by the time our formal education ends, the chances are that we never shall. I cannot expect my readers to know what the difference is if I myself disregard it. In consequence, even where I think I know a good deal, I ought not to take opinions of others for granted.

Generally speaking, when I start a biography I already know something in a scrappy way about my subject. Both my parents, for instance, knew Bernard Shaw and the people who were closely associated with him in his political, as opposed to his dramatic, work. I had read most of his plays, had met him on a couple of occasions, and had seen several of his dramas on-stage, including the original production of *St. Joan*. Nevertheless, when I made up my mind to write about Shaw, I was careful to read his published works in the order in which they were written so that I might look at each in turn as the latest creation of his mind. In this way I formed opinions, though not at all unusual ones, about the development and decline of his talent. Only after this did I turn to what other people said about Shaw's writings, lest I adopt their ideas without realizing that Shaw's actual works were the facts and their value a matter of judgment.

I may in the last few paragraphs have sounded as though I were saying that a fifty-page biography for ten-year-olds requires as much research as a twelve-hundred one for adults. Clearly this is not the case, and I am ready to admit that my own biographies deliberately represent a certain class of effort. If, for instance, I had embarked on a life of Shaw or Gandhi for adults, I would have done so with the idea of adding somewhat to the total of general knowledge on my subject. Either I would have sought unpublished manuscripts or I would have expected to develop some new point of view by examining the known ones. Unless there seemed a fair prospect of doing one or the other, I would not have undertaken the task to begin with. But a young-adult biography is not necessarily trying to add to human knowledge. Only in the case of Edith Wharton does what I say rest on the examination of a good deal of hitherto-unused material. A young-adult biography is basically an attempt to present a life in broad outline for readers who have a great number of other books to study or who bog down in long volumes, but who are intelligent and like ideas.

The Shavian letters

Unquestionably, it is necessary for me to know a great deal more than I can actually put into a book of this kind, but at the same time research has reasonable limits. Let us consider, for instance, the question of Bernard Shaw's letters. Shaw was a voluminous and delightful letter-writer. Indeed his correspondence with the actresses Ellen Terry and Stella Campbell (whom he called "Stella Stellarum"—the Star of Stars) are among the most readable of English letter-collections. People kept Shaw's letters not merely because he was famous, but because they enjoyed them. By the time I came around to writing about Shaw, a great many of them had found their way into print. It would have been possible for me to discover unpublished letters which have since been included in a "complete" edition. Considering, however, the large number and the variety of those already available, it was clear that I might well toil for years to unearth new ones without ever discovering any important enough to include in a book of young-adult length. If I had been writing an adult work, I would have had to make this effort—and several others also—such as studying Shaw's manuscripts in order to look at the corrections he made as a clue to his mind.

Gandhi from afar

In similar fashion, Gandhi was a journalist of almost unbelievable output, writing with equal facility in English and several Indian languages. Essentially, however, he was not a man of letters, but was composing day-to-day articles for people who did not mind repetition of simple ideas. In fact, they welcomed it and, from Gandhi's point of view, even needed it because the re-education of a whole people had to take time. If I had gone to India to study Gandhi's papers in their original languages, I would undoubtedly have gained much. This being in practice impossible, I had to decide whether my upbringing in England during the period when Gandhi was at work in India had given me sufficient indirect contact with the man and the Indian problem to enable me to write something which would be of value for young adults. I thought it would and am pleased with the book, but I could not possibly have undertaken a longer work on the subject. My heap of pebbles would not have been sufficient.

This, then, is another aspect of my struggle with facts. I have to decide in each case how much work is needed to amass them and how much may be dismissed as an unreasonable expenditure of effort. If I had set out to be a scholar, my solutions to this problem would have been quite different. I recognize this, but do not take my own research lightly.

What caused the First World War?

Still another problem with facts which is especially important to the young-adult biographer is raised by his use of background material in broad outline. My books are intended for people who, by and large, have not finished their formal education. Their knowledge is consequently scrappy, and there is very little in the way of historical fact which I can assume that everybody who reads my book is bound to know. Thus in the late Fifties when I was working on a biography of Churchill, I had to face the prospect of explaining the causes of the Boer War, the British parliamentary system, the causes of the First World War, who fought in it on which side, and a number of similarly large subjects. Nobody likes to be lectured, so that I needed to introduce these explanations with great skill and to keep them short. Volumes have been written on the causes of the First World War, some blaming one set of circumstances or people, some another. I found it extremely difficult to outline such a subject, even though I could limit myself to some extent by showing events as they appeared to Churchill at the time. I may fairly say that such pieces of information dropped in with careful casualness or closely woven into my hero's life have nearly always represented a great deal of work. I have often been tempted to envy those who, writing for adults, can blithely assume that anyone interested enough to read their books will have a certain amount of background knowledge. A young-adult biography is designed for people who want to read straight through it, picking up all the background that they need along the way. They do not wish to be interrupted by footnotes or puzzled by the appearance of a character with an unpronounceable Indian name who may or may not have appeared fifty pages before. There is a smoothness required in the writing of such a biography which is extremely difficult to construct out of the hard shape of facts, especially if the author is trying not to impose his own opinions too forcefully.

Sotto voce views

This brings me to the real crux of my own struggle. Of course, I have opinions. Every biographer does, including those who labor to insert everything and pile up footnotes giving pros and cons on every question. Every such author has to arrange his or her material and will reveal himself by how he speaks of it. The young-adult writer, who is making decisions all the time about what to insert, what to explain, and how to compress, not only reveals himself in every line, but runs a very great risk of imposing his opinions on his reader as though they were not his judgments but absolute truth. It is fair to say that any biographer, whether he admits it or not, wants people to understand what he is thinking. He does not, however, wish readers to suppose that his is the only way of thought about his subject. We all know that our personalities limit our points of view and that other people in what we hope are less good books will be needed to give a rounded picture of our hero. We cannot regard our personal answers as final when dealing with another human being.

There is no one solution to this difficulty for the young-adult biographer. I need to impose my views upon the material because its handling requires special techniques. I have to find my solutions as particular ones at particular spots. In one place, I find it possible to debate an issue without actually telling the reader what is the answer. In another I may fling out a suggestion for an eager mind to grasp, but not develop it. Elsewhere I may leave a question hanging. The reception given my hero in his own time may be used to counterbalance what I am doing to him as author. By inserting the right phrase I can often indicate that these opinions of contemporaries are as important as the author's and are closer to my hero. In other words, I must constantly recognize in myself

the desire to "tell people what" and try to counteract it. Where I do not
succeed in being fair, it will be my own fault because my nature has an
obstinate habit of breaking through. I build to my own design, but I do
not try to plaster over the hard-core facts with my personal opinions.
Facts should be left showing and not chipped away to conform with the
shape of my building. I try to work with them in their original form in
order to create a sound structure.

In Biography for Young Readers, Nothing Is Impossible

Elizabeth Segel

Recommendations of Dorothy Aldis's juvenile biography *Nothing Is Impossible: The Story of Beatrix Potter*[1] have been cropping up everywhere
recently. Feminists compiling lists of children's books with competent
female protagonists seem invariably to recommend it. The title appears
in my local library's flyer, "Girls Are People, Too"[2]; in the bibliography
Little Miss Muffet Fights Back, compiled by Feminists on Children's
Media (revised edition, 1974); and in Sandra Styer's article, "Biographical Models for Young Feminists,"[3] to name just a few. I notice also that
in the latest revision of the popular *Anthology of Children's Literature*,[4]
the editors have added a chapter of the Aldis book to the biography section, with the laudable motive, I suspect, of offsetting the traditional
male dominance of juvenile biography.

In addition, the seventy-fifth birthday festivities for *The Tale of Peter
Rabbit* in 1978 have focused attention on the Aldis biography, giving
it a new lease on life. Marilyn D. Button's review of Potter biographies
for the Children's Literature Association *Newsletter*,[5] for instance, mentioned the book favorably.

Because I frequently discuss the book in my children's literature

First published in *The Lion and the Unicorn* 4, no. 1:4–14 (Summer 1980).
Copyright © 1981 by *The Lion and the Unicorn*.

classes as an example of inferior juvenile biography, I decided I'd better read it again.

I preceded my rereading of the Aldis book by reading *The Journal of Beatrix Potter,* transcribed from her code writings by Leslie Linder,[6] and Margaret Lane's adult biography, *The Tale of Beatrix Potter.*[7] I had several reasons for this. The journal is, of course, an invaluable primary source of information about the important years from 15 to 30 in Beatrix Potter's life. What she records and what she chooses not to record in this secret record which she expected no one else to read provide our best clues to the day-to-day reality of her life. The Lane book is the standard biography and one that has been universally praised for its lucidity, accuracy, and intelligence. Dorothy Aldis writes in her preface that she was herself moved to finish and publish her account of Potter's life after reading Lane's book, and she draws heavily on it. In addition, because the Lane biography is written with such clarity and concision (it is only 165 pages long), it can be read and enjoyed by adolescent readers. Thus, although the Aldis book can be read by preadolescents–children from about 9 to 12 for whom the Lane book is probably too difficult–for adolescents, Margaret Lane's biography must be kept in mind as an alternative to Dorothy Aldis's. As such, it has a formidable advantage to begin with in its numerous photographs of its subject, her family and surroundings, and its reproductions of her childhood sketches, fungi paintings, code-writing, picture-letters, and book illustrations. Richard Cuffari's drawings for the juvenile biography are attractive but cannot compete with the wealth of authentic pictorial material enriching the adult biography.

As to the text of *Nothing Is Impossible,* its strengths lie in Aldis's skill at constructing scene and dialogue and in her sensitivity to a young reader's perceptions and preoccupations. She begins her biography:

> Nearly everybody remembers a little of what it was like to be five years old. Quite a few people even remember some things that happened when they were four, or three, or even two.
>
> But most children, when they are five years old, can hardly wait to be six, seven, or eight. When they get to be twelve or thirteen, they long to be grown-up so they can boss themselves. They hurry away from childhood days and soon forget most things about them.
>
> This is a story about a girl named Beatrix Potter who never forgot what it was like to be a child of four or five or six. Perhaps this was because she spent so much of her childhood alone. Until she was almost six, she had no brothers or sisters. She never went to school or had any playmates her own age. Her parents did not seem to be interested in her. At least, they hardly ever saw her. They never gave her parties. They never took her for drives with them in the carriage. They lived in one part of the house, and she lived in another.

She goes on to select those episodes of Potter's childhood that children can best relate to, such as Beatrix's penchant for withdrawing under the parlor table to eat gingersnaps and listen unobserved to grown-up conversation. She often succeeds in creating scenes that can engage the present-day child in the remarkably different life of this genteel Victorian child.

Yet although Aldis does acknowledge the various deprivations Beatrix suffered, as these introductory paragraphs indicate, she apparently felt that she must soften the reality of life in what Potter later referred to significantly as "my unloved birthplace." For example, while portraying accurately the distant, cold figures of Mr. and Mrs. Potter, Aldis provides Beatrix with a loving, encouraging figure in the butler, Mr. Cox. In her book, he helps Beatrix manage her pets, takes her and her brother for long walks, starts her collecting botanical specimens—even gives her the embrace that her parents are incapable of. In the 437 pages of Beatrix Potter's journal, however, there are only three passing references to Cox the butler (pp. 98, 152, 239)—nothing to indicate that her relationship with him had ever been a whit warmer or more personal than her parents' was. (In fact, the journal testifies that as an adolescent, Beatrix shared her parents' snobberies; only later did she forcibly reject them).

This is just one instance of a general pattern. Aldis leaves out of her account what Margaret Lane aptly calls "the two spectres which gloomily haunted [Beatrix] in Bolton Gardens—loneliness and depression" (p. 109). In speaking of Beatrix at 16, Aldis writes sunnily: "Not for a minute did Beatrix think her life was odd or unhappy" (p. 77). Yet in Beatrix's journal of that year we read: "I am up one day and down another. Have been a long way down today" (p. 38). And on her seventeenth birthday: "I, seventeen. I have heard it called 'sweet seventeen,' no indeed, what a time we are, have been having, and shall have—" (p. 47). Whether this refers to overt rows with her parents or to internal struggles with doubts and loneliness we cannot know. No one can read the journal, however, and feel that Mrs. Aldis has been faithful to the emotional reality of the life she chronicles. And in biography, that, it seems to me, is a failure that outweighs factual accuracy and narrative skill.

"How much I have to be thankful for, but these odious fits of low spirits would spoil any life" (Lane p. 52). "Oh, life, wearisome, disappointing, and yet in many shades so sweet, I wonder why one is so unwilling to let go this old year? not because it has been joyful, but because I fear its successors—I am terribly afraid of the future" (*Journal*, p. 161). This last was written on New Year's Eve; Beatrix was 19 years old. Entries like these punctuate the dry, impersonal information and flat, detailed accounts of art exhibitions in the journal of Beatrix's late adolescent years; we find no echo of them in the juvenile biography.

Not only is this omission misleading, it is a mistake in narrative strategy. Many students and writers of biography and historical fiction for children in recent years have recognized that it is more encouraging to a child to know that others shared the doubts and fears he or she feels and yet were able to work out a productive and fulfilled life than to be told that as children the great remained cheerful and confident in the face of all difficulties. Precisely because Beatrix Potter's childhood was so unhappy, Aldis's hewing to the old conventions here is especially damaging.

Marilyn D. Button concluded her brief review of *Nothing Is Impossible* by judging the book "instructive . . . and even inspirational since it tells the story of a seemingly plain, shy girl who, because of hard work and an innate sense of self worth, was able to create something of lasting value in her life."[8] My quarrel with this aspect of Aldis's book is not the prominence of a "moral." Ever since Plutarch chose his subjects "as types of certain virtues and vices and as examples for emulation or avoidance by the young," biographers have aimed to instruct and inspire. Moreover, I'm convinced that the search for models, and the desire to learn from the experiences of others have always been part of the attraction of biography for readers—especially in early adolescence when one faces with trepidation the decisive years ahead.

No, what I object to here is the falseness of this picture of Beatrix Potter's life: ". . . the story of a seemingly plain, shy girl who, because of hard work and an innate sense of self worth. . . ." Button is right. This is the message of Aldis's book. And of hundreds more, of course, as any reader of juvenile biography can testify. ("They all seemed like the same book," a college student once told me, recalling her frustration when the thirst for reading biography hit in junior high school.)

What I deplore, then, most of all in *Nothing Is Impossible* is the squeezing of a unique and fascinating life into a standard mold. To anyone reading the facts of Beatrix Potter's life and her reactions to them in her journal and letters, Button's summary is not the story of that life. An innate sense of self worth was certainly something she did not have as a child or young woman. Hard work did characterize her life, but it did not bear the simple relationship to her success that the book suggests—only indirectly did it contribute by giving her enough financial independence to escape from her parents' home.

What Beatrix longed to be, what she worked steadily and enthusiastically for years to become, was a botanical illustrator. The brief glimpses of happiness in her journal cluster around the holidays in Scotland or the Lake Country, where she could hunt and collect specimens for later painting. When, in her late twenties, she begins to envision this as a lifework, a new enthusiasm and vitality characterize the journal entries. "I have been drawing funguses very hard; I think some day they will be put in a book . . ." she confided to her journal. But it was not to be. The Victorian scientific establishment was not prepared to encourage an amateur, and a young woman to boot. Two hundred seventy of Potter's paintings of fungi survive, most of them done in the years 1893 to 1898. All of this work eventuated in one scientific paper on the spores of moulds, written by Potter but read by someone else at a meeting of the Linnaean Society of London—a meeting that was off-limits to ladies. "The excitement of several years had ended in disappointment," writes Margaret Lane (p. 44).

A major disappointment it was and without a doubt a turning point in Beatrix Potter's life. The voluminous journal kept for fifteen years breaks off forever at this point. In Lane's view, Beatrix now turned to nursery pictures of rabbit families "as an amusement," and "she sometimes regretted the more serious and grown-up work which had been abandoned" (p. 44). That she viewed such work (and the little books that grew out of it, I suspect) as trivial is difficult for us who place a high value on them to accept, but it makes the pains she took with them all the more admirable to my mind. That she seems to have shared to some degree the general attitude of condescension toward children's books also helps us understand her rude impatience with those who in later years lavished praise on her children's book illustrations.

This crucial disappointment in Potter's life is mentioned only in passing by Dorothy Aldis—and the sting has been removed. "Canon Rawnsley . . . had given up begging her to do the mushroom book. They both realized this would take more scientific training than she had" (pp. 111-12). The impression is that the book was Rawnsley's idea and that Beatrix easily acquiesced in giving it up, that she didn't any longer really want to do the book. But the journal tells a different story.

Why would Aldis gloss over and distort what is so clearly a key episode in Potter's life? The answer is obvious: because it doesn't square with her overriding theme, "nothing is impossible."[9] And with this, we arrive at the crux of the problem. This favorite message of juvenile biographers over the years, blithely distilled by them from the diverse lives of ballplayers, statesmen, scientists and artists, is a lie.

If ever there was a life which demonstrates that some things are not possible, it is Beatrix Potter's. She had, in all likelihood, the ability, diligence, and perseverance to succeed in what she set her heart on—winning a small niche in the scientific world as a student of fungi and a botanical illustrator. Yet because of external factors (her parents' unwillingness to give her the formal training she needed, the timidity that resulted from her isolated upbringing, and her society's severe restrictions on women's activities), she did not attain her reasonable goal. Later, Beatrix Potter came to love Norman Warne, the youngest son of the family firm that was publishing her picture books. Calling down upon herself her parents' strenuous objections and accusations of undutifulness, Beatrix engaged herself to marry him. This marriage death decreed impossible, for Norman Warne died within a few months, a victim of acute leukemia.

Pamela Travers once observed that the nursery rhyme "Humpty Dumpty" communicates to small children "that there are some things that all the king's horses and all the king's men cannot put together again; things that, for all our grieving, may be broken beyond mending."[10] Isn't this the honest truth about our life's experience? And is a child of nine or so, who has undoubtedly experienced in some form or other the reality of loss, too fragile to face it?

The nothing-is-impossible formula is in part, I think, a relic of the tendency in late-nineteenth and early-twentieth-century adults to see childhood as a carefree time and to try to postpone for as long as possible the unhappy awakening to the harsh world. In this respect, *Nothing Is Impossible* was somewhat old-fashioned when it was published. (After all, by 1969 the deromanticized view of childhood ushered in by works like *Harriet the Spy* was dominant in fiction for adolescents and preadolescents.) That this softening of unpleasant reality hung on in juvenile biography while it grew rare in adolescent fiction is due probably to the tradition of biography as inspirational literature. More specifically, it stems from the apparent elevation of inspiration (defined narrowly as uplifting, ennobling example) above fidelity to truth as the primary goal of many juvenile biographers. It is this tendency that explains why, as late as 1976, Clifton Fadiman could observe that in contrast to other genres, "no absolutely first-rate history of biography [had] been written for children."[11]

The lesson of Humpty Dumpty "can be a bitter lesson," wrote Pamela Travers. We may with some justification feel that certain lives have been too full of unremitting loss and deprivation to make appropriate biographies for preadolescent children. Yet the life of Beatrix Potter is not such a case. The barren isolation of the early years, the poignant disappointments are not the whole story. Her life, without minimizing the pain of its limited possibilities, does instruct and inspire us—and it need not be falsified to do so. We carry away from it not only an understanding of the rigid definitions of proper behavior imposed by class and gender on the rich diversity of human needs and talents. We see also the solace of having work to do, even if it is not the work one would choose, and the satisfaction of taking pains with it. We glimpse, in Potter's thirty-year marriage, contracted when she was in her forty-eighth year, the joys of love and companionship in a relationship of two people who value each other's autonomy—joys that can come after great disappointment.

All of this is part of the life of Beatrix Potter, along with the depression and restrictions. Dorothy Aldis, in screening out the pain, as too bleak for preadolescent readers, obscured the moving reality, and substituted for it a conventional formula.

Controversy:

An Active, Healthy Skepticism

An information book must communicate facts and ideas to its readers, of
whatever age or capacity, in such a
way that they will develop the will and
the mental equipment to assess these
facts and ideas. In the broadest sense,
an information book is a teacher, and
the role of a teacher is to lead his
pupils towards a considered independence of thought and action. Instruction is important, but freedom of
thought is more important still.

——Margery Fisher[1]

The Problem with Problem Books

Jo Carr

Reading the daily paper has become an uncomfortable challenge. In almost every news story impossible questions seem to be demanding impossible answers: What should be done about the danger of radioactive fallout from a malfunctioning nuclear plant? Should the study of creationism, as well as evolution, be required in biology courses in high school? At what stage does a fetus become a human being? Are people crazy when they say they have sighted UFOs? When is a dying person actually dead? Should industries be required by government to provide clean air and healthful working conditions for their employees, no matter how much these protections might cost? Do dictatorial regimes deserve American support just because they are non-Communist? Does a school board have the right to tell a librarian what books should not be on the shelves of a school library?

Questions of ethical and scientific significance are especially troubling because they tend to be incredibly complex. How many of us know enough about nuclear power to have an acceptable opinion on this subject? Or about genetic engineering? Or about the cost of industrial health and safety measures? Not many of us. Furthermore, an uninformed reaction to any of these issues might actually be worse than no reaction at all.

Fortunately, nonfiction authors, especially those writing for children, have recognized the need for clear information on the complicated issues that affect our lives. In recent years they have written books for children that should go a long way toward making today's children better informed than their parents were in childhood. Naturally some of these books are more successful than others; some are totally ineffective; some are actually misleading. Since nonfiction authors are performing an important function by writing on these complex subjects, we should be sympathetic to the problems they face in trying to deal with controversy. We should also be alert to the twisting of truth that can result.

Although nonfiction writers unquestionably confront more than one challenge with controversial subjects, one problem overwhelms all the others. Somehow an author must walk the fine line between information and inculcation, between passion and prejudice, between teaching and preaching. The way in which an author presents ideas must achieve a balance between conviction and objective truth. Laurence Pringle has discussed this precarious balance in his article "Balance and Bias in Controversial Books." His ideas are worth exploring.

Offhand it would seem reasonable that a nonfiction writer should present a completely balanced view in discussing a controversial subject, but impartial treatment is not actually as desirable as it might seem. In a children's book, giving all sides of an issue is impossible. Either the book would be too long for children to read, or the issues would be treated so superficially that oversimplification and unwarranted generalizations would result.

But even if complete impartiality were possible, it would probably result in a poor book. Here we need to remember that a good nonfiction writer is, above all, a good teacher. A good teacher, as was pointed out in the article on the literature of fact, has a point of view, a philosophical understanding of the subject that gives it unity as well as significance. It is this insight, with the ability to organize and present material selectively, that gives meaning to fact.

Insight often is a product of passion or commitment. A good teacher has a deep commitment to the subject, a kind of passionate enthusiasm. Since enthusiasm is unquestionably a characteristic of good writing as well as good teaching—as has also been pointed out—no writer could hope to intrigue a reader by expounding an uncongenial point of view. Without an author's enthusiasm, the reader must inevitably contend with conscientious shuttling from one view to another: "Although some experts maintain that the danger from radiation is minimal, other authorities contend. . . ." Such "balanced" writing is usually as boring as that encountered in a textbook or an encyclopedia. Certainly it lacks what Barbara Tuchman has called "the pulse beat on the printed page."

An author's exploration of a controversial subject should be made with partiality and passion if a reader is to respond to it. However, the problem with passion is that it sometimes becomes too fervid. The author may become so partial to one point of view that the writing degenerates into propaganda, with no other viewpoints even suggested. Propaganda disguised as information is clearly unacceptable, but how does the reader tell the difference? At what point does passion leave off and propaganda begin?

Let us examine one book in which the author's passion has obviously overwhelmed information. It starts like this: "Like every other girl, you have a lot to learn. And some of the lessons aren't easy. The first, and most basic lesson, is learning to be stupid."[1] Dale Carlson, who must have burned up her typewriter ribbon as she wrote this book, *Girls Are Equal Too,* leaves her reader with no doubt about the evils of a sexist society:

> Do you finally understand what is being done to you just because you are a girl? . . . A sexist society says that a female is less intelligent, inferior, and has to learn to be passive, dependent, gentle, obedient, supportive, motherly; and a boy is more intelligent, superior and has to be

active, independent, aggressive, brave, competitive, successful. . . . Tired of being inferior? Read on.[2]

We would, of course, like to know who it was that said what "a sexist society says . . ." Unfortunately, Dale Carlson fails to tell us. All she provides by way of documentation is this statement: "The major sources for the facts and statistics in the book were: newspapers and magazines, government publications, and books that deal with feminism, the feminist movement, and the lives and thoughts of women."[3]

How can the reader determine from the author's statement whether her facts are to be relied on, whether her views are supported by solid evidence? A bibliography of sources would have helped, although even this would not guarantee that the author's generalizations are warranted. We all are familiar with cases of bias that have been defended by an arsenal of printed one-sided facts. Nevertheless, a list of sources and a balanced, rather than slanted, bibliography for further reading would have been reassuring. The author does include facts and figures in her book, it is true, but only those promoting her view. Balance is not her objective. With the welcome exception of the chapter on early leaders of the women's rights movement, her presentation is almost entirely negative. Little space is given to the good work of NOW and other fine organizations, or to the women who have done and continue to do outstanding work in all fields. The writing itself is loaded with sarcasm and exhortation. Extreme positions are presented so emphatically that they allow for no intellectual response from the reader. Reasoning has been abandoned in favor of emotion. Despite her lively and competent writing, Dale Carlson comes closer to sounding like a fanatic on a soapbox than a creative, exciting teacher engaging children in the process of learning.

Laurence Pringle has suggested that a one-sided book can be justified if there is another book, equally one-sided, with which to balance it, assuming that the reader will read both. It is possible that balance could be so achieved, but unfortunately it doesn't often work that way. A book like *Girls Are Equal Too* reveals the difficulty. Dale Carlson has presented her case with gusto, and most of us would support her all the way, but the other side obviously has a right to be heard as well. Who is there to speak for the other side? Is there anybody about to write a children's version of *The Phyllis Schlafly Report*? No authors have stepped forward, nor are they likely to do so. With an issue as popular as feminism today, a writer is probably going to be as unwilling to sound like a Marabel Morgan as to espouse the cause of a copper company about to strip-mine a wilderness area. Since feminists and environmentalists are "in" at the moment, theirs are the books that tend to get published. It is unrealistic, for this reason, to hope for balance through a mix of opposing ideologies sitting side by side on the shelves in the children's room.

It is unrealistic for another reason to assume that overall balance in the library collection would assure access to opposing points of view. Not only do children and young people read far less than adults, they are tending to read less and less all the time. Therefore, even if contradictory books were available, it would be foolhardy to expect that children would read them, or even some of them. In addition, children are obviously more receptive to what they read than are adults. Since adults bring to their reading greater sophistication and broader intellectual interests, naturally children will be more easily seduced by faulty reasoning and inaccurate but emotional writing. Therefore, any author who writes for children labors under a heavy responsibility, far heavier than any placed on the writer for adults.

For all these reasons, the conscientious children's author, in testing a controversial theme, does have an obligation to give young readers a measure of "con" along with a generous portion of "pro." Daniel Cohen is one writer who has responsibly presented a readable combination of both. In writing *The Ancient Visitors* he has dealt with most fairly the controversy surrounding the existence of ETIs, extraterrestrial intelligences. His balanced presentation contrasts dramatically with *Chariots of the Gods?* by Erich von Däniken, who has done for extraterrestrial visitors what Dale Carlson has done for females. By interpreting curious phenomena according to his own "scientific" theories, von Däniken has made a closed defense of visits by creatures from other planets. His arguments seem absolutely convincing, at least to a reader who is not a scientist and has no way of checking the data. It is only after reading Cohen's account, with other interpretations of the same phenomena, that von Däniken's case is revealed as being one-sided in the extreme. Daniel Cohen is judicious in his discussion of von Däniken, just as he is in his discussion of the mysteries that have stimulated wild theories about Ezekiel and his wheel, gigantic figures etched on a desert in Peru, and strange statues on Easter Island. His tone is low-key and unemotional:

> Even when a writer does not try to beat his readers over the head with a particular point of view, opinions tend to come through. They dictate the choice of evidence, and the very choice of words. The best I can hope to do is to try to present a balanced view of the arguments for and against the theory of ETI visitation.[4]

And this is just what he does in the book. Only in the last chapter does he give his personal reaction to the data, with his reasons for thinking that the evidence supporting extraterrestrial visitations is unconvincing. He ends with a strong bibliography and questions for further investigation.

What do we learn, then, by contrasting a polemic like *Girls Are Equal Too* with straightforward nonfiction like *The Ancient Visitors*? We learn to appreciate, for a start, those authors who support ideas with facts, especially those whose documentation provides evidence for the reliability of those facts. Since bias is inevitable and probably desirable, we appreciate authors who clearly state their point of view at the beginning of the book, while respectfully acknowledging those of others. We also appreciate an author whose writing is lively without being either sensational or propagandistic.

Ideas supported by facts, facts supported by documentation, bias declared while other biases are acknowledged, writing that appeals more to reason than emotion—all these are guidelines we owe to Laurence Pringle. What is more, he follows his own advice; he writes books that could serve as models to demonstrate the delicate balance between conviction and objectivity. In *Nuclear Power, from Physics to Politics*, for instance, he has maneuvered, with his usual skill, between the extremes of anti- and pronuclear energy positions. He states at the beginning of the book that he is not objective: "In this controversy (as well as in others), it is difficult to find a well-informed person who is also neutral. This book is not neutral either."[5] He then explains clearly the major scientific, economic, ethical, and political issues raised by a policy supporting nuclear power. His fear of problems in nuclear reactors, as well as his concern over disposal of nuclear waste, becomes obvious. But he never allows this concern to silence the voice of opposition. After reflecting on the alarming difficulties encountered in storing nuclear waste, for instance, he characterizes the opposite outlook with this statement:

> Nuclear advocates believe that the danger of the wastes—now and in the future—has been greatly exaggerated. Besides, they argue, we have chosen to put other burdens on future generations; for example by burning up so much of the earth's fossil fuels in the past century. We can ease their burden by giving our descendants the gift of nuclear energy.[6]

The final thrust of the discussion is one of caution based on awareness of what both sides contend to be the truth. To increase this awareness, the author has further supplied a bibliography of articles and books, with this advice:

> This list of books and articles includes a wide range of opinions about nuclear matters. The title often reveals whether an author has a pro- or antinuclear attitude. Be especially careful of any publication that claims to be without bias. To keep up-to-date on developments in the nuclear power controversy, I recommend these magazines. . . . In all periodicals watch for follow-up letters commenting on published articles.[7]

In the end, says Pringle, it is people like ourselves who must assume awesome responsibility for weighing the relative benefits and costs of nuclear energy in the future. Our first task, obviously, is to become informed. Laurence Pringle has aided us by writing a responsibly biased exploration of the issues we must face.

At the end of his article on bias and balance in controversial books Laurence Pringle, after having covered the necessity for documentation and declared bias, admonishes readers to keep on asking questions. We must all agree, since probably no aspect of nonfiction writing, either reading it or writing it, is more important. Asking more and more complex questions while continually searching for new answers to old questions is a process that will be increasingly necessary in tomorrow's world. If problems today are complicated, they are probably far less so than they will be ten years from now. Children who will then be adults need to be prepared to reason through complex issues having to do with space stations in orbit, ethical implications of genetic manipulation, responsible utilization of fuel resources, to name only a few. Perhaps a sense of urgency should make us more apprehensive than we are, for none of tomorrow's adults will be equipped as informed decisionmakers unless they have been trained, as children, to think for themselves. Ultimately, then, the process of learning becomes almost more important than what is learned, the exercise in rational thinking more important than the acquisition of information. As Daniel Boorstin said in his speech at the White House Conference, absorbing information is a passive process, while acquiring knowledge requires active participation in a dynamic learning effort. Knowledge, rather than information, will be sorely needed by children from now on.

So the major responsibility of the nonfiction writer becomes that of encouraging sound reasoning from well-informed premises—in other words, to help young readers become independent thinkers. Dale Carlson has denied her readers opportunity for this vital intellectual exercise by her dogmatic way of telling them what to think. It is almost as if she were saying to them: "Since you are so young and inexperienced, I must tell you what is happening to you and what you must do about it." How much better her book would have been had she provided them with the facts and let them discover the truth for themselves.

Obviously Dale Carlson has written a book to promote the truth, but only the truth as she sees it. There are others who seem to be pursuing the same objective. In this context we must ask ourselves honestly about the aims of the Council on Interracial Books for Children (CIBC). They have stated in their article in this collection what they consider to be their function: "We are advocates of a society in which all human beings have the true, not rhetorical, opportunity to realize their full human potential. We therefore frankly advocate books that will help achieve such a society and help prepare children for such a society."[8] With this aim in view each book is examined for its message and for the effect of that message on children. History books, for instance, have been checked for Native Americans with feathers. The illustrators of *Ashanti to Zulu*, although recognized for their artwork, have been criticized for portraying African tribes in their exotic tribal robes, rather than presenting them as they might appear in ordinary life. Illustrations of neighborhoods in which children are at play have been challenged for depicting children of only one color, regardless of whether such neighborhoods might be multi-racial in reality.

After reading countless CIBC reviews of nonfiction books, one begins to suspect that the books advocated by CIBC might be like those prescribed for children in some totalitarian nation. In fact, the *Interracial Books for Children Bulletin* has reported on the value of such books in an article on books in the People's Republic of China that ends with this statement: "A study such as this provides a striking example of what a critical function literature plays in inculcating a society's preferred value and ideals in its children."[9] Anyone who has read *Huang Chi-kuang, a Hero To Remember* (1966) or *Kao Yu-Pao, Story of a Poor Peasant Boy* (1975) or *The Making of a Peasant Doctor* (1976; all published by the PRC's Foreign Languages Press)—books in which all landlords are evil, every Mao soldier heroic, and the state at all times noble—would have a hard time agreeing with this statement. Surely no thoughtful person, even someone committed to the ideals of Mao, would consider such books to be anything but moral treatises and political tracts.

Since we are all sympathetic with the humane ends of CIBC, it is extremely difficult to know how to react to their evaluation of nonfiction books. They are correct in saying that "books carry a message, a moral, a value, or a set of values." The issue becomes one of determining how an author presents this point of view, this set of values. If ideas are to be presented in a spirit of free inquiry, not indoctrination, then the theme of the book, although important, becomes less crucial than sound scholarship and the exploration of opposing points of view treated with respect. Surely we shouldn't have to agree with the conclusions in a book in order to approve of it? CIBC seems to be saying that we must. They seem to be saying, in fact, that they will endorse only those books that carry CIBC-approved messages, only those promoting a society acceptable to them. And this society is not a reflection of the world as it is but the world as CIBC wishes it to be. If we do value free inquiry, then the aims of CIBC are bound to be disturbing; well intentioned, but disturbing nonetheless. In the final analysis we can't help asking ourselves whether such concern for doctrine in books is uncomfortably close to censorship.

On the other hand, perhaps CIBC is right in how they view the role of literature. Most of us see literature as the honest reflection—right or wrong, inspired or pedestrian—of one writer's view of the world. Perhaps literature does have the potential of changing the world, as CIBC contends, if only books with humane values, and those books only, were read by children in their formative years. Whether we condemn CIBC for censoring free ideas or applaud them for attempting to create a better world, how we interpret their controversial efforts depends basically on how we feel about the role of literature in the society. In other words, do we think literature should reflect society or be a means of influencing society? This is something all of us must decide for ourselves.

No matter how we react to the particular aims of CIBC, however, we should continue to reaffirm our faith in the free exploration of ideas through reading. We need to be looking constantly for books that provoke questions and demand intellectual participation on the part of the reader. Quite apart from obvious reasons for encouraging such intellectual activity, we need to supplement those books that inculcate the values of CIBC, Erich von Däniken, Dale Carlson, and all the others who conceive of books as a way to influence behavior. It is extremely satisfying, for instance, to meet the intellectual challenge at the end of Daniel Cohen's book on creatures from outer space:

> The theories of extraterrestrial contact are out in front of the public, and we can make our own judgments upon them. I have made mine— though I certainly hope and believe that I possess the flexibility of mind to change. It would be hard to remain skeptical if that jet plane was found in an ancient tomb or if a spaceship really did land on the White House lawn.
>
> And you—I trust—will make your own judgments as well.[10]

Here the author has left us with the invigorating responsibility of coming to our own conclusions. We need more books like this, books like Lazer Goldberg's *Learning to Choose: Stories and Essays about Science, Technology, and Human Values* (Scribner, 1976), in which children are challenged to discuss social and ethical implications of technological change. Or Joyce Milton's *Controversy: Science in Conflict* (Messner, 1980). We also need more writers like Laurence Pringle, who is brave enough to tackle any subject, even one as prickly as the conflict over industrial health and safety in his book, *Lives at Stake* (Macmillan, 1980).

Throughout this discussion of controversial books one word keeps coming to mind as being deeply significant. It is a word that applies to teachers as well as to writers. That word is *respect*. A good teacher respects the intelligence of students, requiring always that they work hard to pursue ideas on their own. So it is with a good writer. With respect, a writer must demand rigorous intellectual effort from any reader who hopes to become an enlightened citizen of the world. If enough authors can challenge young readers successfully, then these readers will be ready to deal with even the most complicated issues in the future.

Balance and Bias in Controversial Books

Laurence Pringle

During a decade of writing for children and teenagers, some of my books have touched upon unresolved issues in science, and some have dealt directly with such environmental problems as population growth, solid wastes, biocides, food, energy, and nuclear power. My approach to these controversial subjects was intuitive. Now I have been asked to wonder, on paper, about the assumptions lying beneath what has been mostly an unconscious process.

I assume that books can influence children, though the effect of books on them is not to plant seeds in some mythical virgin soil of their minds, but to stimulate and nourish values, interests, feelings, and capacities that are already there.

Also, children deserve some special consideration. They are naive politically and psychologically. They begin with blind faith in such authorities as parents, teachers, and television. This gives them trouble enough; writers shouldn't add more. It is a pleasure to see children grow more sophisticated, to see them recognize the lies and distortions in advertising. They become increasingly aware of life's subtleties and complexities, and learn that commercials do not give the whole story. Neither do teachers or parents.

This healthy skepticism may develop slowly. A child who easily spots the distortions and omissions in a cereal commercial may accept without question an advertisement of an oil corporation. Children and teenagers are more easily fooled than most adults, so the polemics that are sometimes published for adults are unconscionable for younger readers.

The whole story can usually be told, and is usually complex. By "the whole story" I mean the key ideas, not every last detail. Though some people still believe that a nonfiction book is "informational"—wholly made up of facts, statistics, anecdotes, reports of studies, and the like, the real values of the best nonfiction are ideas, insights, and perhaps even wisdom. We gain wisdom partly by sifting through and discarding facts and the best nonfiction writers spare their readers some tedious sifting. A writer can easily loose a torrent of facts about an issue, but this ency-

Reprinted by permission of the Children's Science Book Review Committee from *Appraisal: Science Books for Children* 12, no. 2:1–4 (Spring 1979). Copyright © 1979 by Laurence Pringle.

clopedic approach doesn't help readers who may already be awash with mere information.

One of the most dangerous ideas of our times is that problems are simple and have simple solutions. People would like this to be true, and there's no lack of politicians and others telling us it is so. It isn't. Our fast-changing world grows steadily more complicated. A person who writes for children has a responsibility to dig much deeper than the bumper-sticker level of a controversy and, in some cases, perhaps to choose *not to write* a book because the socio-economic-political factors may be too sophisticated and complex for the youngest readers.

For example, in the early 1970s the problem of litter and solid wastes was presented to young readers in several books which encouraged children to believe that individual efforts, such as saving used bottles, would solve this problem. Children do find such efforts rewarding, but they were done a disservice by authors who most likely did not understand this difficult and highly politicized problem.

One book paid homage to Keep America Beautiful, Inc.—an organization financed by beverage companies, bottlers, container manufacturers, and others who have encouraged a throwaway lifestyle, and whose economic success depends on continuation of that lifestyle. Though this organization would have us believe that "People cause pollution; people can clean it up," others find this simplistic. Individual and community recycling efforts make only a small dent in the huge volume of solid wastes and litter. More effective solutions to this problem deal with the origins of waste, not the end products. Perhaps the youngest readers should have been spared books on this subject if the full complexity of the problem could not be conveyed.

An often quoted standard for children's books about controversies is that they should be "objective and balanced." This is an extraordinary goal, considering that everyone involved in the controversies, including Nobel laureate scientists, is being subjective and biased. I believe bias is usually inevitable and, to an extent, well-informed bias is desirable.

What is a "balanced book?" I don't recall ever reading one, or writing one, if "balance" means giving equal space and equal treatment to both sides (or is it six sides?) of a controversy. My most balanced "issue" book, so far, is probably *The Controversial Coyote* (Harcourt, 1977), which is unabashedly in favor of the coyote species but, by virtue of reporting what biologists actually know about coyotes, managed to upset cherished notions of some extremists on both sides of the western predator control dispute.

It seems unreasonable to expect complete objectivity from a writer who is well-informed about an issue and who cares about the outcome. More realistic goals for a controversial book are that the writer be as objective as possible, and present differing views. Objectivity, or something close to it, comes easily when a writer has little or nothing at stake in the outcome of a controversy. Consider, for example, the on-going reexamination of fossil evidence by paleontologists who wonder whether some or all dinosaurs were warm-blooded. Writing about this (*Dinosaurs and People,* Harcourt, 1978), I found the idea tremendously appealing, probably because I'm warm-blooded myself. But the outcome of this dispute won't have much impact on my life (as it has and will on the careers and status of certain paleontologists), so a fair degree of objectivity was achieved.

"Balance" becomes more difficult when a writer believes that the outcome of a controversy has national or global implications for people and other living things, as in the case of the world's food supply or nuclear power development. It is possible, I suppose, for a writer to bury his or her feelings on such issues and produce a totally unbiased book. But I believe that readers benefit more from a book enriched by the author's views—provided that the author has a good grasp of the whole story and "the other side" is well-represented.

Sometimes a biased book represents balance in a larger context. In controversies about energy, for instance, young people are exposed to many inputs representing views of utilities and energy corporations. These include advertisements on television and in print media, free films and booklets available to schools, tours of power stations and other facilities, and even utility-employed "educational aides" who enter schools and advise on teaching about energy. Against all this, a book that is somewhat biased towards "the other side" can have a vital balancing effect.

Besides offering different views in the text, a writer can urge readers to dig deeper, beginning with a reading list which represents all sides. Beyond that, a writer has the responsibility to desensationalize an issue as much as possible, and to shed some light on its complexity. Part of that light can be simply to ask questions, to reveal the unknown as well as the known. Perhaps the most learned thing we can say about some aspects of today's controversies is "we don't know."

Among the least-understood aspects of today's controversies is *why* people (including authors) choose one side over another. In the increasingly hot dispute over hunting, for example, a University of Michigan study revealed that the presence or absence of certain early family or cultural experiences helped determine a person's attitude towards hunting. To oversimplify somewhat: a city-raised child with no exposure to the process of converting livestock or game to meat on the table is likely to oppose hunting; a rural child who has witnessed the routine killing of animals for food is likely to feel that hunting is all right. Presumably there are other experiences, or lack of them, which influence feelings about other issues. The emotions are often unacknowledged and are masked by a facade of rational arguments.

This is an important idea, with implications for all sorts of conflicts. In what ways do human feelings affect the complex stew of politics, economics, science, technology, and other factors in controversial issues?

One example of their importance is revealed in the history of nuclear power development. A few decades ago, physicists were fascinated by the possibilities of obtaining energy from the fission or fusion of atoms. There were and are many ways of doing this.

How did we come to choose our present troubled nuclear technology? It seems that the choice was made more for psychological reasons than technological ones. People in the United States, or at least their political leaders, felt guilty over the use of nuclear weapons in Japan. To ease the guilt we wanted to do something *fast* to show that nuclear power could be a force for good. Had the goal been to develop a safe, clean, and cheap energy source, a more deliberate and open-minded approach might have led to a different sort of nuclear technology, or none at all.

This illustrates that human emotions can play a major role in matters which are often thought to be mostly scientific and technological. This is a bit of wisdom for people of any age. It also illustrates that the really vital matters of life deal not with "what" questions but with "how" and "why" questions. That's where the wisdom lies. Books about controversies ought to try to answer some "how" and "why" questions, and inspire readers to keep asking.

Bias in Children's Books

Council on Interracial Books for Children

Children's books are not merely a matter of text (which may be lively, entertaining, and stirring, or not) plus pictures (which may be well done or not). Children's books are not merely exciting, imaginative, and full of good characters or the opposite. No; Hugh Lofting's modest *Doctor Dolittle* is actually a very political and colonialist fellow and *Bright April*

Reprinted by permission of the Council on Interracial Books for Children from *Guidelines for Selecting Bias-Free Textbooks and Storybooks for Children*, pp. 7–9, 21–23. Copyright © 1980 by the Council on Interracial Books for Children, 1841 Broadway, New York, NY 10023.

by Marguerite De Angeli sets forth an entire ideology of passively "turning the other cheek" in her quiet way. No writer is just a reporter, and artists put more on paper than their eyes see.

Most of us who work with children's literature know this. We realize that children's books do carry a message—a moral, a value or set of values —and that they mold minds. But how often do we stop to consider the source of those values? Do they come from the personal beliefs of the writer? Do they come from the publisher's mind? If so, then we must ask in the persistent way of children themselves: where do *their* values come from?

We propose that those values are not simply individual, not creatures of a series of vacuums, but that they rise from the total society. In any given society, children's books generally reflect the needs of those who dominate that society. A major need is to maintain and fortify the structure of relations between dominators and dominated. The prevailing values are supportive of the existing structure; they are the dominator's values.

We further propose that children's books play an active part in maintaining that structure by molding future adults who will accept it. Today, we see how such books can also mold human beings with counter-values that may help us to restructure the society. Children's books are both mirror and matrix.

Stop right there, some will say; you are talking about brainwashing. It is only in totalitarian societies that books are used by a class of people to suit its purposes; in a democracy, books just reflect the interests of the majority. Sad to say, examination of thousands of children's books published in the United States over the years does not bear up this belief. The value system that dominates in them is very white, very contemptuous of females except in traditional roles, and very oriented to the needs of the upper classes. It is geared to individual achievement rather than to community well-being. It is a value system that can serve only to keep people of color, poor people, women, and other dominated groups "in their place" because, directly or indirectly, it makes children—our future adults—think that this is the way things should be. So powerful is that system that authors can write *totally unaware* of its influence upon them. More often than not, they are unconscious tools of that system.

If all this seems shocking, let us stop to think: how often have we attended a wedding ceremony and never stopped to think about those words: "I now pronounce you man and wife." Why *man* and *wife*, which reduces the female to a person defined by her relation to another, while the male retains his independent identity? And how many of us speak of a day of woe as "a black day," without realizing that those words equate black with bad and thus help to perpetuate racism? There is a whole world of conditioning and control around us that most people have still to perceive. This is not to say that words in themselves can be the cause of sexism or racism; they only reflect those realities. But they are important, for they condition people—especially children—to accept the maintenance of sexism and racism.

Let's make it also clear that we have no desire to see children's books that would solely help the dominated get a bigger piece of the pie. We don't like the pie, period. Very often, for example, the study of "women's accomplishments" in history has a give-me-more-pie approach and fails to question the very definition of "accomplishments." We should not study merely the few women who have overcome sexist barriers, but examine the very standards that have excluded other women's actions from being considered "accomplishments." We are not interested in seeing different people win a place in the status quo, the present social structure. We are challenging the structure itself because it promotes antihuman values.

There is one more important point, and it is closely related to the previous ones. We propose that most of what has been labeled *human nature* in our society really should be called *culturally conditioned behavior.* There is the popular assumption that jealousy, possessiveness, competitiveness, and war (between nations, peoples, classes, and sexes) are inevitable because of the invisible, all-powerful force called human nature. Yet actual experience, in the United States and other countries, shows that those human tendencies assumed to be immutable are in fact variable. If we did not believe that most *human nature* is in fact *cultural conditioning*, there would be little point in publishing this book. If we assumed that human beings are doomed to continue harming and destroying each other without end, there would be no point at all. But we do not hold that assumption; we firmly believe that when the cultural environment is changed, people will change. We reject that vision of the future which portrays human beings as oxen forever yoked to the painful weight of so-called *human nature.* We reject it for the sake of our own lives and, above all, for the generations of children now and tomorrow.

This view of life is not some impossible dream. History has shown that value-systems, like social systems, are not static. Human values change when society changes, and because society changes.

The last decade in the United States has seen strong pressures on the society to change, to become less oppressive for large groups of people. These pressures, in turn, have brought major upheavals in concepts about social relations. If many people now realize there is something wrong with phrases like a *black day* or *man and wife*, it is because Black people and women, as groups, have strongly challenged the status quo and its values.

Concepts about race and sex relationships are the major areas of upheaval today, but we have also seen other challenges. People—mostly young people—have questioned our dog-eat-dog, materialistic lifestyle. Older people have spoken out against the idea that the word *old* should be equated with the forgotten, the useless, the half-witted. And disabled people have been claiming their right to be mainstreamed into the world of education, work, and recreation.

If we are honest with ourselves, we will admit that our whole structure of relations is rattling and creaking, as people of many, many groups challenge its usefulness to humanity. The demand for a more humane structure and more humane values echoes across the land. Can those of us concerned with children and their books stand passively by? We say no; let us listen to the challenge and reexamine those books.

Toward positive human values

In an age of great and necessary upheaval, new educational materials— including children's books—must be developed. Failure to do so would be a betrayal of our children, for it would leave them stranded and lost in a changing world, unprepared to relate to that process of change. We propose that children's literature become a means for the conscious promotion of human values that will help lead to greater human liberation. We are advocates of a society which will be free of racism, sexism, ageism, materialism, elitism, handicapism and a host of other negative values. We are advocates of a society in which all human beings have the true, not rhetorical, opportunity to realize their full human potential. We therefore frankly advocate books that will help achieve such a society and help prepare children for such a society.

We have named a number of "isms" as our targets. It is important that we offer a definition of each, and some reasons why we feel they must be combatted.

Ageism:
> Any attitude, action, or institutional practice which subordinates people based upon their age. While ageism results in distorted views of older people by young people, its more serious consequences are to keep many older people in United States society severely impoverished, to exclude them from satisfying work, and to treat them as useless, unwanted and unattractive citizens.

Classism:
> Any attitude, action, or institutional practice which subordinates people due to their economic condition. In the United States, poor people and members of the working class are not accorded the dignity and respect (let alone the economic rewards) accorded to wealthy upper-class people. See also "elitism."

Elitism:
> Any attitude, action, or institutional practice which subordinates people due to their social position, economic class, or

lifestyle. The belief held by people in power that they are superior to those without power. Snobbishness.

Handicapism:

Any attitude, action, or institutional practice which subordinates people due to their disability. Handicapist institutional practices prevent the integration of disabled people into the mainstream of society and keep them socially and economically oppressed.

Racism:

Race prejudice *plus* the back-up of institutional *power*, used to the advantage of one race and the disadvantage of other races. The critical concept differentiating racism from prejudice is "the back-up of institutional power." Racism is any attitude, action or institutional practice—backed up by institutional power—which subordinates people because of their color.

Sexism:

Sex prejudice *plus* the back-up of institutional power to impose that prejudice, used to the advantage of one sex and the disadvantage of the other. Sexism is any attitude, action, or institutional practice—backed up by institutional power—which subordinates people because of their sex.

Literary and artistic quality

At this point, one may cry for a halt to all the "isms" and demand some words about *quality* in children's books. After all, children deserve beautiful writing and art; they are values, too. Not only content, but also form, is important.

We could not agree more warmly, and the guidelines we present call for evaluating children's books for form as well as content. Good values in no way justify a poorly written book. Books that are stylistically admirable but that transmit antihuman values causing children harm and pain cannot be justified either. With such books, one can hardly talk about their "beauty"; the inner ugliness of their racism or sexism, ageism, or handicapism, corrupts the very word itself. This type of book is especially venal because, by the very skill of its writing or artwork, it is likely to impress a child more. The more exciting, the more compelling, the more realistic it seems, the more damage it can do; its smooth surface masks its true nature all the more effectively.

There is no automatic correlation between good values and good writing, or bad values and bad writing. Nor is there contradiction between good values and good writing, bad values and bad writing. We seek both good values and good writing. Authors and artists who wish to combat antihuman values in children's books have a responsibility to offer the best quality in their work as well. If we have emphasized content more than form, it is because good form has traditionally been in demand but good content has not. Stylistic values are already recognized; human values are not—at this time. And these are the times that concern us.

To those who argue that it is not the business of children's books to be the vehicle of change, we answer with our opening statement: no writer is just a reporter. All books contain messages and, by tolerating them, we are in effect endorsing those messages. This we cannot do—not when the message is racism or sexism, materialism or ageism, or any other antihuman value.

Books together with television, schools, comics, advertisements, and of course, adult behavior, are the forces that socialize children, mold their ideas. These forces today are almost always sexist, elitist, and materialist. They are often racist, ageist, and handicapist. Far from whimsy —in whose name those forces often appear—they have tenacious societal roots. To combat them requires a constant, difficult, uphill struggle. Along with many other people, we are committed to that struggle for a single reason: we care about the future of our children and of all children.

Book rating instrument

The checklist that follows is for evaluating new children's books or for reevaluating old books. It is worthwhile to repeat the distinction between "non-racist" and "non-sexist" books as against "anti-racist" and "anti-sexist" books. There are many books which, for example, are not sexist, but could never be seen as contributing toward the elimination of sexism. An anti-sexist book would contribute in some way to the elimination of sexism; a sexist book contributes to the maintenance of sexist oppression; and a non-sexist book does neither.

We also consider that building a positive image for a female and/or third world reader is—in our present society—an anti-sexist or anti-racist act, and we define books that achieve such an objective in those terms. Is it also important that white and/or male children perceive those positive images? We answer strongly in the affirmative. We also hope for books calling for another value only previously hinted at: "Inspire action against social oppression." To achieve that objective is one step beyond anti-racism or anti-sexism. Very, very few books fit in that category, but it is the value we wish to encourage most of all.

Naturally there are borderline cases in all the categories, and other complications. No checklist can provide for all the subtleties, all the hidden messages, all the qualities of a book. Reviewers, whether they work as individuals or in teams, must at some point rely on judgments and preferences which are uniquely their own. A subjective element will inevitably enter every analysis.

Book rating instrument

	Art	Words		Art	Words		omission / commission	Art	Words
anti-Racist			non-Racist			Racist			
anti-Sexist			non-Sexist			Sexist			
anti-Elitist			non-Elitist			Elitist			
anti-Materialist			non-Materialist			Materialist			
anti-Ageist			non-Ageist			Ageist			
anti-Conformist			non-Conformist			Conformist			
anti-Escapist			non-Escapist			Handicapist			
Builds positive image of females/minorities			Builds negative image of females/minorities						
Inspires action vs. oppression			Supports status quo						
Stresses cooperation			Stresses competition						

	Excellent	Good	Fair	Poor
Literary quality				
Art quality				
Culturally authentic				

Racist by omission means that third-world people could logically be included but are not.

Racist by commission means that the content or the art is overtly or openly racist in some way.

Non before a negative value means that the book's impact is neutral in that regard and does nothing to challenge the status quo, thereby reinforcing it.

Anti before a negative value means that the book is taking a conscious, deliberate stand to combat that negative value.

Inspires action against oppression means that the book not only describes injustice but in some way encourages readers to act against injustice, preferably to act cooperatively with others.

Who should review books?

While these guidelines were prepared to assist all parents, librarians, teachers, and editors involved in book selection, we suggest a cautionary note. The Council has always followed a policy of involving reviewers who are members of the particular group depicted in any book, and we believe that books about Blacks are best reviewed by Blacks, that books about Chicanos are best reviewed by Chicanos, and books about disabled people reviewed by disabled people, etc. It is extremely difficult for a member of the dominant society to know whether or not a book about a dominated people is culturally authentic or whether or not it is flawed by stereotypes and covert bias. That is why, whenever possible, selection teams for libraries and schools should be strongly pluralistic and include people especially sensitive to third-world, feminist, and other social issues.

The guidelines we present are defined by our present understanding of ourselves and our society. Ridicule of third-world people and women, or putting down or poking fun at any group may be perfectly acceptable in a future society. But these guidelines are intended for the oppressive society that exists today. So our criteria are not timeless, nor are our targets. They do suit today's situation, in which revised values are certainly blowing in the wind and the times are not only changing but profoundly revolutionary. We make no claim to eternal verities; if anything, we look forward to the day when guidelines like this will no longer be relevant.

Any Writer Who Follows Anyone Else's Guidelines Ought to Be in Advertising

Nat Hentoff

Let us suppose that in the early 60s, I had been told by my editor Ursula Nordstrom—or by a librarians' group— that as I wrote, I would have to remember that my book was going to be judged by the following guidelines:

antiracist/nonracist/ racist (by omission/commission)
antisexist/nonsexist/sexist
antielitist/nonelitist/elitist
antimaterialist/nonmaterialist/materialist
antiindividualist/nonindividualist/individualist
antiageist/nonageist/ageist
anticonformist/nonconformist/conformist
antiescapist/nonescapist/escapist
builds positive images of females/minorities
builds negative images of females/minorities
inspires action vs. oppression/culturally authentic . . .

And then down in the corner, almost as an afterthought:

literary quality/art quality.

Had anyone actually shown me such a set of guidelines, my first reaction would have been that I had suddenly been transported to Czechoslovakia or some such utterly stifling state. My second reaction would have been to ignore these externally dictated "standards" entirely because any writer who follows anyone else's guidelines ought to be in advertising.

Yet I did not invent that list. Those are the criteria by which children's books are judged by the Council on Interracial Books for Children, Inc. (CIBC).

Reprinted with permission of Nat Hentoff and *School Library Journal* 24, no. 3:27–29 (Nov. 1977). R. R. Bowker Company/A Xerox Corporation.

Furthemore, these and similar criteria permeate the council's *Bulletin* and their public statements. To what end? Not only to sensitize parents, educators, and librarians to books that are "harmful" to children, but also to mount campaigns to censor those books.

Like certain Orwellian characters, the sepulchral representatives of the council deny that they are censors. For instance, in a letter to *School Library Journal*,[1] Bradford Chambers, director of CIBC—that Watch and Ward Society—declares that he is encouraged at the realization "by many librarians that enlightened weeding and selection policies aimed at reducing racism and sexism do not constitute 'censoring.'"

One librarian's act of weeding can be a writer's shock of recognition that his or her books are being censored off the shelves. That is, if the weeding is not part of the normal process of making room for new books by removing those that kids no longer read but is rather a yielding to such slippery "guidelines" as those of the Council on Interracial Books for Children. The latter is censorship, as even a child can tell you.

Let me stipulate my agreement with the political goals of the council as they are stated on page 4 of *Human (and Anti-Human) Values*. . . . "We are advocates of a society which will be free of racism, sexism, ageism, classism, materialism, elitism, and other negative values." (Such other negative values as censorship, I would add.) I can make this stipulation not out of piety but on the basis of some thirty years of rather dogged if unspectacular work toward these ends as a democratic socialist involved in all kinds of movements to redistribute power in this land.

Politics, however, is not literature. And children ought to have access to the freest literature we can write for them. And literature must be freely conceived or it stiffens into propaganda (no matter how nobly intended) or into some other form of narrowing didacticism.

The council, however, is quite openly working toward the end of having "children's literature become a tool for the conscious promotion of human values that will help lead to greater human liberation."[2] I apologize for being obvious, but literature cannot breathe if it is forced to be utilitarian in this or any other sense. The council fundamentally misunderstands the act of imagination.

Recently, an internationally renowned writer for children commented about the council to me: "Of course, we should all be more tender and understanding toward the aged and we should work to shrive ourselves of racism and sexism, but when you impose guidelines like theirs on writing, you're strangling the imagination. And that means that you're limiting the ability of children to imagine. If all books for them were 'cleansed' according to these criteria, it would be the equivalent of giving them nothing to eat but white bread."

"To write according to such guidelines," this story teller continued, "is to take the life out of what you do. Also the complexity, the ambivalence. And thereby the young reader gets no real sense of the wonders and terrors and unpredictabilities of living. Paradoxically, censors like the council clamor for 'truth' but are actually working to flatten children's reading experiences into the most misleading, simplistic kinds of untruth."

The writer quoted has never been attacked by the Council on Interracial Books for Children but nonetheless asked me not to disclose his or her identity. "Otherwise," the writer said, "they'll go after me. And that, of course, is another chilling effect of their work." In fact, no writer of books for children whom I spoke to in connection with this piece was willing to be identified, for all were fearful of the council.

I also talked—for nonattribution—to several former members of the council who supported CIBC in its early days but who left when the organization began to move toward its current function of righteous vigilanteism. "At the beginning," one of them, a black librarian, said, "the idea was to really open up opportunities for black writers, illustrators, publishers, and minority-owned bookstores. God knows, that needed to be done then, as it needs to be done now. But then the council changed course and turned into censors. That's when I left. I know damn well that if everybody doesn't have the freedom to express himself or herself, I'm going to be one of the first to lose mine."

Yet the council has a ready, if rather devious, rejoinder to such talk of indivisible freedoms. Their contention is that the publishing industry has long practiced "covert censorship." By that, Bradford Chambers says he means the kinds of venerable publishing criteria that result in an "underexposure of the views of women and Third World people." And he's right. For all the belated eagerness of many houses to publish books expressing just such views, the book industry as a whole is certainly still white-dominated. (By the way, that eagerness has so far led to an excess of virtuous pap and scarcely any literature. In the rush to repent, publishers have not sufficiently searched out truly creative tellers of tales who cannot be fitted into neat, sanitized, newly "proper" molds.)

However, the answer to what the council calls "covert censorship" is hardly the council's kind of book "elimination." At base, whatever the reasons of the expungers, all censorship is the same. It is suppression of speech and creates a climate in which creative imagination, the writer's and the child's, must hide to survive.

That the council does not understand the necessarily free ambience for children's literature is regularly evident in its *Bulletin* as well in its procrustean rating systems for "worthy" books. For instance, in a recent issue of the *Bulletin*[3] there is an article about the books that East German children are reading in grades one to six ("What Children Are Reading in GDR Schools" by Donna Garund-Sletack). The author focuses mainly on the "messages" these books convey about sex roles. For the most part, the books get high grades. Women are shown in a wider range of careers than in comparable American readers; children of both sexes exercise real responsibility; individualism is downplayed (no kidding!); all sorts of positive values are inculcated (such as helpfulness); respect for older people is "promoted"; there are plentiful tales of racial discrimination (the East Germans are against it); and by God, "an analysis of poverty and inequality is offered as early as in the first grade reader."

Nowhere in the article is there a hint that East German writers (whether their audiences are adults or children) who offend the state do not get published any more. Some are even given a chance to reflect on their "anti-human values" in prison.

Freedom of expression, however, is clearly not a focal passion of the Council on Interracial Books for Children. Correctness of perspective and attitude are its driving priorities as is stated in the council's pamphlet *10 Quick Ways To Analyze Children's Books for Racism and Sexism:*

No. 7: "Consider the Author's or Illustrator's Background." Look at the biographical material on the jacket. "A book that deals with the feelings and insights of women should be more carefully examined if it is written by a man." If it's written by Phyllis Schlafly, it also ought to be carefully examined. Obviously, blacks are likely to bring more to black themes, as Jews are to Jewish themes. But why not judge each book for itself, rather than order a line up before you read?

No. 9: "Watch for Loaded Words." Like what? "Chairman" instead of "chairperson." I would take twenty lashes rather than be forced to use so utterly graceless a word as "chairperson." And what does that make me, according to the council? A stone sexist, that's what.

And so it goes—"Check the Story Line," "Look at the Lifestyles," "Weigh the Relationships between People," and so on. Fine for East Germany, if that's where you want to write, but no different here from the John Birch Society trying to hammer *its* values into books for children. Such groups are the enemies of any writer with self-respect.

Another dulling, constricting effect of the council's ardent work is that when successful, it produces its own stereotypes. During an appearance by representatives of the council at a February 1977 meeting in New York of the National Coalition Against Censorship, Mary K. Chelton, then consultant on young adult services for the Westchester County Library System, made a good point about the council's addiction to labeling groups. She said that the council's view of racial minorities and women makes the groups emerge as monolithic, with each member of these groups in total accord on any matter that affects them. Describing herself as a feminist, she pointed out that she knows from personal experience that there is no unified perspective among feminists about what is most important to women now, or how best to achieve feminist ends, or even what the term "feminist" means.

The same is true of blacks, Chicanos, and all other so-called "Third World" people. It is no wonder the council considers "individualism" highly suspicious.

Yet there can be no literature without individualism—uncategoriz-
able individualism—sometimes flaky, sometimes complexly rebellious,
sometimes so stubbornly unassimilable as to make the child shout in
recognition of himself. (Or herself. Or the chair he [or] she is person-
ing.)

Collectivism is for politics. And if the council were to marshall its
energies and foundation-financed resources for honestly political ends,
I'd join it. Organize, bring pressure to greatly increase the numbers of
"Third World" editors who will then find more nonwhite writers than
white editors are likely to. (If only because they know a lot more.) Organize support for "Third World" publishing firms and bookstores. And
by all means, hold sessions for librarians and editors on ways in which
the children's booklists ought to be expanded (without censoring other
books). There is still so little of value for children on the jazz life. Or
on the turbulent, desperately complicated history of Puerto Rican independence movements. The list is huge.

But then leave the authors alone. Always leave authors alone. I'm
not talking about editing for grammar and grace. But stay out of
authors' quirkily individualistic heads in terms of what they write.

What it comes down to is that the Council on Interracial Books for
Children not only distrusts individualism ("should be discouraged as a
highly negative force"), but it also greatly distrusts children.

And that is reason enough why the council should not be messing
with children's literature.

The Bible Presented Objectively

Ann Hildebrand

A short time ago a student of mine wrote an essay displaying a fairly
high degree of literacy and a good command of technical matters such
as punctuation, agreement, and spelling. In fact, she skipped over diffi-

Originally published in *Language Arts* 53:69–75 (Jan. 1976). Copyright ©
1976 by the National Council of Teachers of English. Reprinted by permission of
the publisher and author.

cult scientific words like "nuclear thermodynamics," "combustibility," and "electromagnetic radiation" with ease. However, later she made a much less esoteric reference and dismayed me with "Atom and Eve." Her error seemed not a lack of care but rather a lack of exposure to the paired written words. She had apparently not seen them in the Biblical context, this child of the sixties.

In the early days of our country, however, in every colony, the Bible was the basis for a code of manners and morals intended to preserve the religious traditions of the first Americans. It was taught every day in the public schools; indeed, it was often the main textbook either in its unedited form or in excerpts for primer use. Seldom was a "children's version" used, and though children often quaked under the heavy load of weighty Bible fare, they nevertheless know the Bible, its people, and its allusions.

Continuing through the first half of this century, the practice of reading and often discussing the Bible in the classroom was prevalent in our public schools. As supplementary to or substituting for Sunday School or church education, many schools saw it as their role to acquaint children with the people and stories of Bible days. And whether rightly or not, many teachers continued to stress the moral precepts of the Bible in the form of prayers or homilies.

But on June 17, 1963, The Supreme Court of the United States rendered a decision, Abington School District vs. Schempp, which disallowed reading of scripture as part of a religious ceremony in the schools. Many school systems immediately threw out the Bible completely, not only discontinuing daily readings and Bible use in assemblies and gatherings but frowning on the mere mention of Bible characters or allusion to Bible situations or traditions. And yet, in so completely removing the Bible, these schools deprived the students of the most influential literature in the Western world.

Indeed, the school systems which turned their backs on the Bible completely misinterpreted the Court's ruling. For it is clear that the Justices did not intend that the Bible be removed entirely from the classroom. As Justice Clark ruled in the majority opinion,

> It certainly may be said that the Bible is worthy of study for its literary and historic qualities. Nothing that we have said here indicates that such study of the Bible or of religion, when presented objectively as part of a secular program of education, may not be effected consistent with the First Amendment.

Similarly, Justice Brennan noted,

> The holding of the Court today plainly does not foreclose teaching *about* the Holy Scriptures. . . . To what extent and at what points in the curriculum religious materials should be cited, are matters which the courts ought to trust to the experienced officials who superintend our Nation's public schools.

And finally, Justice Goldberg concurred,

> . . . And it seems clear to me from the opinions in the present and past cases that the Court would recognize the propriety of . . . the teaching *about* religion, as distinguished from the teaching *of* religion, in the public schools.[1]

Thus, it is clear that the Supreme Court recognized a study of the Bible for its literary and historical value was appropriate to the secular function of the public schools. The schools could no longer stress the moral teachings of the Bible. But they were charged with keeping alive and accessible its literary richness.

Fortunately, some schools have reviewed and accepted the entire Court mandate. They have experimented and succeeded with ways to fulfill the "when presented objectively" stipulation and have enriched their curricula immeasurably with excellent courses in "Types of Biblical Literature," "Religious Literature of the West," "The Bible as Literature," "Hebrew Literature," and others.[2] Unfortunately, these course offerings seem to be mainly on the high school or junior high school level. There seem to be very few instances of organized elementary school use of Biblical materials. At least one study has been made of the possible use of the Bible in the upper elementary grades, but to my knowledge, the idea has not taken hold. And yet it is important in fulfilling Justice Clark's "complete education" to make elementary children, right from kindergarten through the sixth grade, as aware of Bible literature as the older students.

The Commission on Religion in the Public Schools supports this broader dissemination of Bible study in its statement,

> The desirable policy in the schools . . . is to deal directly and objectively with religion *whenever* and *wherever* it is intrinsic to learning experience in the various fields of study, and *to seek out appropriate ways* to teach what has been aptly called "the reciprocal relation" between religion and the other elements in human culture.[3]

The "whenever and wherever" seems clearly to include the elementary school. Certainly the "directly and objectively" mandate can be fulfilled by a teacher determined to do so. And I suggest that finding "appropriate ways" to present the stories, people, and milieu of the Bible need not present difficulty, if the teacher does make the presentations "intrinsic to the learning experience"; is aware of the vast range of objective, interesting, relevant material available today at the elementary level; and above all, presents the material naturally and unselfconsciously.

In *Children's Literature in the Elementary School*, Charlotte Huck encourages Bible offerings,

> A literature curriculum designed to acquaint children with their literary heritage and develop understandings and skills that will enable them to make continued progress in appreciating fine literature must include

study of the Bible. Other literature cannot be fully understood unless children are familiar with the outstanding characters, incidents, poems, proverbs, and parables of this literature of the Western world of thought.[4]

It is this familiarity of character, incident, poem, and allusion that I stress mainly. Too many children become teenagers and adults without knowing Job, Lot, Esther (or Adam and Eve) and other heroes of Jewish tradition; even Moses, Abraham, David, and Solomon are names only dimly recognized. In fact, with the exception of the increasingly few who acquire religious education from churches, most young people are not at all aware of the significant names in Hebrew literature, the stories and thoughts that influence us today probably more than ever.

Alton C. Capps in his article "A Realistic Approach to Biblical Literature," applauds the introduction, even in the elementary grades, of a "systematic study of Bible stories and the names of Bible characters." But he warns against "a piecemeal, disjointed reading of stories for the sake of name references," and rightly so. However, his remarks seem aimed at the junior high and high school level and do not really address themselves to the realities of the elementary classroom—shorter attention span, more relaxed scheduling, and a lower level of comprehension. The main concern of the elementary teacher should be, not to teach "history," "literature," or "comparative religion," but to introduce and familiarize children with the Biblical characters, major stories, settings, and circumstances of the Bible, thereby preparing them for the more difficult studies they may encounter in the upper grades. If a child learns about heroic David's lifestyle and story in the elementary school, the child will likely bring a comfortable familiarity to the challenging study in high school of the Psalms as literature, or of Samuel I and II as Jewish history. If [the child] learns in elementary school that the myth of Genesis I offers only one of many possible explanations of creation, in high school he [or] she may be able to accept sophisticated scientific explanations of world origins with equanimity. Such an introduction on the elementary level can follow a coherent plan which is intrinsic to the learning experience.

In the past few years, intense interest has centered on retellings of secular traditional tales, including folklore, myths, and epics. This trend is reflected in the realm of traditional Biblical literature, too. There are many excellent and recent books for all ages dealing with Biblical figures as diverse as Elijah, Samson, Daniel, and Solomon on subjects as varied as the Flood, Sodom and Gomorrah, and the Passover. In the classic *Anthology of Children's Literature,* Johnson, Sickels, and Sayers include a chapter on "Sacred Writings" which run the gamut from Bible stories of Joseph, Ruth, and the Prodigal Son to prayers written variously by David, Robert Herrick, St. Patrick, to words of wisdom from Confucious and the Koran, and finally to legends of the Saints. *Cricket,* the new magazine for children, has presented stories based on Bible figures or legends. Scholastic Publications has offered in paperback a book about the Bible hero, Joseph, for public elementary children to buy. The newest literary readers contain retellings of Bible stories. Publishers continue to produce books and recordings about or peripheral to Bible characters. Bible materials are, then, available, accessible, and even abundant. "Appropriate ways" are waiting for the teacher who will seek them out and use them.

The most logical and feasible way, indeed the most natural and un-self-conscious way, to use these critical materials is in tandem with nonreligious materials in the same genre. Thus, I suggest that Bible myths be used with other myths. Today's children are grounded strongly in scientific and rational truths, from the New Math to lab experiments in kindergarten. Because of this emphasis on measurable knowledge, conscientious teachers need more than ever to present man's UN-measurable wisdom. The great psychologist, Carl Jung, reminds us that, "The tree that forgets its roots, dies." The myth-roots are indeed vital to education. Just as the recent upsurge of myth and fable retellings has spurred new versions of the Greek myths, Aesop's Fables, and African legends, so some excellent editions are now available for the Hebrew myths: stories about Noah, Lot's wife, Jonah, and the Hebrew Creation Myth in Genesis. Such retellings could effectively be used along with the creation myths found in Norse mythology, American Indian lore, and Sumerian epic. No creation would be "the right one," neither Glooscap's nor Yahweh's nor that from the *Eddas*, but all could be possible ways of thinking and respecting culturally divergent views at various times. Ideally a child should know what Deucalion, Upnapishtim, Coxcox, and Noah have in common and should be aware how these stories from world legend reconcile with the scientific knowledge of floods in the Tigris-Euphrates valley.

Similarly, Bible heroes can be admired with secular heroes, from Billie Jean King to Frederick Douglass to Joan of Arc to Ulysses and Robin Hood. Why should elementary children not know of Bible examples like Moses, Joseph, Daniel, Ruth, or the apocryphal Judith? Such people should become part of our children's cultural bank and could provide stirring and adventurous reading at the same time. Certainly the marvelous cycle of tales surrounding David is as exciting as any chapter from King Arthur. The persecution of Esther's Jews may stimulate our children to racial tolerance as much as Anne Frank's story.

Then too, the Bible as a source of beautiful poetry is often overlooked by elementary teachers. Such outpourings of song and joy as occur in Psalms, Song of Solomon, Ecclesiastes, the Epistles, and other parts of both the Old and New Testaments are on a par with any nature poetry written. The musicality of these poems makes them delightful to use right along with other lyric poetry for children. Of course, they would not be presented as "literature" to be studied, parsed, and dissected; or as "religion" to be prayed; but as short examples of thought to be heard, felt, and enjoyed.

Just as it is helpful to understand the culture and climate of Greece and Iceland in order to fully value the myths and hero tales of these regions, so an appreciation of Bible customs and lands is helpful in approaching the traditional literature of the Jews. Especially for upper elementary children, related fields such as religious history, music, art, and domestic life enrich the student's sense of the Hebrew culture and hence tolerance of Jewish ideas. The adventures of Moses offer an introduction to modern Hebrew Passover customs; Esther's story gives insight into the beginnings of Purim. The problems of the Middle East are grave, but an understanding of some traditions important to the ancient Jews may help elementary children grapple with the difficulties of modern Israelis. Similarly, books about Bible anthropology, archaeology, biology, and zoology all add dimension to understanding the environment of the Bible and give children another relevant branch to their studies in science.

Since the availability of good objective material from commercial publishers is great, I would caution against the overuse of church house publications in the public classroom. Theological bias may tend to creep into even the best of these publications, or at least the imprimatur of only organized religion may make a retelling seem biased. It is essential for the teacher to be constantly aware of the need for and value of objective presentation. Enthusiasm for presentation of Bible materials is essential; enthusiasm for a particular sectarian point of view is taboo. The teacher has always to remember that the elementary classroom is good ground for teaching *about* religion but not the soil for teaching *of* religion. It would, of course, be wise for the teacher to discuss the use of Bible materials with the Principal in order to reinforce the assurance of objective presentation and to clarify his [or] her intentions.

I would also urge judicious use of New Testament materials. It is impossible not to acknowledge the Christmas Story, and there are even fairly neutral versions of Christ's birth. But these materials should be used only in conjunction with legends of other cultures and religions so as to remove any charge of Christian bias. Certainly Jesus is at least a culture hero, and the children should be made aware of significant details from his life. But here lies trouble if the teacher becomes too zealous in presentation and does not include figures central to other religions like Buddha, Mohammed, or Lao Tse. Perhaps a concentration on the legends surrounding Jesus or Christmas (such as developed in *The Shepherd, Baboushka and the Three Kings,* or the contemporary *A New Day*) would be the least uncomfortable approach, at the same time using legends of the Saints, stories about Hannukah, and accounts of Moslem holidays and American Indian feasts.

When judging any book to be presented to children, one must have standards; the general criteria cited by Arbuthnot and Sutherland in *Children and Books* apply to Bible material, of course. Already inherent in the stories are lively plots, worthwhile themes, distinctive characters, vivid settings, and certainly forceful or beautiful style. However, depending on the genre, one has to ask for certain other distinctions. For instance, is the adaptation of a folktale or myth from the Bible done with imagination, attention to language, and compatibility of spirit? Does it have the oral "ring" of the traditional tale? Or does the myth have the reverence and dignity that it should as an explanation of Truth? Does the religious epic maintain the noble tone of the original hero tale, not trivializing the exploits of the central figure even though adapted and intended for young readers? Is the retelling faithful to Biblical source, fictionalizing only where necessary to enrich the story for children? If conversations have been imagined (as they are in many versions to amplify sometimes terse Bible language), are they consistent with the tone of the event and the character of the speaker? If a Biblical story is embellished, does the style enhance or reinforce the telling? In *The Wicked City*, Isaac Bashevis Singer certainly does give Lot an identity beyond that in Genesis, but his skillful way with Jewish folktale enriches immeasurably this uniquely Hebrew story. Does the poem, whether an entire Psalm or a verse from the Gospels, speak to the child through its subject or its sound? And does the factual account of Bible art, topography, history, or custom present clearly and accurately (not sentimentally or condescendingly) the information it gives? Since many of the books are enriched by pictures, the additional criterion of aesthetic appeal must be considered. One must evaluate the illustrations as art, as well as for their contribution to the text. Happily, there is a wide divergence in media and style for books that give to children an appropriately universal concept about Bible stories. The same story has often been illustrated in so many ways (Moses, for example) that children get a balanced view of a well-known incident, and yet they still have room to imagine.

A Ride across the Mystic Bridge, or, Occult Books: What, Why, and Who Needs Them?

Georgess McHargue

Until recently, members of witch covens, village wise women, gypsy fortune-tellers, and the kings whose touch was believed to cure skin disease got their instructions from local tradition and not from a visit to the local library. Even after the invention of the printing press, occult *books* were most likely to be found in the courtier's private library, the discreet backroom at the bookseller's, the locked study belonging to the respectable Victorian Member of Parliament or merchant of provisions, or more rarely, the collection of the self-avowed magus or the suitably disapproving churchman. Especially in the earlier years, roughly 1450 to 1650, it was as unlikely for the actual practitioner of any of the occult arts (except perhaps alchemy) to read or possess a book on the subject as it would have been for the man behind the ox-drawn plow to be familiar with Virgil's *Georgics*. This is obvious. There were no public libraries, very few books, and even fewer who could read them. Further, many of the titles we would now classify as occult covered subjects that were not merely "hidden," as the root of the word implies, but actually forbidden to western readers by the Church. This prohibition extended beyond the worship of the Devil (more properly called Satanism) and the fertility cults of witchcraft (with which Satanism is persistently confused) to many unrelated practices such as attempting to divine the future (a knowledge reserved for angels) or to summon the spirits of the dead. In the Judeo-Christian world, laws against such activities were at least as ancient as the reign of King Saul, who, in employing the so-called Witch of Endor (actually a medium) to communicate with the spirit of the prophet Samuel, was breaking his own ordinance, made at the express commandment of God.

Reprinted with permission of Georgess McHargue and of *School Library Journal* 19, no. 9:25–30 (May 1973). Copyright © 1973 by Georgess McHargue.

It was natural, therefore, that most early books on these topics, as well as the rare surviving copies of ancient manuscripts, had a somewhat underground existence. From occult books they became cult books, prized and sought after by a very small fraternity of collectors, believers, and unconventional scholars. They thus acquired a highly romantic aura of danger and value.

At a later date, the forbidden nature of occult books led them to be associated, perhaps unconsciously, with another type of proscribed literature, the sex book. Though there was no necessary connection between the two subjects, they sometimes appealed to the same collectors, were sold in the same sort of shops, and were attacked in the same righteous breath by censors.

By the nineteenth century, a general image of the Occult Book had become lodged in the popular mind, influenced largely by the fiction of such writers as Poe, Hawthorne, Le Fanu, Horace Walpole, and the other exponents of the gothic. The ultimate occult book, in this view, was a grimoire, a tome dealing with black magic, especially as it was applied to making pacts with the Devil for the sorcerer's personal advantage. Written in strange tongues or mysterious symbols on parchment or vellum and bound in leather, silver, or the (reputed) skins of dragons or human infants, the grimoires of popular fiction were Faustian volumes which might confer on the reader health, wealth, immortality, and sexual irresistibility, but only at the terrible risk of eternal damnation.

The occult book cult

This evolutionary summary of the image of occult books in western Europe reflects a fact well known to both historians and practicing magicians: in accounting for present conditions, what is important is not so much the *actual* facts as what are *believed to be* the facts. (Thus the person who is convinced he has been put under the evil eye will often become physically ill.) It can hardly be doubted that the current interest in occult books is being influenced by earlier attitudes, as they still affect both readers (favorably, one must assume) and professional bookpeople such as reviewers and librarians (unfavorably, at least in some cases). In other words, this apparent flood of new titles retailing "Sixteen Ways to Know the Future by Examining the Lumps on a Cucumber" or "My Previous Life as Lincoln's Doctor's Dog" are, to some extent, coasting on public relations done in our grandparents' day, although with effects ranging from fascination to multifarious.

Now, in roundabout fashion, we have arrived at the point of acknowledging that there exists something called "the occult book explosion," an event that has inevitably begun to make itself felt in juvenile publishing following the adult trend. This is not a proposition we intend to prove here, if anyone is inclined to dispute it. Let us say only that personal experience has shown a rapid rise in publishers' interest over the last few years and that a lightning-like survey of the review pages of *SLJ* confirmed the fact that from a mere trickle in 1967, books reviewed in the category have increased to well over a dozen in each of the last two years (excluding collections of ghost stories and other weird tales).

What then, if anything, is the import of all this? Should there be occult books for young readers and if so, what kind? Are they, like food, fresh air, and even French grammar, both useful and harmful depending on circumstances, and if so, which books are which?

"Occult" defined

First of all, what *is* an occult book? Or, to be more precise, what is *in* all those books stocked by occult bookstores? The distinction must be made because the word "occult" is hopelessly vague and even an assist from the dictionary gives us only "mysterious," "secret," "hidden," and "supernatural" as synonyms. Under those terms the general reader might well classify the works of James Joyce, the poetry of Wallace Stevens or T. S. Eliot, all mathematics texts, most government files, and even the books of Agatha Christie and her colleagues as "occult."

The fact is that the occult now includes a sweeping variety of subjects, some of which are hardly related at all to the classical occult, in the sense of black magic. As it is used today, the term occult seems to cover five main subject headings, although there are many areas of overlap.

First come books on prediction. All sorts of systems that purport to tell the future or to read character are included here: palmistry, astrology, the Tarot, numerology, the ouija and planchette, crystal gazing and other forms of scrying, the prophecies of Nostradamus, phrenology, the *I Ching*, the *Kabbala*, and many obscure omancies such as hydromancy, ornithomancy, and even onychomancy, which is done by examining the reflections of the sun on the fingernails.

Next there are works on the history and practice of magic, as performed either by primitive peoples today, by the ancients, or in the remarkably eclectic system of thought current among alchemists and learned men of medieval Europe and sometimes referred to as the Great Art.

Third, and obviously related to the above topic, is religion, since one man's faith is another's superstition. Here we find material primarily concerned with religions outside the Judeo-Christian tradition (exceptions are the more obscure early heresies), with preference for the transcendental or mystical beliefs of the orient. Scientology, spiritualism, theosophy and other philosophies and mythologies are also included, as are physical aids to enlightenment such as diet, drugs, meditation, and exercises of the Yoga or self-defense type (the latter only when used as a spiritual discipline).

After these come what might be called occult histories—world views that are more or less minority reports on human, planetary, or universal events of the past. Under this heading are found books of the "hollow earth" school, accounts of lost continents such as Atlantis, Mu, and Lemuria, the "cosmic catastrophe" view of ancient history headed by Immanuel Velikovsky, speculations about the lost tribe of Israel, the Yeti, the Big-foot, and the Loch Ness monster, various nonreligious predictions of the end of the world, and the UFO books, especially those in which influence from other worlds is seen as responsible for events on earth.

The fifth topic is psi, a broad term covering all the phenomena relating to psychic powers, from ESP through psychokinesis, poltergeisting, out-of-body experiences, materialization, precognition, psychic healing, spirit return, ghosts, water and metal divining, and many others. The range is from the most credulous accounts of personal experience to the rigorously controlled and analyzed experiments and observations of J. B. Rhine, Ian Stevenson, and other investigators.

Finally, there are matters peripheral to these five headings, such as abnormal psychology, hypnotism, vegetarianism, world folklore, straight archaeology and anthropology, biofeedback, and acupuncture.

Taken all together, this is certainly a fine kettle of fish, a bouillabaisse from the table of Shakespeare's Weird Sisters. Why in the world would any sensible person devote more than ten seconds to such a mishmash? When the semantics is stripped away, all these topics have one characteristic in common: they are in some sense the rejected hypotheses of our culture, unpopular opinions about the nature of our minds and of the world we live in.

The occult in history

Many of the beliefs we now classify as occult are simply ideas whose time has past. Yet they have left their traces on every surface of modern life. Attend a performance of *Faust,* reread *The Tempest,* visit Delphi or Stonehenge, delve into the history of the court of Louis XIV or Scotland under the Stuarts, read Fowles's *The Magus* or Tolkien's *The Lord of the Rings.* Think, too, about the origins of such words as "nightmare," "pixillate," "bugaboo," "glamor," "hermetic," "sinister," and "scapegoat." Then try to tell yourself that the history of occult thought is irrelevant to present-day experience.

The position of the historian is that of an outsider, cataloging and interpreting in the hope of adding to the sum of human knowledge. This has its own rewards, but it is not at all the sole, or perhaps even the principal attraction of occult studies. The occult holds out the alluring possibility of finds that possess more than historical value. Like golden fibulae tossed out among potsherds, there are certain areas of occult that *may* turn out to be deserving of serious consideration.

Just what those areas are is, of course, a matter of opinion. It would imply some obvious contradictions to accept *all* the propositions classified as occult, so that some must be rejected even by the believer, to say nothing of the person who merely tries to keep an open mind. For myself, the topics that hold out the most hope of eventual verification are those concerned with delimiting more exactly the powers of the mind, such as telepathy, precognition, and psychokinesis. Furthermore, I consider the existence of life in other solar systems (though not necessarily in the form of little men in shiny silver saucers) to be a near mathematical certainty. I think it very possible that there is some large, previously unknown creature living in Loch Ness and the other lochs of Scotland and Ireland, and I am convinced that we have a great deal to learn about the power of the mind over the body, both conscious and unconscious. On the other hand, I am not a believer in astrology, and I am unconvinced of the existence of a "soul" that either transmigrates from body to body or returns from the dead to communicate through mediums. So much for the size and shape of the limb onto which I am personally willing to venture.

The point of this confession of faith and the lack thereof is not to make pronouncements about the relative validity of various occult beliefs, since the one thing nearly every reader will agree on is that I have gone either too far or not far enough. Its only legitimate use is to put the reader on notice as to the degree of the writer's involvement with the subject, because the question of objectivity becomes so extremely important as soon as one ceases to speak exclusively as a historian.

Yet objective though we may be in one sense, in another we are less so. It seems that the phrase most noticeably lacking in nonfiction writing for children is "we don't know." Textbooks and reading books alike are filled with comfortable certainties that tell, at best, an incomplete story: "George Washington was the Father of his country." "The desert is a very hot place." "Richard III murdered the little Princes in the Tower." All these statements are generally accepted as true, although each is open to debate, qualification, or further explanation. To be sure there are exceptional books that give the child any sense of the *gaps* in our knowledge of the universe; but they are few.

This discussion points out an important possible function of occult books for young readers. A *known* fact is at best only a stepping-stone to another fact, previously unknown; at worst it is a stumbling block on a list to be memorized. Unfortunately, our educational system often produces adults who view known facts as merit badges while anything unknown is a threat, a possible failing mark on a phantom examination. The best way to kill curiosity is to make it humiliating for students to admit that *they* don't know, and impossible for them to imagine that *we* don't know. Thus occult books, like another despised branch of literature, science fiction, can be mental can openers. If the can in question turns out to be a can of worms, so much the better. No one learns to judge between the false and the true without having had experience of both.

Modern Canutes

We have seen, in a brief and unsystematic way, what is generally meant by occult books and why it may be unwise to reject the whole gallimaufry as either useless or merely trashy. Yet the bald fact is that "we"—writers, educators, editors, librarians—can no more turn back the occult tide than King Canute could command the waves of the English sea. (And the reasons why an Anglo-Saxon ruler believed himself to have power over the waters are to be sought—where else?—in the history of occult thought.) We are not going to be able to dam the occult flood for three reasons. First, it's already here. Second, it is natural and inevitable for kids to want to know about whatever interests their elders, and right now that's the occult; we have already passed that time-lag point after which the juvenile readership starts demanding to catch up with the adult. Last, and perhaps most compelling, occult books are fun. They are exciting and sometimes a little bit scary, and only the most arteriosclerotic mind is so rigid as to find those emotions altogether painful. Witches are fun, werewolves are fun. Mysteries, mummies, and magicians are fun, like all things that allow us to pretend they are more dangerous than they are. So the popularity of occult books is going to run its course regardless, and the only useful question to ask about it is not, "What is to be done about it?" but "Why has it happened and how can we understand it better?"

Of course, questions beginning with *why* are among the slipperiest fish in the language, as children are all too adept at demonstrating. Nevertheless, we can certainly make some reasonable suggestions.

A sense of loss

It is not necessary to have recourse to catch-phrases like "counter-culture" or "alienation" to perceive that there are many individuals today who find something seriously lacking in the civilization that has shaped their lives. In a recent newspaper interview, Captain Edgar Mitchell, the astronaut who conducted psychic experiments while on a moon mission, had this to say about increasing interest in psi phenomena: "I think it is a fear on the part of people that they're losing identity and that the course of world history is not conducive to ultimate survival. They're concerned about it. I see this fear of deepening planetary crisis. People are just damned concerned and they're looking for answers. The mind, the spirit, is just one area they're looking."

To some extent, of course, this same pattern has held true for centuries. The witch cults of medieval Europe appealed principally to the powerless, the individualist, the outcast, and those who had no other socially sanctioned outlet for their energies (the prime example of the latter being women). Today, however, discontent has grown deeper, not only because of the increasingly technological direction taken by western culture but because more people have time to spare from the bare business of survival and because they are freer to express their doubts. One will not, for example, be burned at the stake for reading the *Grand Grimoire*.

For many, the symptom that requires an antidote is materialism, so that it is the otherworldliness or nonworldliness of Buddhism, Hinduism, Taoism, or other eastern religions that beckons. Or it may be the machine, especially the computer, that is seen as the principal evil, and then the cure is often sought in the psychic and magical. The seductive thing about magic is that it restores to individuals the sense that they have some direct control of their lives. (How often have you wanted to turn an obstructive bureaucrat into a toad or a typewriter ribbon?)

The negative side of occult belief is that it can produce a narrow anti-intellectualism that is just as doctrinaire, petty, and repressive as the conditions it claims to be reacting against. Still, as has been said of politics, "The trouble with any good cause is the company one is forced to keep." Certainly there are loudmouthed, opinionated, irrational astrologists, Krishna people, or Tarot enthusiasts. But then there are the Republicans, Democrats, Dolphins fans, car nuts, bird lovers, bridge players. . . .

A more moderate view of occultism would take it to be, not a studied attempt to overthrow all rationalism and orderly thought, but a needed corrective for a culture that has come to honor things and the manipulation or possession of things above human values and intuition. It will not do for us to overlook the fact that magic is in itself a coherent system of thought, shaped by its own internal logic and capable of great flexibility, precision, and communicative power. In this it is parallel to, though utterly different in structure from the system of thought we use every day and which (sometimes without much justification) we name rational. Magical thought describes a universe, or one of the universes, termed by Carlos Castaneda's Don Juan "a separate reality." To view this universe, no matter how briefly and imperfectly, is to be forced to abandon the sort of psychological provincialism that insists on believing its own propositions to be the only possible ones. Anthropologists of recent decades were made to learn this lesson in a hard school, having found that all their carefully preserved field notes presented an excellent reflection of the minds of western anthropologists but bore almost no relation to the realities of life as perceived by members of other (often magical) cultures.

Because the operations of ancient or primitive magic are not predictable and orderly in the manner of a chemistry experiment, the mistake is often made of thinking magic is arbitrary and irrational. It would be more nearly true to describe it as nonrational or pararational. The reason is that the standard of success for a magical operation is not how closely it adheres to some measurable external standard but rather how well the individual magician has combined the symbolic values of the words in the spell or the ingredients in the charm. For example, there are certain chemical procedures that will, when performed with the right equipment and materials under standard physical conditions, invariably produce, say, potassium iodide as an end product, any other result being traceable to an error in technique. The success or failure of the process does not depend on the chemist's name, history, and frame of mind, or whether he or she has fasted before setting to work; neither is it relevant to know the moral purpose for which the potassium iodide is wanted.

On the other hand, although it should be possible to give a detailed explanation of the magical purpose of each ingredient used by Macbeth's three weird ladies in their much-quoted potion, we would first have to know the exact purpose of the brew and also certain details such as the time of year and phase of the moon. Into such an explanation matters like the protein content of eye of newt or the nature of the colloids in toe of frog would not enter (although as rationalists we might speculate on the toxic effects of conine and taxine from the root of hemlock and slips of yew). However it *would* be of the utmost importance that the "toad that under cold stone . . . . sweltered venom sleeping got" should have done so for 31 days and nights as specified, rather than for 30 or 32. We may be sure that if the sisters lived up to their reputation they would not proceed merely by rote, a very low form of magic, fit only for amateurs and outsiders. Probably never again would the conditions be such that the brew could be prepared in an identical manner, so that method and ingredients would have to vary accordingly.

Magic as art

To have made these statements about magic is to have said that it is truly an art, since all art is concerned with the arrangement of symbols, whether of color, form, sound, words, textures, movement, or a combination. The painter who creates a scene of the Nativity, for example, is working with a rather limited set of visual symbols—mother, father, child, Magi, shepherds, stable, star, angels—which have been combined and recombined in the same basic scene for centuries. The difference in our intellectual and emotional response to a Nativity by Leonardo and one by a fourth-rate Victorian book illustrator is precisely the difference between a good and a bad magical spell. In each case no one but the artist/magician can fully justify or even account for the particular intuition that gave form to the work, nor can a work of the same power be produced solely by application of rational formulas. This last fact is the despair both of aspiring creative artists and sorcerer's apprentices.

Magic not only partakes of the nature of art in general but is closely allied with the specific art of poetry. It is not a coincidence that a magic *spell* and *spell* in the ordinary sense come from a Germanic word root meaning simply to speak or discourse, nor that something en*chant*ed has been placed in the magician's power by virtue of *chant*ing about it. Indeed it might be suggested that the development of words and language was the original magical event in human history, for to *name* a thing is to control it in a very special way, so that the name *stands for* the thing and in a certain sense *is* the thing named. This is one of the two or three universal laws of magic, which are seen to underly the most diverse magical undertakings in every kind of culture. It is likely that the first poetry was pronounced for ritual rather than for artistic purposes. Intuitively we know that magic is additive and that repetition of a name or command makes the magical effect stronger. Thus repetition produces its own rhythms and variations and a simple invocation such as, "Let the game come to the hunter," becomes a hunting chant, a thing of much greater psychological force.

We undertook this short discourse on the nature of magic, and thereby of all occult thought, knowing that we were speaking of times far beyond the reach of recorded history, and open only to speculation. We did so, too, in the hope of showing that there is a dimension in occult studies that goes beyond the question of whether specific occult claims—levitation, precognition, spirit survival, or what have you—should turn out to be "true" in the conventional sense. Magic is a mode of thought that may represent nothing more than a phase in the history of our species. Yet it is certainly with us still, nor is it entirely clear that magical thought, as applied to the quality and forms of life, is merely a superstition to be rooted out, even supposing that could be done.

Serious vs. solemn

If this profile of the nature of occult thought has succeeded at all, it will have provided a basis for understanding why we now state that a large percentage of books on the occult, both for young readers and for adults, are guilty of failing to take the subject seriously. By "seriously," of course, we do not mean "solemnly." There has been enough portentously solemn writing for both audiences to last several generations. But, by failing to be serious in the sense of recognizing that the subject is not simply quirky or ridiculous, the writer does a disservice to his audience and demonstrates that he or she would have done better to choose another topic. It has been shown to be perfectly possible to write about Hitler without being a Nazi, about Japan without advocating ritual suicide, or about Columbus without sharing his conviction that India lay directly west of Spain. Yet for some reason the prevailing attitude among both writers and public seems to be that one cannot write about the occult without being forever labeled as a new sort of fellow traveler. For this reason qualified researchers often avoid the subject as if they were afraid of catching creeping astrology.

The general disrespect that is felt for the occult contributes, perhaps, to the formation of another unfortunate attitude, this time among those who *do* write about it. We have all seen occult books so sloppily researched and sketchily written that they seem to carry the message, "This stuff is all a fake anyway, so why bother to get the facts straight?"

Deliberate fakery, as opposed to misguided credulity, is a factor that certainly must be reckoned with in writing about the occult, from the earliest times to last week. The history of the more practical aspects of occultism, such as foretelling the future, reading the past, and communicating with the dead, is riddled with cases of proven (sometimes self-confessed) fraud. This fact *seems* to reinforce the conclusion that all occult claims are bunk, and therefore not worth proper investigation. Logically, however, the existence of fraud is as irrelevant to the validity of occult experience as is the existence of an Elmyr de Hory (the notable art forger) to the greatness of Rembrandt.

Fraud is a fascinating topic in its own right, and nowhere is it seen to better advantage than in the psychic world of the last two or three centuries, where at times the unconscious desire of the public to be fooled was so intense that we can only be amazed that fakes and opportunists were not even more numerous. All of us, not least those who consider themselves hardheaded, have an immense talent for believing what we want to believe. Thus the whole question of belief becomes one of considerable interest, even for the skeptic. Why, for example, does a whole population bow to the persuasions of a Savonarola while another adamantly refuses to believe in vaccination or fluoridation? The fact of belief often makes the difference between history and oblivion, and forms a rather neglected aspect of intellectual history, especially the history of science, which seems often to overemphasize the role played by logic. Fraud is an interesting scholarly sidelight, but certainly not a blanket condemnation of the field.

It would not be fair to imply that the defects in many current occult books are all due to misconceptions about the subject and frivolous treatment by authors. The field in general has been held in such low esteem that tools of research such as specialized bibliographies, indexes, and library collections are few or nonexistent. Of the three major encyclopedias of the occult and related topics in my possession,[1] two are un-systematic and riddled with errors of fact and spelling, while the third is of limited scope, and all are in need of updating.

There is another factor that increases the difficulty of writing good occult books. The occult is a live topic. That is, people seem to hold more passionate opinions on it than on anything except sex and politics. Even from the perspective of one author's very limited experience as a writer and reviewer of occult books, it seems that one cannot publish a word on the subject without exciting the wrath of both opposing camps. Prominent psychic writers leap to denounce the "antipsychic bias" of the same work cited by unbelievers as evidence of rank gullibility. American history or art appreciation simply does not call forth such intense reaction. It is no wonder that some excellent writers have shied away from becoming involved in this kind of circus. We can only hope that increasing interest and a wider market will attract better research-ers and encourage both writers and editors to require of themselves the same degree of accuracy and objectivity that would obtain in other fields, and that librarians will not buy bad books simply to fill a demand. Certainly, some aspects of the occult are sensational, some are incredible (from the point of view of the depth of human folly if from no other), some are titillating, and some are marked by fraud ranging from blatant to brilliant. But that may be said of other topics and is really no excuse for simply producing a pastiche of startling instances and reputed hap-penings in the manner of Ripley's Believe-It-or-Not.

This is not to say that some first-rate juvenile books have not been produced on occult subjects. The topic of UFOs has been well cov-ered as have those perennial favorites, the Abominable Snowman and haunted houses. There are two or three good books on ghosts and per-haps too many on witchcraft. Magic and lost continents have been given at least a once-over, and there is a good supply of collections of tales, both from folklore and from alleged personal experience which are far too numerous to mention. However, there are many noticeable gaps. In only two or three cases are there enough good books on a topic so that an interested reader can get an informed and, what is more important with a controversial subject, a varied and objective view of, say, secret societies, telekinesis, or the life of Mme. Blavatsky.

Rationalists will have to live with the fact that occult books are here, at least for a while. After all, our society has certainly not lost its appe-tite for the impossible. It is only that circumstances have conspired to deprive us of a genuine sense of mystery, thus forcing us to pretend to find prodigies in the prosaic. Come, take a little trip in search of the evidence. Just dab a little "Tabu" or "Sortilege" behind your ears and don't forget the Secret deodorant. Put on your best clothes (freshly washed in Miracle White) and your charm bracelet. We'll start out across Boston's Mystic Bridge. Shall we head for Hell's Canyon, Devil's Lake, or the Garden of the Gods? The kids in the back seat are happily drawing with Magic Marker. Later we'll stop for sandwiches made with Wonder Bread and Miracle Whip. For dessert some angelfood. And, if we're lucky, tonight's motel may have beds equipped with Magic Fingers. Now turn on the radio for an analysis of the Apollo flights. What about some music? Are they playing the Beatles "Magical Mystery Tour," or is it just "That Ol' Black Magic"?

The Impossible Book

Harry C. Stubbs

There is a widespread feeling that mankind is in a mess, and that science is what got him there. I concede the first statement without debate, and even though I am a scientist by choice and taste, I will admit that there is something—not a great deal, but something—to the second. It is admittedly true that Earth would not have its present exploding human population, with its fallout of environmental pollution and ecological instability, if man had not learned so much about the laws of nature. Most of our ancestors would have died in infancy. Most of our ability to manipulate the environment is a direct result of our knowledge, and the people who claim that we are prostituting that ability can certainly make a very strong case. I must point out, though, in defense of science and technology, that neither this nor any other form of prostitution has ever gotten or will ever get very far without a large, dependable supply of customers.

People complain loudly about the sulfur dioxide from fossil-fuel power stations, or radioactive wastes from nuclear ones; but the same people howl even more loudly when the power fails. It will be fun—grim fun, but still fun—to listen to them when electricity is rationed and they can only run their washers between noon and two P. M. and their electric lights until nine in the evening. They will, of course, blame someone else.

The teenager sneers at the 350-horsepower status symbol of his Establishment-supporting elder, but when criticized about the smoke from his own jalopy he asks who is going to pay for the ring job it needs

Reprinted by permission of the Children's Science Book Review Committee from *Appraisal: Science Books for Children* 4, no. 3:1–3 (Fall 1971). Copyright © 1971 by Harry C. Stubbs.

(personal experience of a friend of mine). The thought that he shouldn't drive until the job is done is unacceptable; it isn't *his* fault that the car smokes.

The *excuse* has become the mainstay of life for too many of us. If we don't have the time, or the money, or the knowledge to correct whatever we are doing wrong, that's enough. *We* can't be blamed for doing it. We shouldn't even have to suffer the consequences.

Mother Nature, of course, does not share this attitude. I am reminded of the tourist who was standing at the edge of the Grand Canyon admiring the view when a drunk lurched into him and sent him over. He kept screaming, truthfully and with feeling, "It wasn't my fault!" all the way down, but this had no measurable effect on his impact velocity.

This general attitude, I would judge, contributes to the panic-type reaction so common when trouble does force itself on our attention. We promptly pick a scapegoat, preferably Establishment-related if we are young, and long-haired if we aren't, and piously insist that some single thing should be banned or regulated or changed. It's always, let me repeat, some *single* thing—DDT, or atomic power plants, or the auto manufacturers.

Occasionally, perhaps, some single factor may be a key to a given trouble; but generally speaking, I would suggest this aphorism as the Axiom for Ecological Activists: *It's impossible to do anything one at a time.* I know the grammar is off-base, but that just makes an aphorism more ear-catching

More serious than the picking of a single scapegoat is the tendency to make it someone else. *They,* who generate the electricity, are poisoning the air with sulfur dioxide, not *we* who use the current. *They* are killing off our wild life with pesticides, not *we* who eat and complain about high food prices. *They* are building unsafe automobiles, not *we* who drink the alcohol responsible for half our traffic deaths (in that connection, why is the Big Business which manufactures cars, rather than the Big Business which produces liquor, the chosen scapegoat? They're both Establishment!). This childish explosion of resentment against someone else whenever our own actions get us into trouble is starting to make me embarrassed to be a member of the human species.

Hitler's selection of the Jews as a scapegoat for Germany was disgraceful and unimaginative, and the willingness of the German people to follow his lead was disgusting; but Americans at this point have forfeited whatever right we ever had to criticize them for it. We are doing exactly the same thing. Our current public behavior is just as disgraceful, unimaginative, and disgusting. Changing the scapegoat to "The Establishment" or "Big Business" is not a significant difference, and certainly not an ingenious or imaginative improvement.

Our population has expanded to the point—well beyond the point, in fact—that we can no longer survive without a high-energy technology. It seems clear to me that whatever solution there may be to our mounting problems must lie in science, even if we want to blame science for getting us here. We must learn more, since going back to muscle-powered dirt farming and "natural" fertilizers would mean starving most of humanity, and our present knowledge won't support a culture which is living on its energy capital for more than a few decades. At the moment, though, this is a highly unpopular notion in many quarters, and writers who want to get children interested in science are bucking a strong head wind. Science, like Business and The Establishment, is a good, easy scapegoat.

I am looking, therefore, for a book or a set of books able to set our brighter youngsters onto a line which may reasonably lead to a solution of our survival problems. I don't know whether I have any right to be hopeful that such a book can or will be written.

I don't mean another *Silent Spring*, with all respect to Rachel Carson. Her work admittedly pointed out some important and serious facts, which did and still do call for our best thought; but it did so in a way which also saddled us with the panic reaction I mentioned earlier. Even Mario Salvadori's *Building: The Fight against Gravity* isn't the whole answer. I was one of the judges who awarded this book the New York Academy of Sciences prize for the year, and concurred unreservedly in the opinion of the body. It is interesting, rich in information and ideas, and well stocked with suggestions for challenging and attention-trapping activities. It can reasonably be expected to get a lot of young readers interested, at least for a time, in architecture and structural engineering, and I certainly don't belittle the importance of these fields to human welfare in general. However, it does not seem likely to arouse the deep-rooted curiosity about the fundamental rules of the universe of which we are a part, a curiosity that is a necessary characteristic of the real, basic researcher. This, I think, is what we need.

The book, then, should not encourage people to go off on one line. We already have enough "Ban DDT" bumper stickers around; and as the late John Campbell pointed out in a recent *Analog* editorial, it seems a little hasty to substitute organic carcinogens in antiknock gasoline for lead bromide, when we can treat lead poisoning much more effectively than we can cancer. Narrow-line reasoning, to flatter it, has caused us to panic over lead. And mercury. And sulfur dioxide. And (some of us) fluoride ion. And—you name it. If you don't have your own personal and favorite panic item, you are a very unusual individual.

The book will have to be factual and accurate, of course. It will have to arouse that imaginative curiosity which is humanity's most human quality (personal opinion; sorry). It will have to point out the essential simplicity of scientific (or natural, if you prefer) laws, without losing sight of the enormous complexity of the game being played under those laws. It will have to make clear that being a scientist, engineer, or technician can be rewarding fun, and comparable in spiritual value to art or music, and far superior as a method of self-expression to breaking windows in Harvard Square; at the same time, it must avoid conveying the false notion that science does not involve hard, challenging, and sometimes boring work.

The book will, I hope, make clear both the risk of acting on too little information and the risk of not acting at all, even though information is never complete. Perhaps it should even afford a glimpse of the possibility that not all human problems can be solved—at least, not for four billion people—if this can be done without scaring the readers into hippie-type withdrawal from all problem-facing.

It should appeal to readers young enough so that there is still hope of influencing their attitudes, without using a style which slightly older readers will dismiss as childish.

I don't think the book has been written yet. This is not to say that there are no good children's science books; on the contrary. I can think of only two which I have encountered in the past several years which I decided not to pass on to my school library. Most are extremely good, and I must take this opportunity to express my compliments to children's science book editors as a class; they seem to be doing a remarkable job of filtering.

Maybe I am hoping for too much. It is discouraging, but unfortunately not difficult, to suppose that combining all these qualities in a single book is in fact impossible. Still, it remains a challenge; and however a writer may go about solving it, the problem of presenting science and its associated human problems in such a way that children will react with thought instead of panic is certainly one worth tackling. We have certainly missed the boat with too many of their elders.

Awards for Nonfiction: Where All the Prizes Go

> I would guess that some of the novels given the
> prize [Newbery Award] in the past might easily have
> been matched or surpassed in literary quality by works
> of nonfiction, if only the judges had not swallowed
> the nonsense that fiction alone can be called literature.[1]

Until such time as Newbery committees begin to consider the best nonfiction books as worthy of the Newbery Award, nonfiction authors will have to be grateful for recognition by institutions that have established special awards for nonfiction. This is a list of these awards. It includes only those that are currently active.

The American Book Awards

The American Book Awards, sponsored by the Association of American Publishers, were created in 1979. A prize of $1,000 is to be awarded to the author of an outstanding book in many literary categories, children's books included. 1980 awards were given, not only to authors of hardcover and paperback books for children, but also for a children's nonfiction book. The selection committee has not determined at this time whether there will be a nonfiction award in the future. For further information write to:

The American Book Awards,
Joan Cunliffe, Director,
1 Park Avenue, New York, NY 10016.

1980 Nonfiction Award:
  Oh, Boy! Babies! by Alison Craigin Herzig and Jane Lawrence Mali (Little, Brown)

Boston Globe–Horn Book Award

Since 1976 awards have been given for outstanding nonfiction, along with fiction and illustration. The award is $200 to the winner in each category.

1976
  Voyaging to Cathay: Americans in the China Trade by Alfred Tamarin and Shirley Glubok (Viking)

Honor Books:
> *Will You Sign Here, John Hancock?* by Jean Fritz (Coward)
> *Never to Forget* by Milton Meltzer (Harper)
> *Pryamid* by David Macaulay (Houghton)

1977
> *Chance, Luck, and Destiny* by Peter Dickinson (Little)

Honor Books:
> *From Slave to Abolitionist* by Lucille Schulberg Warner (Dial)
> *The Colonial Cookbook* by Lucille Recht Penner (Hastings)
> *Watching the Wild Apes* by Bettyann Kevles (Dutton)

1978
> *Mischling, Second Degree: My Childhood in Nazi Germany* by Ilse Koehn (Greenwillow)

Honor Books:
> *Settlers and Strangers: Native Americans of the Desert Southwest and History as They Saw It* by Betty Baker (Macmillan)
> *Castle* by David Macaulay (Houghton)

1979
> *The Road from Home: The Story of an Armenian Girl* by David Kherdian (Greenwillow)

Honor Books:
> *The Iron Road: A Portrait of American Railroading* by Richard Snow; illus. with photographs by David Plowden (Four Winds)
> *Self-Portrait: Margot Zemach* by Margot Zemach (Addison)
> *The Story of American Photography: An Illustrated History for Young People* by Martin Sandler (Little)

1980
> *Building: The Fight against Gravity* by Mario Salvadori (Atheneum)

Honor Books:
> *Childtimes: A Three-Generational Memoir* by Eloise Greenfield and Lessie Jones Little (Crowell)
> *How the Forest Grew* by William Jaspersohn (Greenwillow)
> *Stonewall* by Jean Fritz (Putnam)

Carter G. Woodson Award

First presented in 1974, the Carter G. Woodson Award honors the contribution of the distinguished black historian and educator. The award is intended to "encourage the writing, publishing and dissemination of outstanding social science books for young readers which treat topics related to ethnic minorities and race relations sensitively and accurately." It is sponsored by the National Council for the Social Studies. Eligible for the award are thematically appropriate nonfiction books with a United States setting, published in the year preceding the presentation of the award, a plaque.

1974
> *Rosa Parks* by Eloise Greenfield (Crowell)

1975

> *Make a Joyful Noise Unto the Lord: The Life of Mahalia Jackson, Queen of Gospel Singers* by Jesse Jackson (Crowell)

1976

> *Dragonwings* by Laurence Yep (Harper)

1977

> *The Trouble They Seen* by Dorothy Sterling (Doubleday)

1978

> *The Biography of Daniel Inouye* by Jane Goodsell (Crowell)

1979

> *Native American Testimony*, ed. by Peter Nabokov (Crowell)

1980

> *War Cry on a Prayer Feather: Prose and Poetry of the Ute Indians*, ed. by Nancy Wood (Doubleday)

Christopher Awards

Although there is not a separate category for nonfiction, The Christophers have honored so many nonfiction writers over the years that it is reasonable to list them here. Candidates must be published in the calendar year for which the award is given, must enjoy a reasonable degree of popular acceptance, and must be representative of the highest level of human and spiritual values. Children's books has been a recognized category since 1969. The number of books selected each year varies. The award is a bronze medallion. Address: The Christophers, Father John Catoir, Director, 12 East 48th Street, New York, New York 10017.

1969

> *Brother, Can You Spare a Dime?* by Milton Meltzer (Knopf)

1970

> *The Erie Canal* by Peter Spier (Doubleday)
> *A Moment of Silence* by Pierre Janssen, trans. by William R. Tyler (Atheneum)
> *Sea and Earth, the Life of Rachel Carson* by Philip Sterling (Crowell)

1971

> *On the Day Peter Stuyvesant Sailed into Town* by Arnold Lobel (Harper)
> *The Rights of the People: The Major Decisions of the Warren Court* by Elaine and Walter Goodman (Farrar)

1972

> *Tracking the Unearthly Creatures of Marsh and Pond* by Howard G. Smith (Abingdon)
> *Vanishing Wings* by Griffing Bancroft (Watts)

1973

> *Gorilla, Gorilla* by Carol Fenner (Random)
> *The Wolf* by Michael Fox (Coward)
> *The Right To Know: Censorship in America* by Robert Liston (Watts)

1974
> *First Snow* by Helen Coutant (Knopf)
> *Save the Mustangs* by Ann E. Weiss (Messner)

1975
> *Pyramid* by David Macaulay (Houghton)

1976
> No nonfiction award

1977
> *Where's Your Head? Psychology for Teen-Agers* by Dale Carlson (Atheneum)

1978
> No nonfiction award

1979
> No nonfiction award

1980
> *The New York Kid's Book*, ed. by Catherine Edmonds et al. (Doubleday)

1981
> *All Times, All Peoples: A World History of Slavery* by Milton Meltzer (Harper)
> *The Hardest Lesson: Personal Accounts of a School Desegregation Crisis* by Pamela Bullard and Judith Stoia (Little)

Eva L. Gordon Award for Children's Science Literature

Given by the American Nature Society in memory of Eva L. Gordon, author, reviewer, and professor of children's science literature at Cornell University. A certificate is awarded to an author whose works exemplify Eva L. Gordon's "high standards of accuracy, readability, sensitivity to interrelationships, timeliness, and joyousness while they extend, either directly or subtly, an invitation to the child to become involved." The address is: Helen Russell, Secretary, 44 College Drive, Jersey City, New Jersey 07035.

1964
> Millicent Selsam

1965
> Edwin Way Teale

1966
> Robert McClung

1967–1969
> No award

1970
> Jean Craighead George

1971
> Verne Rockcastle

1972–1973
>   No award

1974
>   Phyllis Busch

1975
>   Jeanne Bendick

1976
>   Helen Ross Russell

1977
>   Herman and Nina Schneider

1978
>   George Mason
>   Dorothy Shuttlesworth

1979
>   Ross E. Hutchins

1980
>   Glenn O. Blough

Garden State Children's Book Award

Established in 1977 by the Children's Services Section of the New Jersey Library Association, awards in three categories are given to authors and illustrators in recognition of fine books written for children in the early and middle grades. Only books published three years prior to the award are considered. The award is a certificate. The winners in the Younger Nonfiction category are as follows:

1977
>   *On the Track of Bigfoot* by Marian T. Place (Dodd)

1978
>   *How Kittens Grow* by Millicent Selsam, with photographs by Esther Bubley (Four Winds)

1979
>   *A Very Young Dancer* by Jill Krementz (Knopf)

1980
>   *The Quicksand Book* by Tomie de Paola (Holiday)

The Golden Kite Award

Presented by the Society of Children's Book Writers. Since 1977 a golden kite statuette has been presented annually to the author of an outstanding nonfiction book, in addition to a statuette for the author of an outstanding work of fiction. The authors must be members of the Society of Children's Book Writers. One honor-book certificate is also awarded in each category.

1977
>   *Peeper, First Voice of Spring* by Robert McClung (Morrow)

Honor Book:
>   *Evolution Goes on Every Day* by Dorothy Hinshaw Patent (Holiday)

1978
>   *How I Came to be a Writer* by Phyllis Naylor (Atheneum)

Honor Book:
>   *Bionic Parts for People* by Gloria Skurzynski (Four Winds)

1979
>   *Runaway Teens* by Arnold Madison (Elsevier/Nelson)

Honor Book:
>   *America's Endangered Birds* by Robert McClung (Morrow)

1980
>   *The Lives of Spiders* by Dorothy Hinshaw Patent (Holiday)

Honor Book:
>   *Finding Your First Job* by Sue Alexander (Dutton)

The New York Academy of Sciences Children's Science Book Awards

Instituted in 1972 by the New York Academy of Sciences with the intention of encouraging the writing and publishing of more books of high quality in the field of science for children. In 1973 the award was divided into two categories: for younger children (YC); for older children (OC). In the list below, the year cited is the year in which the book was published. A citation, plus $250, is awarded to the winning author in each category.

1971
>   *The Stars and Serendipity* by Dr. Robert Richardson (Pantheon)

Honor Books:
>   *Gobble, Growl, Grunt* by Peter Spier (Doubleday)
>   *Insect Behavior* by Philip Callahan (Four Winds)
>   *Invitations to Investigate* by Dr. Paul Brandwein and Hy Ruchlis (Harcourt)

1972 (YC)
>   *City Leaves, City Trees* by Edward Gallob (Scribner)

Honor Books:
>   *Wharf Rat* by Miska Miles (Little)
>   *Make a Bigger Puddle, Make a Smaller Worm* by Marion Walter (Evans)
>   *8,000 Stones* by Diane Wolkstein (Doubleday)

1972 (OC)
>   *Reading the Past* by Leonard Cottrell (Crowell)

Honor Books:
>   *Track Watching* by David Webster (Watts)

*What Makes It Go? What Makes It Work? What Makes It Fly?
What Makes It Float?* by Joe Kaufman (Golden)

Life in a Log by George and Bernice Schwartz (Natural History
Press)

1973 (YC)

The Web in the Grass by Berniece Freschet (Scribner)

Honor Books:

From Afar It Is an Island by Bruno Munari (World)

Discovering Cycles by Glenn O. Blough (McGraw-Hill)

City Rocks, City Blocks, and the Moon by Edward Gallob (Scribner)

1973 (OC)

A Natural History of Giraffes by Dorcas MacClintock and Ugo
Mochi (Scribner)

Honor Books:

It's Fun to Know Why by Julius Schwartz (McGraw-Hill)

Vultures by Ann W. Turner and Marion G. Warren (McKay)

X-Raying the Pharaohs by James E. Harris and Kent R. Weeks
(Scribner)

Special Honorable Mention for an outstanding series:

The Walck Archeology Series, Henry Z. Walck, Inc.

1974 (YC)

See What I Am by Roger Duvoisin (Lothrop, Lee, Shepard)

Honor Books:

Circles, Triangles, and Squares by Tana Hoban (Macmillan)

Handtalk by Remy Charlip, Mary Beth and George Ancona
(Parents Magazine)

Sunlight by Sally Cartwright (Coward)

1974 (OC)

Hunters of the Whale by Ruth Kirk and Richard K. Daugherty
(Morrow)

Honor Books:

Fever by John G. Fuller (Reader's Digest)

Gypsy Moth by Robert M. McClung (Morrow)

Summer Gold by John N. Dwyer (Scribner)

Treasure Keepers by John FitzMaurice Mills (Doubleday)

Wrapped for Eternity by Mildred M. Pace (McGraw-Hill)

Special Honorable Mention for an outstanding reference work:

The Rand McNally Atlas of World Wildlife (Rand)

Special Honorable Mention for the continued excellence of the Walck
Archeology series:

Ancient China and *The Archeology of Ships*

1975 (YC)

Emperor Penguin by Jean-Claude Deguine (Stephen Greene)

Honor Books:

Spring Peepers by Judy Hawes (Crowell)

The Desert Is Theirs by Byrd Baylor, illus. by Peter Parnall
(Scribner)

Paper Movie Machines by Budd Wentz (Troubador Press)
The Lobster: Its Life Cycle by Herb Taylor (Sterling)
The Blue Lobster: A Life Cycle by Carol Carrick, illus. by Donald Carrick (Dial)

1975 (OC)
Doctor in the Zoo by Bruce Buchenholz (Viking)
Honor Books:
A Life of Their Own by Aylette Jenness and Lisa W. Kroeber (Crowell)
Sounds and Signals: How We Communicate by Charles T. Meadow (Westminster)
The Story of Oceanography by Robert E. Boyer (Harvey)
Look How Many People Wear Glasses by Ruth Brindze (Atheneum)

1976 (YC)
Corn Is Maize by Aliki (Crowell)
Honor Books:
Iceberg Alley by Madelyn Klein Anderson (Messner)
The Milkweed and Its World of Animals by Ada & Frank Graham (Doubleday)
A Foal Is Born by Hans-Heinrich Isenburt (Putnam)

1976 (OC)
Watching the Wild Apes by Bettyann Kevles (Dutton)
Honor Books:
Window into a Nest by Geraldine Lux Flanagan and Sean Morris (Houghton)
The Cave Bear Story by Bjorn Kurtén (Columbia Univ. Pr.)
Potatoes by Alvin and Virginia B. Silverstein (Prentice-Hall)
Exploring the World of Leaves by Raymond A. Wohlrabe (Crowell)
Special Award on the twentieth anniversary of this publication:
The Cosmic View by Kees Boeke (John Day)

1977 (YC)
Wild Mouse by Irene Brady (Scribner)
Honor Books:
Anno's Counting Book by Mitsumasa Anno (Crowell)
Hanging On by Russell Freedman (Holiday)
Castle by David Macaulay (Houghton)

1977 (OC)
Grains by Elizabeth Burton Brown (Prentice-Hall)
Honor Books:
Epidemic! by Jules Archer (Harcourt)
Three-Dimensional Optical Illusions by Larry Evans (Troubador Press)
The Versatile Satellite by Richard W. Porter (Oxford)
The Microbes, Our Unseen Friends by Harold W. Rossmoore (Wayne State Univ. Pr.)
Special Award to a book resulting from an exhibit:
Human Biology—An Exhibition of Ourselves by British Museum, Natural History (Cambridge Univ. Pr.)

1978 (YC)
> The Smallest Life Around Us by Lucia Anderson, illus. by Leigh
> Grant (Crown)

Honor Books:
> Hyena Day by Robert Caputo and Miriam Hsia, photographs by
> Robert Caputo (Coward)
> Dr. Beaumont and the Man with the Hole in His Stomach by Sam
> and Beryl Epstein (Coward)
> The Bakery Factory by Aylette Jenness (Crowell)
> Winning with Numbers by Manfred G. Riedel (Prentice-Hall)

1978 (OC)
> Laser Light by Herman Schneider (McGraw-Hill)

Honor Books:
> Worlds within Worlds by Michael Marten, John Chesterman,
> John May, and John Trux (Holt)
> Color in Plants and Flowers by John and Susan Proctor (Everest
> House)
> Insect Magic by Michael G. Emsley, photographs by Kjell B.
> Sandved (Viking)
> The Magic Orange Tree and Other Haitian Folktales by Diane
> Wolkstein (Knopf)

Special Award for an outstanding series on engineering and technology
to the Viking Press:
> Jet Journey by Mike Wilson and Robin Scagell
> Space Frontiers by Heather Couper and Nigel Henbest
> Supermachines by Ralph Hancock
> Television Magic by Eurfron Gwynne Jones

1979 (YC)
> A Space Story by Karla Kuskin, illus. by Marc Simont (Harper)

Honor Books:
> What Do Animals Do When It Rains? by J. Fred Dice, illus. by
> Teppy Williams (Crescent Pubs.)
> Natural Fire by Laurence Pringle (Morrow)
> The Wild Inside by Linda Allison (Scribner/Sierra Club)
> Bubbles by Bernie Zubrowski, illus. by Joan Drescher (Little)

1979 (OC)
> Building: The Fight against Gravity by Mario Salvadori (Athe-
> neum)

Honor Books:
> The Crab Nebula by Simon Mitton (Scribner)
> Archosauria by John C. McLoughlin (Viking)
> Time and Clocks for the Space Age by James Jespersen and
> Jane Fitz-Randolph (Atheneum)
> Morse, Marconi and You by Irwin Math (Scribner)

Special Award for a reference book series to Harry N. Abrams, publishers, for a series "which have exceedingly beautiful photographs and
which are unusually affordable":
> Wildlife of the Forests by Ann and Myron Sutton
> Wildlife of the Mountains by Edward R. Ricciuti
> Wildlife of the Oceans by Albert C. Jensen

1980 (YC)
>   *Bet You Can't!* by Vicki Cobb and Kathy Darling (Lothrop)

Honor Books:
>   *Max, the Music Maker* by Miriam B. Stecher and Alice S. Kandell (Lothrop)
>   *Sunflower* by Martha M. Welch (Dodd, Mead)
>   *Unbuilding* by David Macaulay (Houghton)

1980 (OC)
>   *Moving Heavy Things* by Jan Adkins (Houghton)

Honor Books:
>   *Careers in Conservation* by Ada and Frank Graham (Sierra Club/ Scribner)
>   *Magic in the Movies: The Story of Special Effects* by Jane O'Connor and Katy Hall (Doubleday)
>   *Our Urban Planet* by Ellen Switzer (Atheneum)
>   *Stones: Their Collection, Identification, and Uses* by R. V. Dietrich (W. H. Freeman)

Times Educational Supplement Information Book Awards (British)

Established in 1972 by the *(London) Times Educational Supplement,* this is an award given for distinction in content and presentation in non-fiction trade books originating in the United Kingdom or Commonwealth countries. Since 1973, awards are offered for books in both Junior (up to age nine) and Senior (ages ten to sixteen) categories. £100 to the winner in each category.

1972
>   *Introducing Archeology* by Magnus Magnusson (Bodley Head)

1973, Junior
>   No award
>   Senior
>   *Human Populations* by David Hay (Penguin)

1974, Junior
>   *Frogs, Toads and Newts* by F. D. Ommanney (Bodley Head)
>   Senior
>   *Understanding Art* by Betty Churcher (McDougall)

1975, Junior
>   *Spiders* by Ralph Whitlock (Priory)
>   Senior
>   *Window into a Nest* by Geraldine Lux Flanagan and Sean Morris (Kestrel)

1976, Junior
>   *Wash and Brush Up* by Eleanor Allen (Black)
>   Senior
>   *Macdonald's Encyclopedia of Africa* (Macdonald)

1977, Junior
>   *Street Flowers* by Richard Mabey (Kestrel)
>   Senior
>   *Man and Machines* (The Mitchell Beazley Joy of Knowledge Library)

1978, Junior
>   *Tournaments* by Richard Barber (Kestrel)
>   Senior
>   *Butterflies on My Mind* by Dulcie Gray (Angus and Robertson)

1979, Junior
>   *The Common Frog* by George Bernard (Whizzard/Deutsch)
>   Senior
>   *Make It Happy* by Jane Cousins (Virago)

1980, Junior
>   *Earthquakes and Volcanoes* by Imelda and Robert Updegraff (Methuen)
>   Senior
>   *The Oxford Junior Companion to Music* by Michael Hurd (Oxford)

Washington, D.C., Children's Book Guild Nonfiction Award

This annual award, originating in 1977, is presented to a nonfiction writer for a total body of creative work. Winners are selected by a committee of Children's Book Guild members. Honor winners were not chosen after 1979. The prize is $200, with a certificate.

1977
>   *Winner:* David Macaulay
>   *Honor winners:* Olivia Coolidge and Laurence Pringle

1978
>   *Winner:* Millicent Selsam
>   *Honor winners:* Jean Fritz and Milton Meltzer

1979
>   *Winner:* Jean Fritz
>   *Honor winners:* Laurence Pringle and Milton Meltzer

1980
>   Shirley Glubok

1981
>   Milton Meltzer

Appendix B:
Professional Books and Journals

Although the professional books listed below cover nonfiction primarily, they are not the only selection tools professionals will find useful in buying nonfiction. Standard review journals can be valuable, as can chapters in children's literature textbooks, general bibliographies, and notable lists. Charlotte Huck's chapter on nonfiction in *Children's Literature in the Elementary School*, for instance, is an excellent introduction to nonfiction writing. The chapter on nonfiction in the sixth edition of *Children and Books* by Zena Sutherland, Diane L. Monson, and May Hill Arbuthnot is also first-rate.

All books in the bibliography have been published since 1970. Some are in print; some are not. All cover books for children and young people, with those for children in the elementary through the intermediate grades predominating. The choice of titles has been selective.

For detailed annotations of these professional books and journals, refer to *Children's Literature: A Guide to Reference Sources*. This invaluable scholarly work has been compiled by Virginia Haviland and Margaret Coughlan at the Children's Literature Center, Library of Congress. The work is in four volumes.

Books

American Association for the Advancement of Science. *AAAS Science Book List Supplement.* ed. by Kathryn Wolff and Jill Storey. Washington, D. C.: The Association, 1978. This updates *AAAS Science Book List*, 3rd ed., 1970. 457p.

————. *Science Book List for Children.* ed. by Hilary Deason. 3rd ed. Washington, D. C.: The Association, 1972. 253p. A supplement is in preparation.

Byler, Mary Gloyne. *American Indian Authors for Young Readers: A Selected Bibliography.* New York: Assn. of Indian Affairs, 1973. 26p.

Coughlan, Margaret. *Creating Independence, 1763–1789.* Washington, D.C.: Library of Congress, 1972. 62p.

Fisher, Margery. *Matters of Fact: Aspects of Non-Fiction for Children.* New York: Crowell, 1972. 488p.

Hotchkiss, Jeanette K. *African-Asian Reading Guide for Children and Young Adults.* Metuchen, N.J.: Scarecrow, 1976. 269p.

————. *American Historical Fiction and Biography for Children and Young People.* Metuchen, N.J.: Scarecrow, 1973, 318p.

————. *European Historical Fiction and Biography for Children and Young People.* 2nd ed. Metuchen, N.J.: Scarecrow, 1972. 272p.

Information Center on Children's Cultures. United States Committee for UNICEF. *Near East and North Africa: An Annotated List of Materials for Children.* New York: The Center, 1970. 98p.

Irwin, Leonard B. *A Guide to Historical Reading: Non-Fiction; For the Use of Schools, Libraries, and the General Reader.* 9th rev. ed. Brooklawn, N.J.: McKinley Pub. Co., 1970. 276p.

Johnson, James P., comp. *Africana for Children and Young People; A Current Guide for Teachers and Librarians.* Westport, Conn.: Greenwood Periodicals Co., 1971. 172p.

Kister, Kenneth. *Encyclopedia Buying Guide.* New York: Bowker. 389p. Revised every three years.

Kulkin, Mary-Ellen. *Her Way: Biographies of Women for Young People.* Chicago: American Library Assn., 1976. 449p.

Lass-Woodfin, Mary Jo, ed. *Books on American Indians and Eskimos: A Selection Guide for Children and Young Adults.* Chicago: American Library Assn., 1977. 360p.

Metzner, Seymour. *World History in Juvenile Books: A Geographical and Chronological Guide.* New York: Wilson, 1973. 357p.

Nicholsen, Margaret E. *People in Books, First Supplement: A Selective Guide to Biographical Literature Arranged by Vocations and Other Fields of Reader Interest.* New York: Wilson, 1977. 792p.

Peterson, Carolyn Sue, and Fenton, Ann D. *Reference Books for Children.* Metuchen, N.J.: Scarecrow, 1981. 273p.

Schmidt, Nancy J. *Children's Books on Africa, and Their Authors: An Annotated Bibliography.* New York: Africana Pub. Co., 1975. 291p.

————. *Supplement to Children's Books on Africa and Their Authors: An Annotated Bibliography.* New York: Africana Pub. Co., 1979. 273p.

Silverman, Judith. *Index to Collective Biographies for Young Readers; Elementary and Junior High School Level.* 3rd ed. New York: Bowker, 1979. 405p.

Stanius, Ellen J. *Index to Short Biographies for Elementary and Junior High Grades.* Metuchen, N.J.: Scarecrow, 1971. 348p.

Stensland, Anna L. *Literature by and about the American Indian: An Annotated Bibliography for Junior and Senior High Students.* Urbana, Ill.: National Council of Teachers of English, 1973. 208p.

Wenzel, Evelyn L., and Arbuthnot, May Hill, comps. *Time for Discovery, Informational Books; A Collection of Representative Selections.* Glenview, Ill.: Scott, Foresman, 1971. 293p.

Wynar, Christine. *Guide to Reference Books for School Media Centers,* 2nd ed. Littleton, Colo.: Libraries Unlimited, 1981. 377p.

Journals and Notable Lists

Appraisal: Science Books for Young People. Boston: Boston Univ. School of Education and New England Roundtable of Children's Librarians. Published three times a year. Recently expanded.

Children's Science Books, 1981. Chicago: Museum of Science & Industry. Notable list, including titles published prior to 1981, available from the Museum, 57th & S. Lake Shore Dr., Chicago, Ill. 60637.

The Horn Book Magazine. Boston: The Horn Book, Inc. Published six times a year. Special science review articles by Sarah Gagné and Harry C. Stubbs.

The Kobrin Letter, 732 Greer Road, Palo Alto, Calif. 94303. Monthly newsletter for "parents and other educators, concerning children's books about real people, places and things."

"Notable Children's Trade Books in the Field of the Social Studies." Washington, D. C.: National Council for the Social Studies. Published each year in one of the spring issues of *Social Education.* Also available from the Children's Book Council, New York.

"Outstanding Science Trade Books for Children in 19   ." Published each year in one of the spring issues of *Science and Children.* Also available from the Children's Book Council, New York.

Science and Children. Washington, D.C.: National Science Teachers Association. Published eight times a year. Reviews science books for children in the elementary grades.

Science Books and Films. Washington, D.C.: Association for the Advancement of Science. Published five times a year. Reviews science books, films, and filmstrips for children and young people, as well as for adults.

The Science Teacher. Washington, D.C.: National Science Teachers Association. Published nine times a year. Reviews science books for young people in intermediate and high school.

Scientific American. New York: Scientific American, Inc. December issue. Philip and Phylis Morrison discuss the best children's science books of the year.

Contributors

Jo Carr, who has been a librarian in both schools and public libraries, teaches children's literature at the University of Virginia in Falls Church and at George Washington University in Washington, D.C.

Olivia Coolidge is the author of many books for children and young adults on classical and historical subjects.

The Council on Interracial Books for Children has been created to oppose sexism, racism, and other forms of prejudice in children's books. Its address is 1841 Broadway, New York, New York 10023. The Council offers a free catalog listing many antisexist, antiracist teaching materials.

Margery Fisher is the editor of *Growing Point*, a journal of literary criticism of children's books published in England. She has written a number of books on children's literature. One of them, *Matters of Fact; Aspects of Non-Fiction for Children*, is now unfortunately out of print. Margery Fisher lives in Northampton, England.

Dennis Flanagan is the editor of *Scientific American* and the husband of Ellen Raskin.

Carol Gay is an associate professor of English at Youngstown State University in Ohio. She has published numerous articles and monographs on scholarly subjects related to children's literature, especially American children's literature before 1865.

Pamela R. Giller reviews and writes about children's books. She is the editor of *Books, Children & Parents*, a periodic newsletter. She also teaches children's literature at Middlesex Community College, in Lexington, Massachusetts.

Nat Hentoff is a staff writer at *The New Yorker* and *The Village Voice*, as well as author of numerous books for young readers—both fiction and nonfiction—including *Jazz Country, This School Is Driving Me Crazy*, and *Does This School Have Corporal Punishment?* His latest nonfiction book has special relevance to his article in this collection. It is called: *The First Freedom: The Tumultuous History of Free Speech in America*.

Ann M. Hildebrand is a member of the Department of English and teaches children's literature at Kent State University. She is a former public school teacher, the author of several articles, and the initiator of the Religious Studies Program at Kent State University.

Georgess McHargue is a writer and reviewer. She has written books on the occult, as well as many books of fiction and other nonfiction.

Milton Meltzer has written outstanding books, both for adults and young people, on history and biography. His special contribution is in writing the history of minorities, as will be evident from the selections printed here.

F. N. Monjo was editorial director of Books for Boys and Girls at Coward, McCann & Geoghegan before his death. The many books he wrote for children include both biographies and historical fiction.

Laurence Pringle studied wildlife conservation at Cornell University and at the University of Massachusetts, where he received an M.S. For seven years he edited *Nature and Science,* a children's science magazine published at the American Museum of Natural History. Since 1970 he has been a free-lance writer and photographer. Mr. Pringle has written nearly forty highly praised books for young people on biological and environmental subjects.

Frances Clarke Sayers, now retired, taught children's literature at the University of California–Los Angeles after years as superintendent of work with children at the New York Public Library. She has always been a prolific writer and lecturer in the children's literature field.

Elizabeth Segel, who holds a Ph.D. in English literature from Brandeis University, teaches children's literature at the University of Pittsburgh. She is currently working on a study of gender and children's books and is collaborating with Margaret Kimmel on a guide to reading aloud to school-aged children.

Millicent Selsam is one of the most prolific and highly respected science writers for children.

Harry Stubbs, in addition to teaching science at Milton Academy, regularly discusses recent titles in "Views on Science Books," in *The Horn Book* and reviews for *Appraisal.* He has served as one of the judges for the awards given by the New York Academy of Sciences for the best children's science book of the year. He also writes science fiction under the pseudonym Hal Clement.

Zena Sutherland is an associate professor at the Graduate Library School of the University of Chicago, as well as editor of the *Bulletin of the Center for Children's Books* and children's book review editor of the *Chicago Tribune.* She is the author of numerous books on children's literature, including *Children and Books* and *The Best in Children's Books.*

Dr. Evelyn L. Wenzel teaches children's literature in the Department of Elementary Education at the University of Florida, Gainesville.

Denise Wilms is a children's books reviewer for *Booklist,* published by the American Library Association.

Kathryn Wolff, formerly a chemist and teacher, is now managing editor of publications at the American Association for the Advancement of Science. Her responsibilities include supervising the publication of scholarly books, as well as overseeing the reviewing of science books, films, and filmstrips.

Notes

Nonfiction Writing: Books as Instruments of Intelligence

1. Helen Haines, *Living with Books: The Art of Book Selection* (New York: Columbia Univ. Pr., 1950), p. 5.

Writing the Literature of Fact

1. Frances FitzGerald, *America Revised: History Schoolbooks in the Twentieth Century* (Boston: Atlantic/Little, 1979), p. 47.
2. Ibid., p. 27.
3. Barbara Tuchman, "The Book," *The Washington Post Book World* 9:14 (30 Dec. 1979).
4. Milton Meltzer, "Where Do All the Prizes Go? The Case for Nonfiction," *Horn Book* 52:21 (Feb. 1976).
5. Mike Wilson, Robin Scagell, and contributors, *Jet Journey* (New York: Viking, 1978), p. 50.
6. Paul Murray Kendall, *The Art of Biography* (New York: Norton, 1965), quoted in Margery Fisher, *Matters of Fact: Aspects of Non-Fiction for Children* (New York: Crowell, 1972), p. 302.
7. Deborah Crawford, *Four Women in a Violent Time* (New York: Crown, 1970), p. 48.
8. Robert J. Hastings, *A Nickel's Worth of Skim Milk: A Boy's View of the Great Depression* ([Carbondale, Ill.]: University Graphics and Publications, Southern Illinois University at Carbondale, 1972), pp. 2–3.
9. John McPhee, *The McPhee Reader* (New York: Farrar, 1976), pp. 211–12.
10. Theodora Kroeber, *Ishi, Last of His Tribe* (Berkeley, Cal.: Parnassus Pr., 1964), p. 26.
11. Peggy Thomson, *Museum People: Collectors and Keepers at the Smithsonian* (Englewood Cliffs, N.J.: Prentice-Hall, 1977), p. xiv.
12. Francis Ross Carpenter, *The Old China Trade: Americans in Canton 1784–1843* (New York: Coward, 1976), p. 23 and p. 26.
13. Kendall, as quoted in Margery Fisher, *Matters of Fact*, pp. 302–3.
14. Hal Borland, *The Golden Circle: A Book of Months* (New York: Crowell, 1977), p. 43.
15. Henry Steele Commager, *The Great Constitution: A Book for Young Americans* (Indianapolis, New York: Bobbs-Merrill, 1961), pp. 9–10.

Introduction to Matters of Fact

1. *The Bookseller* 3158:28 (2 July 1966).
2. Robin Bateman, "Children, Teachers and Librarians," *The School Librarian* 18:139 (June 1970).

Historical Backgrounds

1. Mrs. E. M. Field, *The Child and His Book* (London: Wells Gardner, Darton, 1892; reissued, Detroit: Singing Tree Press, 1968), p. 8.
2. Ibid., p. 19.
3. Ibid., p. 23.
4. Ibid., pp. 64–65.
5. Virginia Haviland, "The Travelogue Storybook of the Nineteenth Century," in Siri Andrews, *The Hewins Lectures, 1947–1962* (Boston: Horn Book, 1963), pp. 58–63. *Note:* Dates and publishers do not always agree with listings by other authors. Many editions of these books existed. Copyright and publication dates are not always the same, and writers frequently list the edition available to them for examination.
6. Herbert S. Zim, "Informational Books—Tonic and Tool for the Elementary Classroom," *Elementary English* (March 1952), p. 131.
7. Haviland, p. 54.
8. Richard L. Darling, *The Rise of Children's Book Reviewing in America, 1865–1881* (New York: Bowker, 1968), p. 42.
9. Ibid., p. 145.
10. Ibid., p. 84.
11. Ibid., p. 207.
12. Ibid., p. 226.
13. Ibid., p. 45.
14. K. Ushinsky, *How a Shirt Grew in the Field* (New York: McGraw-Hill, 1967).
15. Haviland, p. 28.
16. Mary Liddell, *Little Machinery* (Garden City, N.Y.: Doubleday, Page, 1926).
17. Lillian Hollowell, ed. *A Book of Children's Literature* (Little & Ives, 1939), pp. 903–8.

Science: The Excitement of Discovery

1. Lillian Smith, *The Unreluctant Years* (Chicago: American Library Assn., 1953), pp. 178–79.

Clarity in Science Writing

1. Laurence Pringle, *Death Is Natural* (New York: Four Winds, 1977), p. 46.
2. Robert M. McClung, *Lost Wild Worlds* (New York: Morrow, 1976), p. 262.
3. Kim Marshall, *The Story of Life, from the Big Bang to You* (New York: Holt, Rinehart, Winston, 1980), pp. 17–18.
4. Victor B. Scheffer, *The Seeing Eye* (New York: Scribner, 1971), p. 7.
5. *Appraisal* 13, no. 3:22 (Summer 1980).
6. Virginia Buckley, "Editing Science Books," *Appraisal* 11, no. 1 (Winter 1978), unpaged.
7. *Appraisal*, 12, no. 2:33 (Spring 1979).

Reviewing Science Books for Children

1. Richard K. Winslow, *Publishing for Scientific Literacy: A Report for*

the *Public Understanding of Science* (AAAS Miscellaneous Publication 72–11 [Washington, D.C.: American Assn. for the Advancement of Science, May 1972]). *See also,* Ruth V. Byler, ed., *Teach Us What We Want to Know* (New York: Mental Health Materials Center, Inc., 1969).

2. Hilary Deason, "Evaluating Science Books for Children," *Science and Children* (Nov. 1965), pp. 9–11.

3. Bentley Glass, speech to Thomas Alva Edison Foundation (Dearborn, Mich., 11 Feb. 1969).

Writing about Science for Children

1. Millicent Selsam, *Terry and the Caterpillars* (New York: Harper, 1962).

2. George Gaylord Simpson, Colin S. Pittendrigh, and Lewis H. Tiffany, *Life: An Introduction to Biology* (New York: Harcourt, 1957), p. 22.

3. George Sarton, *The History of Science and the New Humanism* (Cambridge. Mass.: Harvard Univ. Pr., 1937), pp. 129–301.

4. Lucretius, *De rerum naturae* 823–26, 832–36. Set in English verse by Alban Dewes Winspear (New York: S. A. Russell, Harbor Press, 1956), p. 170.

5. Norman L. Munn, "The Evolution of the Mind," *Scientific American* (June 1957), p. 140.

6. Eva L. Gordon, "Reviewing and Selecting Nature Books for Children," *School Science and Mathematics* 49:604–5 (November 1949).

Selecting Science Books for Children

1. Known as Hal Clement to science fiction readers.

Science and the Literary Imagination

1. C. P. Snow, *The Two Cultures and the Scientific Revolution* (New York: Cambridge Univ. Pr., 1959).

2. F. R. Leavis, *Two Cultures? The Significance of C. P. Snow* (London: Chatto and Windus, 1962).

3. Aldous Huxley, *Literature and Science* (New York: Harper, 1963).

Science as Literature

1. Victor B. Scheffer, *Little Calf* (New York: Scribner, 1970), p. 13.

2. Ibid., p. 25.

3. Aileen Fisher, *Valley of the Smallest: The Life Story of a Shrew* (New York: Crowell, 1966), p. 4.

4. _____, *Feathered Ones and Furry* (New York: Crowell, 1971), p. 3.

5. Jean G. George, *Spring Comes to the Ocean* (New York: Crowell, 1965), pp. 28–29.

6. Lillian Smith, *The Unreluctant Years* (Chicago: American Library Assn., 1953), pp. 178–79.

History: The Past Realized, Remembered, and Enjoyed

1. Leon Garfield, "Bookmaker and Punter," in Edward Blishen, *The Thorny Paradise: Writers on Writing for Children* (Harmondsworth, Middlesex, Eng.: Kestrel Books, 1975), p. 85.

History: Factual Fiction or Fictional Fact?

1. Jane Austen, *Northanger Abbey*, in *The Complete Works of Jane Austen* (New York: Random, n.d.), p. 1123.
2. Jill Paton Walsh, "History Is Fiction," *Horn Book*, 47:22 (Feb. 1972).
3. Ibid., p. 23.
4. Ibid.
5. Michiko Kakutani, "Do Facts and Fiction Mix?" *New York Times Book Review* (27 Jan. 1980), p. 3.
6. Constance Irwin, *Strange Footprints on the Land: Vikings in America* (New York: Harper, 1980), pp. 32–33.
7. Rosemary Sutcliff, *Blood Feud* (New York: Dutton, 1976), p. 66.

History Books for Children

1. Jacques Barzun, *Clio and the Doctors: Psycho-History, Quanto-History and History* (Chicago: Chicago Univ. Pr., 1974), p. 144.

History Books: Making America's Past Come Alive

1. Paul Hazard, *Books, Children and Men* (Boston: Horn Book, 1944), p. 42.
2. Available in reproduction from Horn Book, Inc., Boston, Mass.
3. Cited in Abraham S. W. Rosenbach, *American Children's Books* (New York: Dover, 1971).
4. Available in *Randolph Caldecott's Picture Book*, vol. 1 (New York: Frederick Warne, n.d.).
5. Rosalie V. Halsey, *Forgotten Books of the American Nursery: A History of the Development of the American Story-Book* (Boston: Charles E. Goodspeed, 1911), p. 123.
6. Available from Dover Publications, New York, New York.
7. For the years preceding 1776: *Young Man from the Piedmont: The Youth of Thomas Jefferson*; for the Revolutionary years: *A Dawn in the Trees*; for the years 1789–1801: *The Gales of Spring*; for his later years: *The Time of the Harvest*. All published by Farrar, Straus & Giroux.

Biography: Facts Warmed by Imagination

1. Helen Haines, *Living with Books: The Art of Book Selection* (New York: Columbia Univ. Pr., 1950), p. 252.

What Do We Do about Bad Biographies?

1. Helen Haines, *Living with Books: The Art of Book Selection* (New York: Columbia Univ. Pr., 1950), pp. 266–67.
2. Margery Fisher, "Life Course or Screaming Farce?" *Children's Literature in Education* 22:114 (Autumn 1976).
3. Patrick Groff, "Biography: The Bad or the Bountiful?" *Top of the News* 29:210–17 (Apr. 1973), and "Biography: A Tool for Bibliotherapy?" *Top of the News* 36:269–73 (Spring 1980).
4. Michael Collins, *Flying to the Moon and Other Strange Places* (New York: Farrar, 1974), pp. 133–34.
5. Marilyn Jurich, "What's Been Left Out of Biography for Children," *The Great Excluded: Critical Essays on Children's Literature* [*Children's Literature*] 1:143–51 (1972).

6. Jane Yolen, *Writing Books for Children* (Boston: The Writer, 1973), pp. 78–79.
7. Jean Fritz, *Where Was Patrick Henry on the 29th of May?* (New York: Coward, 1975), pp. 37–38.

Biography

1. Dennis Potter, "The Art of Trespass," *The Times Saturday Review* (29 Nov. 1969).
2. Paul Murray Kendall, *The Art of Biography* (New York: Norton, 1965), p. 17.
3. André Maurois, quoted in James L. Clifford, *Biography as an Art: Selected Criticism, 1560–1960* (New York: Oxford Univ. Pr., 1962), p. 168.
4. Edmund Gosse, "The Ethics of Biography," quoted in Clifford, ibid., p. 115.
5. Dryden's Preface to *Plutarch's Lives, 1863–66,* quoted in Clifford, ibid., pp. 18–19.
6. John Drinkwater, *The World's Lincoln* (New York: Bowling Green Press, 1928), pp. 7–8.
7. Mary K. Eakin, "The Changing World of Science and the Social Sciences," in Virginia Haviland, *Children and Literature: Views and Reviews* (Glenview, Ill.: Scott, Foresman, 1973), p. 321.

In Biography for Young Readers, Nothing Is Impossible

1. Dorothy Aldis, *Nothing Is Impossible: The Story of Beatrix Potter* (New York: Atheneum, 1969). All page references are to this edition.
2. Carnegie Library, Pittsburgh.
3. Sandra Styer, "Biographical Models for Young Feminists," *Language Arts* 55, no. 2:168–74 (Feb. 1978).
4. Edna Johnson, Evelyn R. Sickels, Frances Clarke Sayers, Carolyn Horovitz, eds., *Anthology of Children's Literature*, 5th ed. (Boston: Houghton, 1977), pp. 1016–18.
5. Marilyn D. Button, *Children's Literature Association Newsletter* 2, no. 4: 7–9 (Winter 1978).
6. Beatrix Potter, *The Journal of Beatrix Potter*, ed. by Leslie Linder (London: Warne, 1966). All page references are to this edition.
7. Margaret Lane, *The Tale of Beatrix Potter*, rev. ed. (London: Warne, 1968). All page references are to this edition. A new book by Margaret Lane, *The Magic Years of Beatrix Potter*, was published in 1978 by Warne. This volume, which focuses on Potter's years of literary productivity, draws heavily on the earlier work. It provides additional reproductions of Potter's drawings and paintings, but it does not supplant the earlier work, which remains the standard biography.
8. Button, p. 9.
9. This phrase has its source in fictionalized dialogue between the child Beatrix and her governess, Miss Hammond (p. 47). A scene of the sympathetic, wise adult encouraging high aspirations in the child protagonist is a standard feature of conventional juvenile biography.
10. Pamela Travers, "The Shortest Stories in the World," *The [London] Times Literary Supplement* (15 July 1977), p. 858.
11. Clifton Fadiman, "The Case for a Children's Literature," *Children's Literature* 5:18 (1976).

Controversy: An Active Healthy Skepticism

1. Margery Fisher, *Matters of Fact: Aspects of Non-Fiction for Children* (New York: Crowell, 1972), p. 474.

The Problem with Problem Books

1. Dale Carlson, *Girls Are Equal Too: The Women's Movement for Teen-agers* (New York: Atheneum, 1973), p. vii.
2. Ibid., pp. xii–xiii.
3. Ibid., verso of title page.
4. Daniel Cohen, *The Ancient Visitors* (Garden City, N.Y., Doubleday, 1976), p. 8.
5. Laurence Pringle, *Nuclear Power: From Physics to Politics* (New York: Macmillan, 1979), p. 1.
6. Ibid., p. 73.
7. Ibid., p. 125.
8. Page 171 of this work.
9. *Interracial Books for Children* 7:11 (1976).
10. Cohen, pp. 200–201.

Any Writer Who Follows Anyone Else's Guidelines
Ought To Be in Advertising

1. *School Library Journal* 23:5 (January 1977), p. 4.
2. Council on Interracial Books for Children, *Human and Anti-Human Values in Children's Books* (New York: The Council, 1976), p. 4.
3. Ibid., *Interracial Books for Children Bulletin* 8, no.3.

The Bible Presented Ojectively

1. Reprinted from a pamphlet published by the Religious Instruction As-sociation (now PERSC), Fort Wayne, Ind., 1966.
2. *See also* Robert F. Hogan, "The Bible in the English Program" and Alton C. Capps, "A Realistic Approach to Biblical Literature," both reprints from *English Journal*. *See also* James V. Panoch, "Why Not Inaugurate a Course?" *Religious Education* (March/April 1969).
3. Commission on Religion in the Public Schools, *Religion in the Public Schools* (New York: Harper, 1965), p. 3.
4. Charlotte Huck, *Children's Literature in the Elementary School* (New York: Holt, 1968), p. 199.

A Ride across the Mystic Bridge, or Occult Books:
What, Why, and Who Needs Them?

1. Nandor Fodor, *Encyclopedia of Phychic Science* (Hyde Park, N.Y.: Uni-versity Books, 1966). Useful but spotty and not always accurate.
   Fossell H. Robbins, *The Encyclopedia of Witchcraft and Demonology* (New York: Crown, 1959). Excellent but inherently limited in scope.
   Lewis Spence, *Encyclopedia of Occultism* (Hyde Park, New York: University Books, 1960). More systematic but often less comprehen-sive than Fodor.

Appendix A

1. Milton Meltzer, "Where Do All the Prizes Go? The Case for Nonfiction," *The Horn Book* 52:22 (Feb. 1976).

Designed by Ellen Pettengell

Cover photograph by Peter Jones

Composed in Linotype Primer and
Cairo by FM Typesetting.
Display type, Avant Garde,
composed by Eddie Price, Inc.

Printed on 50-pound Antique
Glatfelter, a pH-neutral stock, and
bound in 10-point Carolina cover
stock by the University of
Chicago Printing Department